The Atlanta Rhythm Section

THE AUTHORIZED HISTORY

Willie G. Moseley

Foreword by Gloria Buie

Schiffer Publishing Ltd

4880 Lower Valley Road • Atglen, PA 19310

Other Schiffer Books by the Author:
The Bass Space: Profiles of Classic Electric Basses
  (978-0-7643-5522-6)
Vintage Electric Guitars: In Praise of Fretted Americana
  (978-0-7643-1361-5)

Other Schiffer Books on Related Subjects:
Paul Yandell, Second to the Best: A Sideman's Chronicle
  by Norm Van Maastricht (978-0-7643-5048-1)
Unstrung Heroes: Fifty Guitar Greats You Should Know
  by Pete Braidis (978-0-7643-5088-7)

Designed by Justin Watkinson
Type set in Bello Pro/Aachen BT/Minion Pro
ARS logo courtesy of Mike McCarty

ISBN: 978-0-7643-5564-6
Printed in China

Published by Schiffer Publishing, Ltd.
4880 Lower Valley Road
Atglen, PA 19310
Phone: (610) 593-1777; Fax: (610) 593-2002
E-mail: Info@schifferbooks.com
Web: www.schifferbooks.com

For our complete selection of fine books on this and related
subjects, please visit our website at www.schifferbooks.com.
You may also write for a free catalog.

Schiffer Publishing's titles are available at special discounts for
bulk purchases for sales promotions or premiums. Special editions,
including personalized covers, corporate imprints, and excerpts,
can be created in large quantities for special needs. For more
information, contact the publisher.

We are always looking for people to write books on
new and related subjects. If you have an idea for a book,
please contact us at proposals@schifferbooks.com.

Obviously, this is for the members, associates, and fans of the Atlanta Rhythm Section, but it's also in memory of George Harper, H. F. "Jim" Levy, and Kathleen Moseley.

Contents

Foreword

The Atlanta Rhythm Section was a unique and interesting band, and it is my pleasure to introduce their story.

I grew up in Dothan, Alabama, and was aware of Bobby Goldsboro and the Webs, who were managed by my late husband, Buddy. His involvement with that group was the beginning of Buddy's commitment to writing songs and managing bands, and that commitment was part of his personality for the rest of his life.

Buddy's enthusiasm and drive would lead him to Atlanta, where he garnered a lot of success as a songwriter, created a recording studio in Doraville that was then state of the art, and helped create one of the most unusual bands in rock music history.

The Atlanta Rhythm Section's original members already had years of concert experience when the band formed in 1970, but they were mainly known for their abilities in recording studios. The idea that they could create their own band (to include songwriting and touring) had never been done before.

By the time Buddy and I married, the Rhythm Section was going strong, and I watched with pride as their reputation as professionals continued to expand. Once I began working at Studio One myself, I was able to monitor how they meticulously crafted their music. While there were many other bands and singers who recorded at Studio One, our own "house band" was the most dedicated group of musicians I've ever seen and heard.

Each member of the Rhythm Section had his own personality traits, and they all had different lifestyles, but the one thing that held them together was their dedication to the music. It was as simple as that, and they would be awarded gold and platinum albums for their efforts.

As is the case with any famous band, there were good times and bad times, and Willie has done a good job of covering all the bases via his methodical research and dozens of interviews. I've discovered new stories about some of members of the band and have found myself wishing that I'd been out on the road with them myself at certain times.

The current edition of the Rhythm Section is just as dedicated to its music as the original members were, and that music is continuing to be presented in an admirable manner. This book is also a worthwhile tribute to the Atlanta Rhythm Section and its legacy.

—Gloria Buie

Introduction

Call it "integrity," indeed.

I can't think of another term that better describes what the Atlanta Rhythm Section was seeking to accomplish during its heyday, even though such a "quest" by the band was more or less unspoken or perhaps even subliminal.

The genesis of this book was an inquiry in mid-2016 to the *Vintage Guitar Magazine* home office from Terry Spackman, a former A.R.S. roadie—and that term now seems to be antiquated, having morphed into "tech."

Spackman hadn't been onboard during the heyday of the band in the 1970s, but he was simply requesting that the magazine consider doing an article about Barry Bailey.

I'm not sure to what extent Mr. Spackman was motivated to contact *VG* because of Barry's physiological challenges in recent times, but, as it turned out, the guitarist's health issues didn't really figure into a decision to do a profile of him, since I've always been enthusiastic about interviewing veteran musicians who fit the magazine's format.

The Barry Bailey article in *Vintage Guitar* soon begat—as might have been expected—a J. R. Cobb profile (couldn't have one without the other), as well as a comparison profile of the same-brand, same-model, same-year, same-color Gibson Les Paul Deluxe guitars owned by Barry and 38 Special founding lead guitarist Jeff Carlisi.

So it's not surprising that the idea of chronicling the previously untold and unique history of the highly underrated band in which Messrs. Bailey and Cobb were the highly underappreciated founding guitarists began to develop.

In the late 1960s and early 1970s, I'd been fortunate enough to see and hear iconic bands and singers such as Cream and Joe Cocker, as well as the original incarnations of the Allman Brothers Band, Santana, and the Chicago Transit Authority (the Allmans had played at my college in southeastern Alabama a month before they recorded the legendary *Live at the Fillmore East* album in 1971).

And as I began to do the research for this project, I wondered what my thoughts would have been had I experienced an Atlanta Rhythm Section concert back in the 1970s.

What few archival concert videos that can be sussed out on YouTube confirm that while the A.R.S. didn't put on much of a show, their music was impeccable. And the concentration of the band members when crafting their sonic presentations (live and in the studio) did indeed validate bassist Paul Goddard's forthright attitude and advocacy—bordering on ferocity—about favoring sound over visuals, as recalled by his sister herein.

For that matter—and to their credit—other legendary musicians have always had the same laudable point of view. Peter Frampton, who has constantly diversified throughout his career, is on record as insisting that "for me, it's always 'what does it sound like,' not 'what does it look like.'" And Frampton's highly listenable music underlines his point of view.

It was gratifying that so many persons critical to the story agreed to contribute recollections, photos, and memorabilia. It took a lot of months of interstate miles—and even a couple of trips on a dirt road or two—to meet with central and ancillary characters, but every interview was accomplished with a sense of courtesy and mutual respect. It seemed that every interviewee agreed that the story of the Atlanta Rhythm Section needed to be told.

The band's focus on the integrity of their music has indeed been validated by the longevity of their songs, as Dean "Ox" Daughtry and others have summarized in the final chapter. The Atlanta Rhythm Section was, and is, an iconic Southern band with a definitely different style and approach, and their compositions and recordings have indeed stood the test of time.

Acknowledgments and Contributors

O nce again, the first person I need to thank is my wife, Gail, for her patience and understanding, as is always the case whenever I take on a new book project.

I appreciated the eager participation of those who were and are involved in the chronicle of the Atlanta Rhythm Section—musicians, roadies/techs, business personnel, and fans, who provided beaucoup recollections and beaucoup photos. What was interesting and gratifying about the "research and development phase" of this book was the "domino" effect of referrals for interviews ("I can put you in touch with _____"; "You really ought to talk to _____").

Special acknowledgement, as always, goes to Alan Greenwood, founder and publisher of *Vintage Guitar Magazine*, for the ongoing writing opportunities.

Ditto to the folks at Tallapoosa Publishers for the "emeritus" writing status and perks concerning their regional periodicals.

Many persons who were interviewed also did a decent amount of research regarding archival photos and memorabilia, so here's another tip of the headstock to those individuals (the aforementioned Terry Spackman needs to be singled out in this category). I also appreciated the research efforts of several knowledgeable music fans (i.e., non-interviewees) such as Shap Ashley, Bill Schaum, Robert Register, Andy Patterson, and David Strickland.

Special thanks for research access also goes out to Mazie Bowen and Mary Linnemann at the University of Georgia Special Collections Library, and to Chantel Dunham at the main library at the same institute of higher learning.

Ditto: Kevin Fleming at the Georgia State University Library.

Ditto: Mandi Johnson and Amanda Pellerin at the Georgia Tech University Library.

Ditto: Lisa Love (Georgia Department of Economic Development).

A tip of the headstock also goes to Tatyana Warrick (National Safety Council).

"Out-in-the-audience" fans who shared their egalitarian recollections included Tom Brantley, Charles Casmus, Greg Henderson, Dan Lipson, Mitch Sneed, and Ham Wilson.

Likewise, I'd like to express my appreciation to Col. Glenn Mackey, USAF (ret.) for his usual presubmission perusal and input regarding the text.

And here's the perpetual "read-between-the-lines" salute to the Messrs. Spilman for motivating me to become a full-time writer all those years ago.

Contributors:

Andy Anderson: lead singer for the Atlanta Rhythm Section

Barry Bailey: founding guitarist of the Atlanta Rhythm Section

Rusty Banks: technician/roadie for the Atlanta Rhythm Section

Bruce Brown: lead guitarist of the Charlie Daniels Band

Ben Buie: son of Gloria and Buddy Buie

Buddy Buie (1941–2015): songwriter/promoter/producer and founder of Studio One in Doraville, Georgia (Note: Buddy's remarks were culled from his spoken-word commentaries on his personal two-CD anthology, *Music of My Life.*)

Gloria Buie: Buddy Buie's wife, and business manager for Studio One and the Buie-Geller Organization, as well as other enterprises

Jerry Buie: Buddy Buie's brother

Rick Campbell: technician/roadie for the Atlanta Rhythm Section

Jeff Carlisi: founding lead guitarist of 38 Special

Mike Causey: guitarist for Stillwater

Craig Chaquico: lead guitarist for Jefferson Starship

J. R. Cobb: songwriter/guitarist for the Classics IV, founding guitarist of the Atlanta Rhythm Section

Jerry Coody: truck driver / technician / roadie for the Atlanta Rhythm Section

Wendell Cox: lead guitarist for the Travis Tritt Band

Dean "Ox" Daughtry: keyboard player for the Candymen and Dennis Yost & the Classics IV, founding keyboard player of (and concurrent member of) the Atlanta Rhythm Section

Elliot Easton: lead guitarist of the Cars

Mark Egan: founding bassist of the Pat Metheny Group

Tinsley Ellis: Atlanta-based blues guitarist

Arnie Geller: music industry executive; partner in Buie-Geller Organization

Emory Gordy Jr.: veteran musician and producer

Steve Hammond: brother of Atlanta Rhythm Section lead singer Ronnie Hammond (1950–2011).

Dave Hope: founding bassist of Kansas

Jeff Jackson: lighting director / production manager for the Atlanta Rhythm Section

Nan Jacobs: sister of founding Atlanta Rhythm Section bassist Paul Goddard (1945–2014)

Rodney Justo: lead singer for the Candymen, founding lead singer of the Atlanta Rhythm Section

Ed King: guitarist for Lynyrd Skynyrd

Spencer Kirkpatrick: lead guitarist of the Atlanta Vibrations and Hydra

Chuck Leavell: keyboard player for the Allman Brothers Band and Sea Level

Mylon LeFevre: gospel songwriter/singer/musician

Butch Lowery: Atlanta music industry executive

Tommy Mann: lead singer for the K-Otics

Greg Martin: lead guitarist of the Kentucky Headhunters

Jack Martin: Atlanta promoter and musician

Rick Maxwell: Studio One studio manager

Mike McCarty: graphic artist/designer for the Atlanta Rhythm Section

Steve McRay: keyboard player for Mose Jones

Rodney Mills: engineer and producer at Studio One

Kyle Mooty: general manager, the *Eufaula Tribune*

Mark Pucci: Atlanta public-relations executive

Greg "Fern" Quesnel: front-of-house soundman for the Atlanta Rhythm Section

Darryl Rhoades: Atlanta-based comedian/drummer

Justin Senker: bassist for the Atlanta Rhythm Section

Lynn Sinclair: music director / program director for radio stations in Georgia and South Carolina

Terry Spackman: technician/roadie for the Atlanta Rhythm Section

Larry Steele (1952–2017): stage manager for 38 Special

Steve Stone: guitarist for the Atlanta Rhythm Section

Marvin Taylor: guitarist for the K-Otics and the second incarnation of Mose Jones

Rob Walker: guitarist for Stillwater

Bill Wendt: engineer/tech for Stillwater and the Atlanta Rhythm Section

Richard Williams: founding guitarist of Kansas

CHAPTER 1
Wiregrass Roots

Named after a native and common wild grass, *Aristida stricta*, the Wiregrass region of Alabama is located in the southeastern corner of that state. Its informal "border towns" include Eufaula to the north, Troy to the northwest, and Opp to the west, with the state lines of Georgia and Florida also serving as boundaries (although portions of those two states are also referenced when a multistate "Wiregrass region" is being considered).

The Alabama Wiregrass area includes Ft. Rucker, a sprawling US Army installation of over 63,000 acres, which is the primary training facility for army aviation (almost exclusively helicopters). The cities of Enterprise, Ozark, and Daleville all have entrance gates to Fort Rucker, and those communities count on the Army and its personnel stationed in the area for economic support.

Enterprise also has what is thought to be the world's only official (modern-day) statue dedicated to an insect. In the days before insecticides were able to control crop pests, the boll weevil devastated innumerable acres of cotton fields across the Deep South.

Many farmers in southeastern Alabama switched to raising peanuts, and that crop was so successful that a monument acknowledging the boll weevil as the inspiration for the agricultural shift was erected in downtown Enterprise. Visitors to that city who are unfamiliar with the regional legend might not know what to make of a statue of a goddess-like figure holding a bug aloft.

The largest city in the Wiregrass is Dothan, situated about fifteen miles north of the Florida state line and about twenty miles west of the Georgia state line. Dothan has become known as "Circle City" in citizens band (CB) radio lingo; Ross Clark Circle, built in the early 1960s, had surrounded most of the town when it was completed, but Dothan's city limits would expand far beyond that circuit in the ensuing decades.

Not surprisingly, Dothan is also peanut-centric regarding regional agriculture and has hosted an annual festival honoring that crop since 1938 (except for the World War II years). The speaker at the first event was George Washington Carver of Tuskegee Institute, who had discovered hundreds of uses for the unique legume.

"Circle City" ultimately developed its celebration into a gargantuan National Peanut Festival that is held each fall, replete with exhibits and concerts at the local fairground.

And around the time Ross Clark Circle was being constructed, the earliest musical "seeds" of what would evolve into a multifaceted, successful musical venture in Atlanta, Georgia, were planted and nurtured in Dothan.

●●●●●●

The story of the Atlanta Rhythm Section can't be told without including a (condensed) biography of Buddy Buie.

Perry Carlton "Buddy" Buie was born on January 23, 1941, in Marianna, Florida, about thirty-five miles south of Dothan. His father drove a bread truck, and when Buddy was about six months old, his family relocated to Dothan as owners-operators of a restaurant called the City Café, which would eventually move elsewhere downtown and become known as Buie's Restaurant. Buddy would refer to Dothan as his hometown.

Buddy, his older sister, Gloria, and younger brother, Jerry, were compelled to work at the family business, but Buddy's gregarious personality included an always-in-gear creative drive that was musically oriented. Even though he didn't necessarily aspire to be a bona fide performing musician, he knew at a young age that he had a knack for songwriting, and he set out to prove it.

Jerry stayed more down to earth, working his way up to becoming part owner of the restaurant.

As a student at Dothan High School, Buddy befriended Bobby Goldsboro and John Rainey Adkins, both of whom would become members of what Buie recalled as "Dothan Alabama's original rock band, the Webs."

"My cowriters are one of the primary reasons for the success I've enjoyed," he recounted. "The first one was John Rainey Adkins; he was a guitar hero of mine when we were in high school. He was the first person I told that I was gonna be a songwriter who didn't snicker. We'd sit in my '55 Chevrolet in front of his house on Main St. I'd sing my ideas a capella, and he'd pick them out on his guitar. Without him, I might still be working in my family's business."

As for Buddy's own musical abilities, "he could play the guitar, but he wasn't very good," Jerry Buie said of his older brother, "and he could sing. I think he hired a lot of singers like [future Atlanta Rhythm Section lead vocalists] Ronnie Hammond and Rodney Justo because he wanted them to sing a song like he would sing it himself."

Buddy developed a teenage romance with a petite blonde girl named Gloria Jean Seay, who was three years younger. Their families attended Grandview Baptist Church. Gloria wasn't allowed to "car date," so Buddy would drive over to the Seays' home on a regular basis. It helped that the family owned a pool table.

"I didn't get to go to a lot of the places where other kids went," Gloria remembered. "My parents were Southern Baptist and were very strict. Buddy went to hangouts like Porter's Fairy-Land all the time because of the bands. I didn't get to go there much, but I saw Bobby Goldsboro and the Webs when they played at the bowling alley one night, on the back of a pickup truck."

The relationship of Gloria and Buddy was, like many stereotypical teenage romances, doomed from the start, primarily due to parental concerns. Buddy's parents fretted that his musical aspirations meant that he wasn't oriented toward a "real job," and Gloria's parents didn't think Buddy would end up with a successful occupation, either. The Seays didn't encourage their daughter's romance, and the twosome eventually went their separate ways.

"Buddy and I were childhood sweethearts, but we broke up," Gloria said. "He just wanted to be in music. One of the last things he said to me back then was 'You're gonna be sorry, because one day I'm gonna be a famous songwriter, and you're gonna hear about me.' I didn't even know where that came from—other than John Rainey, he had stopped telling anyone else he wanted to be a songwriter, because he thought they might make fun of him.

"In 1962, when I graduated from high school, I married someone else, left town, and went to Tuscaloosa. That's where I became a huge [University of] Alabama fan."

Gloria also asserted that Buddy's energetic, go-get-'em personality was caused by a then-undiagnosed medical disorder. She speculated about how his working life would have turned out had a diagnosis and treatment been available in those times.

"I know for a fact that he was ADD [Attention Deficit Disorder]," she said, "but back then they didn't know about that. If they had treated him with the drugs they have now, Buddy would never have become a songwriter. Thank God they didn't."

Buddy had already begun booking bands while he was still at Dothan High School. He graduated in 1959, and attended Auburn University for a brief time, but soon left. The same thing happened when he later enrolled at Troy State College, about fifty miles up Highway 231 from Dothan. Higher education didn't seem to appeal to Buie, who was itching to make his big ideas become reality.

By the early 1960s, Buddy had his own artist booking business, Southland Talent Agency, set up in suite 25 of the Merrill-McRae Building, located at 200½ North Foster St. in downtown Dothan. A slogan in an "All-Star Revue for '62" brochure proclaimed that his agency was "Serving the South with the Best."

Buddy's parents had reservations about their middle child being in the music business, but they saw how his energetic personality suited such an occupation, and they already knew he was a decent songwriter as well.

"He booked a lot of acts back then, said Jerry Buie. "I'd go around town and help put up posterboards; we'd sell tickets out of a cigar box at the restaurant, and my aunt, uncle, and parents would take up tickets at shows. It was kind of a family thing."

As Buddy's booking business expanded, Jerry would be the liaison who actually went to some of the venues to represent the agency at performances.

While most of the singers and musicians featured in Southland Talent Agency's 1962 brochure were solo artists (including Charlie Rich, Ace Cannon, and Bruce Channel of "Hey Baby" fame), it wasn't surprising that the Webs—consisting of Bobby Goldsboro on vocals and guitar, John Rainey Adkins on lead guitar, Amos Tindall on bass, and Paul Garrison on drums—were also in Buie's lineup of performers. The quartet even recorded a few primitive-sounding singles in Birmingham.

Concert trends during such times included name singers using local talent as a backup band for a particular appearance. A big break for the Webs happened when Buddy booked singer Roy Orbison to play in Dothan, with the Webs slated to perform the backing music for the legendary vocalist.

When Orbison performed at that show, he was astounded at how well the local boys had learned his material, and offered the Webs an opportunity to go on the road with him as the backup band for all of his performances. Buddy signed on as Orbison's tour manager.

Primitive 8 mm home movies by Amos Tindall show the young musicians and Buie hamming it up for the camera while on the road. Orbison's appearances in the movies consist of a couple of bemused gestures of acknowledgment that he's being filmed. His reaction seems to be in sync with his somewhat-enigmatic stage presence.

The Webs, as seen in the 1962 Southland Talent brochure. Left to right: Amos Tindall, John Rainey Adkins, Bobby Goldsboro, Paul Garrison.

The Webs' equipment trailer was also filmed; in addition to the band's name displayed on the side of the trailer (emblazoned in large logo-style letters), the name, address, and phone number of the Southland Talent Agency were also seen.

"Roy would come to our home in Dothan when he was in town," said Jerry, "and would eat at my family's restaurant. He was one of the nicest guys you'd ever want to meet."

As is always the case with professional musicians, the band began to experience turnover in membership.

Goldsboro would depart the Webs to pursue a solo career when a self-penned single of his, "See the Funny Little Clown," was released in 1963 and became a huge national hit. Likewise, Buddy left his job as Orbison's tour manager and fastened his fortunes to Goldsboro's efforts.

"United Artists took an interest in Bobby," Buie detailed. "He and I went to New York; Bobby signed an artist deal with UA, and I was offered a writer's contract for $75 a week. Here I was, fresh out of Dothan, Alabama, staying in a cheap motel off Broadway.

"Everybody who knows me knows that food is very important to me. I would pass a deli and press my nose up against the glass, knowing that I couldn't afford what I saw. I was hungry and I was homesick, and I wrote the song 'Georgia Pines' from my heart."

Buddy didn't complete writing that song in New York, however. He eventually returned to Dothan and began working with Roy Orbison and the Webs again. Bassist Amos Tindall had left the Webs around the same time as Goldsboro and had been replaced by Bill Gilmore.

"When I got home, John Rainey and I finished 'Georgia Pines,'" Buddy recalled. "Later, my friend Wilbur Walton and I put together the James Gang, and Wilbur's version of 'Georgia Pines' is near and dear to my heart to this day."

Walton, a burly soul singer who was promoted with a "Jr." suffix added to his name, would become another Wiregrass legend. Buie helped create the James Gang with Walton in the fall of 1964, after he'd returned from the Big Apple. The band's moniker was later changed to "Wilbur Walton Jr. and the James Gang." While that aggregation quickly became popular performers at high-school dances and National Guard armories in Alabama, Florida, and Georgia, Wilbur's group would disband later in the 1960s. The James Gang of Dothan had no connection with the Cleveland, Ohio, band of the same name that formed in 1966, and was ultimately fronted by guitarist Joe Walsh.

The K-Otics in 1965, clad in stereotypical-for-the-times matching outfits. Clockwise, from bottom: Marvin Taylor, Glenn Griffin, Tommy Mann, Ray Goss, Kim Venable.

CHAPTER 2
Jacksonville and Tampa Connections

By the time Buddy had settled back in Dothan again, the Webs had become known as the Roy Orbison Band when they backed the famous singer, but they soon became known as the Candymen, a reference to Orbison's early 1960s hit, "Candy Man." It wasn't the most masculine/macho moniker—"candy ass" being a redneck slur—and for a time, they retained the Webs name when they weren't on tour with Orbison, but eventually decided to use the Candymen name for shows that they did without Orbison, as well.

In the spring of 1965, Buie began planning a large show at the Houston County Farm Center in Dothan that was headlined by Orbison. Included in the lineup was a quintet called the K-Otics, whose members were from Tallassee and Tuskegee, in central Alabama. That band was experiencing a moderate amount of area success with a single called "Charlena," and Buddy saw an opportunity to expand his band management a bit beyond the Wiregrass.

The K-Otics' lead singer, Tommy Mann, was a student at Troy State College, majoring in business, and he was also managing the band's business affairs. The upcoming Dothan show would be their first booking with Buddy, and Mann recalled meeting with Buie at the promoter's parents' house to discuss plans for the event.

"Buddy was already working on his vision of what might be called 'the perfect American dream,'" Mann remembered. "He'd get an idea, would dig into it, and would really cover the whole picture. And, of course, his huge ideas included writing songs, producing the recording of those songs, managing bands, and personal management of individuals. I don't think anyone had ever done it that way before he did. He talked about how he had worked with the Webs and had developed a business process to follow up for future bookings at the same place. I thought I could apply a lot of what he taught me to the K-Otics."

Poster for a 1965 Buie-promoted concert in Dothan with Roy Orbison as the headliner. *robertoreg.blogspot.com*

Soon after the Houston County Farm Center show, Mann met with Buddy in Dothan again, this time accompanied by K-Otics drummer Kim Venable. The enthusiastic promoter attempted to sign the band to a management contract, but the K-Otics declined.

Around the same time, Buddy was getting to know a fellow promoter named Paul Cochran in Clearwater, Florida, west of Tampa. A former teacher and basketball coach from Johnson City, Tennessee, Cochran had migrated to the Sunshine State to work for the Clearwater Recreation Department.

In late 1961 and early 1962, Cochran had staged concerts featuring nationally known recording stars at Clearwater's Municipal Auditorium. Such an event would usually be promoted as a "Star Spectacular." Other times, dances featuring local talent were presented.

The multiple-act concert concept clicked for Cochran, and he opted to pursue that facet of the entertainment field. When he and Buie met, Cochran was managing the Roemans, a Tampa-based band that had started out as the Romans, but their name had been slightly changed when they began backing up teen idol Tommy Roe. They still performed on their own, however, and later toured Europe with English singer P. J. Proby. At one point, future Allman Brothers Band bassist Berry Oakley was a member of the Roemans.

Cochran also managed the Classics IV, a combo from Jacksonville, and other bands.

When it came to business, Buie and Cochran were kindred spirits, and they formed the Buie-Cochran Management Company, combining their rosters and expanding their performance opportunities throughout Alabama, Florida, and Georgia. In late 1965, they moved their business to Atlanta and formed a publishing company with Atlanta music industry legend Bill Lowery called Low-Sal Publishing.

· · · · · ·

In the spring of 1966, the K-Otics finally signed on with Buie-Cochran Management, around the time they had released "Double Shot," a cover of a "beach music" song by Dick Holler and the Holidays.

However, the band from central Alabama would end up duking it out nationally with the Swingin' Medallions, a horn band from Greenwood, South Carolina, which had recorded and released another version the same song around the same time.

While the K-Otics' rendition was more popular in certain locations, such as the metropolitan Miami area, the Medallions ultimately won the national battle. Decades later, more than one erstwhile member of the K-Otics was still speculating about whether music industry machinations of the under-the-table type were involved in the Swingin' Medallions' "win."

Buie and Orbison on the road in 1966.
robertoreg.blogspot.com

Buie-Cochran wasn't involved in that controversy, and the K-Otics disbanded in 1967. Kim Venable and guitarist Marvin Taylor later migrated to Atlanta to further their respective musical aspirations, and both would eventually succeed.

••••••

When Paul Garrison left the Webs / Roy Orbison Band in the mid-sixties for a career in advertising, Orbison found a replacement drummer in Jacksonville, Florida.

Born in Blakely, Georgia, in 1944, Robert Nix had come of age in Jacksonville listening to numerous pop and soul singers, but he also liked jazz drummers such as Joe Morello, Buddy Rich, and Hal Blaine. Nix was playing at a club called the Golden Gate Lounge when Orbison showed up one evening at midnight, dressed in black and wearing his impenetrable thick glasses. After listening to Nix's combo for a brief time, Orbison invited the young drummer to join his band, which was about to embark on a tour of England. Nix accepted, and he would recall that this new assignment was his legitimate start in the music business.

Like Buddy Buie, Robert was known for having a type A aggressive personality, which was enhanced by his imposing stature—he was well over six feet tall.

••••••

New York City native Rodney Justo is of Spanish heritage and was brought up in a multicultural section of Tampa, Florida (although "multicultural" didn't exist as a term back then). A cool and confident vocalist, Rodney was the singer for a band called the Mystics. He described that combo's approach as somewhat innovative, noting, "We did songs that other bands wouldn't do. I've never learned a Chuck Berry song in my life; that was too easy for us, and there was no challenge."

And like the Webs in Dothan, the Mystics would back up famous singers that came to the Tampa-Clearwater area during the era of "teen idol" singers. They also played (on their own) at more than one of Paul Cochran's early shows at the Clearwater Municipal Auditorium. Rodney would ultimately sign a solo personal management contract with Cochran.

"He was an extremely close friend of mine," Justo said of Cochran. "My parents had to sign the contract, but Paul treated me like I was his son."

Rodney recounted that the Mystics supported "essentially everyone that ever had a hit record until 1965. Obscure singers all the way up to Neil Sedaka, Freddy Cannon, Lou Christie, Gene Pitney, Fabian, Bobby Rydell, Johnny Tillotson. We worked with Ray Stevens a *lot*. We learned their songs for the performance in advance. Usually, those singers would come into town by themselves, but occasionally, they'd bring another person; maybe they'd have a guitar player with them. One time, the Four Seasons brought along a drummer.

"The singers would do their own hits, and also other current hits like 'Peppermint Twist' and Ray Charles's 'What'd I Say' or maybe a Bo Diddley song. I don't think any of them played more than forty minutes."

As the lead singer for the Mystics, Justo would often sing a couple of songs before a nationally famous crooner was introduced. Rodney would then shift to a backup role, which included singing harmony parts.

And among the famous singers who hired the Mystics was Roy Orbison, who was so imbued with Justo's singing that he produced a record of Rodney performing as a solo artist.

Justo vividly recalled the first time he met Buddy Buie, which happened to be the same occasion at which Paul Cochran met Buie:

"Same time, same place. Paul was promoting those dances at the Clearwater auditorium. Buddy was wearing a brown jacket, and when he got excited, he stuttered and stammered. He had the demeanor of Jackie Gleason; he was bigger than life. He said, 'I like the way you sing and I'm gonna write you a song!' And he hadn't written any hits yet. The first song of any significance that I recall that he wrote was 'Party Girl' with Bill Gilmore, for Tommy Roe."

Early lineup of the Candymen, left to right: Bobby Peterson, John Rainey Adkins, Robert Nix, Bill Gilmore, Rodney Justo. This photo was taken in Roy Orbison's house.

However, it was through Orbison that Rodney ultimately got to know the talented musicians from Dothan, whose band had undergone some personnel changes.

"By the time I came along, they had pretty much stopped calling themselves the Webs," he remembered. "When they went out with Roy, they were called the Roy Orbison Band. Paul Garrison had left and was replaced by Robert Nix. So it was John Rainey Adkins, Robert, Bill Gilmore, and Bobby Peterson on keyboards; he came onboard a few weeks before I did. When I joined, the band was already called the Candymen; John Rainey and Nix came to Tampa to talk to me about coming with them. Of course, I'd already known Roy, who was committed to have a band perform prior to his taking the stage."

As for the Candymen breaking off from Orbison to become a self-contained band, Justo remembered that he was in a minority:

"I was content with Roy; it was a regular-enough job where I was raising my family, but the others were intent on being on our own. We tried all kinds of names—like the 'Hustlers' when we played in Miami—because we thought Roy wasn't going to let us have the [Candymen] name. We even recorded a single for MGM under the name of the Webs. Roy got us the deal, but it wasn't much; I think it was his way of controlling us because he didn't want us to leave."

Bobby Peterson departed the Candymen around the time the band went out on its own, and he would later have a brief tenure with the McCoys, of "Hang On Sloopy" fame. His replacement would be yet another musician from the Alabama Wiregrass.

• • • • • •

Dean "Ox" Daughtry was born in the small community of Samson, Alabama, located on Highway 52 just west of Geneva. His parents split up before he was even a year old, and the youngster and his mother would temporarily reside at her parents' home.

Most of his childhood was spent in small communities in the same area, since his mother was an itinerant mill worker.

"She worked in shirt factories around the area, like in Florala," he recalled, "and at the Micolas cotton mills in Opp. And there was also a shirt factory in Kinston, where I graduated from high school. Kinston's population was about 500 at the time."

Dean took formal piano lessons, becoming an accomplished purveyor of hymns and gospel music in church at a young age. He would end up also playing in what he termed as "juke joints" when he got older, and he cited early influences that included Floyd Kramer, Ray Charles, and Jerry Lee Lewis. He would listen to hit songs on WBAM Radio ("The Big Bam"), a 50,000-watt station broadcasting out of Montgomery.

Dean had a beefy physique and a squarish face, and the nickname of "Ox" was bestowed on him by a guitar player named Howard Martin during a performance at a club in Crestview, Florida.

"He came up to sit in with us," Daughtry remembered, "and took one look at my long hair and said, 'How am I supposed to play with this lady ox sittin' beside me?'"

The pianist eventually made his way to Dothan, but he already knew about the Webs before that band evolved into the Candymen.

"They were the 'Wiregrass stars,'" he recalled appreciatively. "When I ran across them in Dothan, it was like running across Elvis."

When Peterson left the Candymen, Daughtry was quickly hired as an immediate replacement, but Bobby met with Dean to impart the band's song arrangements to the band's new keyboard player.

"He only had to show me once," Dean said of the instructions from his predecessor. "I was so anxious to learn because the Candymen were *the stuff*. As soon as he played it for me one time, I played it back exactly like he played it, which kind of freaked him out."

······

The Candymen's touring schedule got off to an exciting start in 1967, when the band (sans Rodney Justo) backed up Roy Orbison in Australia in late January. The Yardbirds, featuring future Led Zeppelin guitarist Jimmy Page, were on the same tour, as was an American band, the Walker Brothers. Daughtry recalled a performance on an Australian television show where Page reportedly refused to turn down his amplifier. In addition to the Yardbirds, Orbison and the Candymen also played on the same broadcast.

Ox particularly enjoyed the tour Down Under, noting "I've been back to most of the places I've played except Australia, and I'd like to go there, too."

The spring of 1967 saw the Candymen going to England, also to support Orbison, and this time Justo was included. Their tour package included the Small Faces, Paul and Barry Ryan, the Searchers, P. P. Arnold, and a group called Sonny Childe and the TNTs.

"Sonny went on to record 'Take a Letter Maria' as R. B. Greaves," Rodney detailed.

The Candymen also met numerous British music heroes of theirs. Graham Nash, then of the Hollies, took a shine to the band and supervised a recording session for two songs, "Hope" and "I'll Never Forget." The songs were recorded at Abbey Road Studios, using the Beatles' equipment (Nash reportedly got an okay from Paul McCartney to use the gear, since the Candymen's instruments were on their tour bus). The Hollies singer/guitarist also contributed background vocals.

The boys from Dixie were particularly fascinated by John Lennon's Mellotron, a primitive electronic keyboard device that played actual tape recordings of a certain instrument or human voices playing/singing a certain musical note (but only for several seconds).

One of the most widely heard uses of Lennon's Mellotron was the somewhat-mournful flute introduction to "Strawberry Fields Forever." The Mellotron would be rendered obsolete in a few years by technologically superior devices, but during the late 1960s, Dean would be compelled to adjust his keyboards and amplifier to emulate a Mellotron-generated flute sound when the Candymen performed "Strawberry Fields Forever" themselves.

Another tour going on at the same time in England was the Stax/Volt tour, a revue of Memphis singers and musicians associated with those record labels. The two tours ended at the same time, and the Candymen returned to the States on the same flight as Otis Redding, the Mar-Keys, Carla Thomas, Rufus Thomas, Arthur Conley, Booker T. and the M.G.'s, and Fats Domino and his band, whom Justo and Robert Nix had seen in concert at the Saville Theatre in the West End of London.

Justo recalled Otis and Orbison ("the two big Os") sitting next to each other on the flight, as well as a memorable moment regarding a then-popular song:

"Arthur Conley had a song out at that time called 'Sweet Soul Music.' I don't know if it happens to everyone, but sometimes I get a song in my head and I can't stop singing it. I got on the plane singing 'Do you like James Brown, y'all,' and I heard, 'He's the king of 'em all, y'all' sung back to me by Otis, with a big grin on his face."

Conley and Redding were the cowriters of "Sweet Soul Music."

●●●●●●

The Candymen would finally acquire the rights to use their band's name and would record two albums, an eponymous 1967 release and 1968's *The Candymen Bring You Candy Power*, both produced by Buddy Buie. Not surprisingly, the majority of the songs on both albums were written or cowritten by the producer.

As for the beginnings of his songwriting efforts with Buie, Dean recalled that he would usually work with Nix at the outset.

"Robert and I would piddle around with each other," Ox said, "then we would get with Buddy to get everything together, because Buddy was a good organizer of songs. That was part of his skill. Usually, he would think of lyrics and Robert and I would think about the music and arrangement."

The Candymen's first album included the band's only hit, which was their version of "Georgia Pines." There were also covers of "Stormy Monday Blues" and Don Covay's 1965 hit "See Saw." The second album included a version of "Candy Man."

As for the two tracks recorded by the Candymen at Abbey Road with Graham Nash supervising, "Hope" was never used, but a different version of that song would be recorded for the band's first album. "I'll Never Forget" appeared on the second album ("Graham's voice is very easily identified on the recording," said Rodney).

Robert Nix seemed to have the biggest aspirations to be a rock star, and, for a time, teenage-oriented media nurtured his dreams.

"We looked like, acted like, and believed we were pop stars," Justo explained. "We didn't really have hit records, but there was something about us. A lot of that had to with a wonderful publicist, Dominic Sicilia. He told us, 'I'll do it for free; that's how good I think you guys are.' You couldn't pick up a teen magazine without seeing our picture in it. Robert would actually carry issues with him to show to people—'Here's the new *16* magazine; here's the new *Datebook* magazine.'"

It was the live performance facet, however, for which the Candymen would be remembered by many if not most of their fans. The band was known for astounding reproductions of Beatles and Tom Jones hits, among others, in concert. Their impressive repertoire

1967 publicity photo of the Candymen. Left to right: Dean "Ox" Daughtry, Robert Nix, John Rainey Adkins, Rodney Justo, Bill Gilmore.

would be lauded from throughout the Deep South to clubs in New York City and the surrounding area.

A somewhat similar and innovative concept was being pioneered at the same time by a Long Island, New York, band called the Vanilla Fudge, who reworked popular songs with classical music interpolations played on rock instruments, as 1960s music slowly began to evolve beyond cutesy pop songs.

The Candymen concentrated on note-for-note presentations of original versions of songs in concert, which was no small feat, considering how primitive many electric musical instruments were in the 1960s.

Fans who had seen them backing Roy Orbison already knew the band had chops, but the technique and finesse of the Candymen in covering complex songs such as "A Day in the Life," "What's New, Pussycat?," "I Am the Walrus," and "Strawberry Fields Forever" was mind-blowing, particularly for teenage males who were in "garage bands" themselves.

Some youngsters would arrive at venues early just to watch the band set up, eagerly seeking playing advice from their heroes, and the band members took the time to talk to the kids and offer tips whenever possible.

One fan recalled the in-concert concentration of John Rainey Adkins on guitar, remembering, "He wasn't a flashy player, but every note he played on his guitar was exactly what was needed."

Justo's energetic manipulations of his microphone stand were also impressive, and would-be keyboard players marveled at how Ox Daughtry got such magnificent sounds out of a cheesy Farfisa Combo-Compact organ and a Wurlitzer electric piano.

"[Musician/producer] Emory Gordy once told me that I could play string parts like the record and sing at the same time was because I didn't know any better," said Dean. "I didn't know it was supposed to be impossible."

Daughtry sang "Stone Blues Man" (written by Buddy Buie and John Rainey Adkins) on the band's first album and would also sing lead on "Sgt. Pepper's Lonely Hearts Club Band" and Little Richard's "Long Tall Sally" in concert.

"But almost everybody in the Candymen sang on almost everything," he clarified. "I sang on anything that needed a high voice."

And the band would learn their selected cover songs soon after the original versions had been released. One longtime fan recalled going to a high school dance where the Candymen were booked two weeks after the Beatles had released *Sgt. Pepper's Lonely Hearts Club Band*. The then student heard the title track of the album playing as he entered the gym, thinking the record album was being piped through a public address system, only to discover the Candymen were performing the song live.

"Everybody in the band had very complicated parts," Dean said, "because the Candymen didn't go for simple stuff. We even did 'MacArthur Park,' that Jim Webb song. That one wasn't easy."

As for potential "carbon copy arrangement" criticism, Justo said, "Back then, how else were you *supposed* to do them? As for singing a Tom Jones song or a Beatles song, I don't *sound* like those guys but I *sing* like them. There's a difference.

"And what I did for the vocal parts, John Rainey Adkins did for the music, and he was wonderful at doing it, considering the sound equipment. Same for Dean— what he used to do was nothing short of remarkable. He had to change a setting on his Farfisa, his Wurlitzer, or his Fender Super Reverb (amplifier) on virtually every song, back and forth—he'd make something sound like trumpets or strings. The vocal parts were easier, in a sense, because they followed a certain formula, but you could sometimes add an extra bit of harmony vocals."

"The Candymen were a fantastic band," said Chuck Leavell, whose boyhood musical aspirations in Tuscaloosa, Alabama, during the Sixties ultimately resulted in his becoming the pianist for the Allman Brothers Band in the early Seventies, as well as membership in the Rolling Stones' touring band in later decades. "While Rodney was the lead singer and sounded great, I remember Dean singing 'Long Tall Sally' and a couple of other tunes. He was also an excellent keyboard player, mostly on 'Wurly' back then, but perhaps some organ as well.

"They were a very tight band and were one of my favorites growing up. They would play at the Fort Brandon Armory, where other bands like [Allman Brothers Band precursor] the Allman Joys played. Those of us who were just starting out and were a good bit younger than the bands playing there thought the Candymen and the Allman Joys were the best bands around. Later, when I was 'on the scene,' Dean and I got to talk, and I got to tell him about seeing them 'way back in the day.' He was a sweet guy and seemed quite humble. Ox was certainly an early influence for me."

••••••

The initial 1967 booking of the Candymen at the Scene, a club in New York City owned by music entrepreneur Steve Paul, would be a watershed event in the band's relatively brief history, as it happened prior to the band signing a record deal with ABC. Just before the quintet journeyed to the Big Apple, the Doors, who had a huge national hit with "Light My Fire," had performed at the venue. The up-and-coming Southern band knew the multinight gig didn't pay much, but they also knew how important the opportunity was.

The band opted to open with cover songs when they took the stage at the Scene, cranking off with "Right String, Baby, but the Wrong Yo-Yo," followed by "Good Vibrations." The strategy of bombarding the New York audiences with impeccable note-for-note versions of hit songs worked.

Justo recalled that the first person he met on the sojourn to New York was Al Kooper, erstwhile singer / keyboard player for the Blues Project. That band had split up, and Kooper was in the process of forming a horn band that would be named Blood, Sweat & Tears. He praised the Candymen's performance and advised them that they would quickly find out how "the New York underground" worked, and that within a week, they'd be the number one group in the city.

"When he said 'underground,' I thought he meant something like 'underworld'— gangsters," Justo said. "But he was right. Within four days you couldn't get in the place. By the end of the fifth day, every musician in town was showing up."

While musicians rarely jammed with the band, there were some notable exceptions in New York.

"The Candymen played very strict arrangements, so it didn't really make sense for people to sit in with us," Rodney explained. "However, Steve Paul's the Scene was just a different place, and virtually all of the top musicians in the US and even England would come to see the Candymen when we played there."

Said musicians included a flashy black guitarist named Jimi Hendrix.

"Jimi loved us," said Justo, "and would always come up to the stage and request one of two songs, 'A Day in the Life,' and 'The Sun Ain't Gonna Shine Anymore.' One day he comes up and says, 'Can I sit in with you cats?' Now, Jimi was big! Probably the biggest act in the country at that time. So we just said sure, and we did 'Stormy Monday Blues.'"

"My first impression was 'Damn, he's good,'" Dean remembered. "He was also the coolest dresser for the time; he was wearing a cool hat with a rooster's feather in it."

The only other musicians who sat in with the Candymen were Hendrix's bassist and drummer, Noel Redding and Mitch Mitchell, Who bassist John Entwistle ("the greatest bass player I ever played with," said Dean), and Al Kooper ("We did an old Ray Charles number, 'I've Got News for You,'" Rodney remembered).

The Candymen played the Scene for three bookings, for around ten days each time. They also played a celebrity-oriented nightclub called Arthur twice; that venue had been founded by actor Richard Burton's ex-wife Sybil. Other New York City venues where the Candymen performed included the Electric Circus in the East Village, and the Bitter End. The band also played clubs on Long Island such as the Action House in Island Park, which had nurtured the careers of the Vanilla Fudge, the Young Rascals, the Vagrants (in which future Mountain guitarist Leslie West played), and the Hassles (in which Billy Joel played keyboards).

The fascinating performances by the southern quintet and their impeccable musicianship took the Big Apple and Long Island by storm.

"It was a special time, and we were on top of the world, in many respects," said Rodney.

● ● ● ● ● ●

Following the breakout of "Georgia Pines" from the first album, the Candymen would also appear on television, performing on Dick Clark's *American Bandstand* as well as regional shows such as Cleveland's *Upbeat*, which was syndicated to other markets.

The Candymen perform at Jefferson Davis High School in Montgomery, Alabama, in the fall of 1968. The visible musicians are, left to right, Robert Nix, Dean Daughtry, John Rainey Adkins, and Rodney Justo. The neck of Bill Gilmore's bass is seen just above Adkins's guitar neck. *The Cavalier*

Several songs for a proposed third album were recorded in Atlanta in the summer of 1969, but such a record didn't happen.

No "formal" live recordings of the Candymen are known to exist, which means that their amazing prowess in concert was never officially documented. For decades afterward, however, many professional musicians as well as music fans would assert that the Candymen were the best and most professional band they'd ever seen and heard.

The Candymen might be portrayed in the pantheon of popular music as a stereotypical One-Hit Wonder, cited for their version of "Georgia Pines," but Justo is even more analytical (and assertive):

"When you really get down to it, it was almost like we were *No*-Hit Wonders! But I don't mind telling anybody there was no band in America better than us."

••••••

"It wasn't an orphanage," James Barney "J. R." Cobb said of the Florida Baptist Children's Home, where he spent several years of his childhood.

Born in Birmingham, Alabama, J. R. was the oldest of seven brothers and sisters and was seven years old when the next sibling was born. His parents moved to Jacksonville when J. R. was a baby; his father had recently been discharged from the military, and several of his relatives who were truck drivers lived in that town. J. R.'s father chose the same occupation and was on the road a lot. Such a job made the marriage shaky, and after more than one separation and reconciliation, the Cobbs divorced.

"I was fourteen when the last child, my only brother, was born—there were five girls in between," J. R. recalled. "I was in the Baptist Home at the time. Most of the children there were from broken homes, where a parent was not able to take care of them. Through the church, they could get into the Baptist Home. We had a couple of hundred of kids, max. Two of my sisters eventually went there, as well."

The layout of the Baptist Children's Home campus had separate housing for boys and girls, with a dining hall in between. Cobb adapted to what he termed as the "reasonable" discipline of the quasi-military lifestyle for children at the facility.

"I respected it and appreciated it a lot more after I got out," he said. "It came along when I really needed it. I could easily have gone the other way. I got out when I was almost sixteen; I went to work and moved back home to support my mother, because she was there with all of those kids."

••••••

As for music, J. R. recalled, "No one in my family was particularly musical, but the radio was on all the time when I was a child, and I was exposed to lots of different kinds of music."

He first became interested in guitar due to an uncle.

"He played some when he was in the navy, but he was not a professional musician," said J. R. "He gave me my first 'beater' guitar and showed me a couple of chords. I'd play it for a while, then stick it in the closet and not touch it for three or four months. That went on until I was in high school."

J. R. began playing after school with friends, and his first electric setup was a Sears Silvertone guitar and amplifier. He later upgraded to a Fender Jazzmaster guitar and a borrowed Fender amp.

"I was influenced by the Ventures, Duane Eddy, Chet Atkins, Buddy Holly, and just about anybody I heard on the radio," Cobb recalled. "Later on, I got in a band with a couple of high school friends called the Emeralds. We played mostly instrumentals at what were called 'sock hops,' supermarket openings, and 'cocktail lounges' or 'nightclubs,' which, in Jacksonville at the time, were just fancy names for bars with a little stage and a dance floor."

He recalled interpolating British music after what he termed a "sea change" happened when the Beatles appeared on *The Ed Sullivan Show* in February 1964.

"We dropped most of the instrumentals," J. R. said, "and started to discover R&B and traditional blues. Nobody played much country music, and 'standards' weren't cool anymore."

The Emeralds didn't last long, but the brief association included an encounter with a famous personality from early spaceflight history.

"I met [Mercury astronaut] Gus Grissom at the Satellite Lounge in Cocoa Beach," he recalled. "Nice guy."

J. R. had a day job with the Florida Steel Company as an apprentice welder but ultimately left that trade to become a full-time musician.

"I think I realized that my chances for advancement as a welder—if I ever became one—were pretty slim," he said, "and I thought I could probably make at least as much money as I was making if I was playing in a band . . . any band, really."

One of the biggest bands in Jacksonville was called the Classics, and J. R. saw and heard them at the Golden Gate Lounge and other clubs. Their lead vocalist was Dennis Yost, who also played drums standing up.

"Their guitar player either got drafted or quit," Cobb remembered, "and they asked me if I'd like to work with them. I had worked forty hours a week for Florida Steel, making $47.50 a week, if I remember correctly. The Classics said they'd pay me $80 for five nights a week at the Golden Gate. That was like stealing, so it was a no-brainer to me."

The lineup of the Classics included two saxophones, a trumpet, an organ, a bass, drums, and a guitar. The band's repertoire included a lot of Four Seasons songs.

After Cobb had been in the Classics for about a year, the band made a decision to go on the road. Traveling expenses figured into the move, and the horn section was culled, leaving Cobb, Yost, bassist Wally Eaton, and keyboard player Joe Wilson. They would soon change their name to the Classics IV to refer to the number of members in the band. The band began playing lounges and dance clubs along Florida's Atlantic Coast and eventually began playing venues on the Gulf Coast side as well.

J. R. met Buddy Buie for the first time in Jacksonville. Buie was getting his venture with Paul Cochran underway, and while Buddy would give credit to Cochran for discovering the Classics IV, he began frequenting numerous clubs in the Sunshine State himself. The pudgy motormouth impressed Cobb pretty much in the same way he impressed Rodney Justo.

"Buddy had the gift of the gab and was a top-notch salesman," Cobb recalled with a chuckle. "He'd come into clubs, always wearing a sports jacket, and most of the musicians knew who he was. He'd find somebody singing or playing that he liked, and he'd tell them he wanted to cut a demo with them, or that he wanted to write a song for them. He said that to Dennis Yost in Jacksonville."

J. R. and Joe Wilson were roommates when the band traveled, and they began discussing songwriting.

"The whole idea of writing songs just really appealed to me," Cobb said of his rapid evolution as a songwriter. "I'm sure the Beatles and artists like Roy Orbison, the Beach Boys, and some of the other singer-songwriters coming along then sort of fueled that; I had listened to Roy Orbison on the radio before I ever played a lick. While most of the Classics IV hits were 'mellow' or 'ballad-ish'-type tunes, that isn't necessarily my preferred writing style."

Buie heard about the two musicians' songwriting aspirations and talked with them about that facet of music when the Classics IV were performing at a club in Clearwater. Buddy showed up again at a later performance at the Daytona Plaza Hotel in Daytona Beach, this time with some associates of the Bill Lowery music empire in Atlanta. He invited the band to record in the Peach State capital.

This publicity photo was printed during the brief time frame when the Classics had trimmed its lineup down to a quartet, but before "IV" had been added to the band's name. Left to right: Dennis Yost, Wally Eaton, J. R. Cobb, Joe Wilson.

Management:
Paul Cochran
Allan Diggs

THE CLASSICS

For Bookings Contact:
NATIONAL ARTISTS ATTRACTIONS
OF GEORGIA, INC.
3379 Peachtree Rd, N.E.
Suite 234
Atlanta, Georgia 30326

CHAPTER 3
Atlanta Rising

During the 1960s, Atlanta, Georgia, was an obvious focal point of the original Civil Rights Movement. In spite of the presence of Civil War memorial sites such as Stone Mountain and the Cyclorama, the largest city in the "Old South" was lurching through an inevitable sociological transformation from segregation to integration in a very public manner, as white elected officials waged a defiant and doomed campaign against race mixing.

That decade saw Martin Luther King Jr. serving as copastor of Ebenezer Baptist Church on Auburn Ave. (alongside his father), with the younger King diligently involved in ongoing activism.

In 1964, King was awarded the Nobel Peace Prize. That same annum, Atlanta restaurateur Lester Maddox became nationally notorious due to his refusal to serve black customers at his Pickrick Restaurant, brandishing an axe handle to intimidate would-be diners. He would be elected Georgia's governor in 1967.

Atlanta continued its sluggish stumble toward integration as it simultaneously evolved into a modern-day metropolis. Its airport would become the busiest in the world.

Other restaurants such as Pitty Pat's Porch (named for a character in the iconic movie *Gone with the Wind*) flourished. The popular Varsity restaurant, which had been established in 1928, was proclaimed to be the world's largest drive-in and was noted for its greasy onion rings and vociferous employees.

The Milwaukee Braves, a major-league baseball team, moved to Atlanta in 1966, and the city welcomed a new National Football League expansion team, the Falcons, in the same year.

When the hippie movement blossomed across the country in the latter half of the decade, most of the head shops and psychedelic clothing boutiques in Atlanta were found in the 10th and 14th Street / Piedmont Park area downtown. The portion of Peachtree Street between 10th and 14th became known as "the Strip." Free performances featuring area bands would often be staged in Piedmont Park.

Outdoor concerts by touring rock bands would be held at locations such as the Chastain Park Amphitheatre, which resembled a downsized Hollywood Bowl. Downtown's Municipal Auditorium also hosted rock concerts as well as Friday-night professional wrestling matches. In 1970, that building would be the site of boxer Muhammad Ali's first fight following a ban of over three years for declining to be drafted into the US military.

And during those times of racial tension and unprecedented growth, Bill Lowery presided over the local music scene.

Bill Lowery early in his career in the 1950s.

Lowery, originally from Louisiana, moved to Atlanta in the mid-twentieth century. He became the manager of a new radio station, WQXI, and rapidly carved out a place in the local entertainment field as a nationally-known disc jockey and Atlanta television show host.

Bill's son Butch noted that his father was also "a mentor to songwriters," recalling how the elder Lowery had dominated electronic media in Atlanta.

"Dad was an early cancer survivor," Butch recounted, "and he was determined to provide for his family. He used to have Ray Stevens and Jerry Reed as regulars on his radio show and got along with them so great that he got into music publishing. In 1956, his first hit was 'Be Bop a Lula' by Gene Vincent, and in 1957, there was Sonny James's 'Young Love.'"

Lowery later branched out into music recording, a booking agency, and artist representation and promotion. He was successful in those facets as well. He also founded radio stations and a television station. Butch noted, however, that his father relinquished the booking agency due to some potential conflicts of interest with artists who were signed up with other facets of the Lowery empire.

If Atlanta beckoned to the Deep South in toto, Lowery's Master Sound Recording Studios was a mecca for Southern musicians. The facility was located inside an old schoolhouse (along with other divisions of the Lowery enterprise) in the northern section of the city.

"Officially, Master Sound was owned by Bob Richardson and was separate, businesswise, from Lowery," said veteran producer and musician Emory Gordy Jr. "They had some kind of deal going, and most all of the Lowery stuff was done at Master Sound."

"Bill Lowery was *the* music mogul of Atlanta," said J. R. Cobb, "and we'd been hearing that for a long time, before we'd even moved there. A lot of people had gotten their start with him—Tommy Roe, Jerry Reed, Mac Davis, Ray Stevens, and others. Bill was the guy to know in Atlanta at the time.

"You might call him a 'developer'; he was an old-school publisher. He was also a songwriter himself, so we'd take songs to him and would let him critique them. He'd say things like 'You've got a good idea here,' 'I think it would be better here or there,' or 'Go back and try it again.' He did that with Joe South, Buddy [Buie], me, and a lot of others."

Butch Lowery also noted his father's influence on Buie, who was usually fixated on writing hit songs that lasted around three minutes.

"Buddy wrote with a lot of other folks, or sometimes by himself," said Lowery. "Back in the day, short songs were what were in demand as hits. [Buddy] knew that was his forte, and I think he got a lot of his direction from Dad."

* * * * * *

Another renowned recording facility in Atlanta was LeFevre Sound Studios, located on the west side of town and owned by Meurice LeFevre of the fabled gospel music family. His brother, singer / guitarist / future prodigal son Mylon LeFevre, would ultimately interact, musically and otherwise, with other local musicians.

"We were making mono[phonic] records, even before stereo," Mylon recalled. At age seventeen, Mylon wrote his first song, a gospel hit called "Without Him," which would eventually be recorded by Elvis Presley and numerous other singers.

* * * * * *

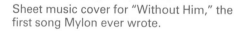

Sheet music cover for "Without Him," the first song Mylon ever wrote.

Barry Bailey recalled that he had "a pretty typical middle-class—not upper-class—home life" in the Atlanta suburb of Decatur. His father had a large big-band record collection and later supplemented his assemblage with an assortment of Dixieland jazz albums.

Those two genres were early influences on Barry as a youngster, as was a trip to the Lenox Square shopping center to check out a primeval "battle of the bands" contest circa 1958. Family outings to view *Rock around the Clock* at a local movie theater as well as attending a concert by surf music singers Jan and Dean were also memorable and influential events in his childhood.

"I was always exposed to music," he remembered. "Both of my parents were musically inclined."

He received his first guitar for his twelfth birthday in 1960. The budget instrument was a Sears Silvertone archtop model, made in Chicago by the Kay company.

Barry soon began playing in teenage garage bands, including the Imperials, the Mystics (no relation to Rodney Justo's band in Tampa; Bailey played bass in the Decatur band), the Vons, and others. They would play teen sock hops, purveying cover songs of numerous hits, as was the case with countless teenage bands in communities all across the country.

While playing with the Vons, he met the love of his life, Dawn Vanderlip, when his band played at her high school in 1965.

"She was always my biggest fan," Barry remembered.

••••••

In 1965, Spencer Kirkpatrick was a fifteen-year-old lead guitarist in a band called the Atlanta Vibrations. That combo was the opening act for a concert by the Beatles on August 18 of that year at Atlanta Stadium (three days after the Fab Four's legendary Shea Stadium concert in New York). The Atlanta Vibrations had won a local battle-of-the-bands contest to garner the leadoff slot.

And Spencer was a fan of Barry's playing as far back as the Vons era. "I heard them warming up for a dance after a football game at Decatur High School—Barry's own school—and it was like listening to a verbatim version of what the Beatles did. Even then, he already had wonderful finesse and touch."

Kirkpatrick recalled that another influence on his own playing was John Rainey Adkins of the Candymen, "in the same way that Barry was. Both of them really had style. The Candymen played Atlanta a lot, at places like Jefferson Park out in East Point, the College Park Auditorium, the regular circuit."

Spencer would continue to consider Barry to be a musical role model and would later become the lead guitarist for Hydra, one of the South's earliest hard-rock bands. That aggregation formed in 1969.

••••••

From the outset, Barry's interest in guitar involved intense concentration on his playing; he would focus on making the music work, eschewing any onstage antics or showboating. That said, he would soon end up in a musical aggregation whose lead singer was a dynamo—at least, visually.

Wayne Logiudice and the Kommotions were fronted by a manic white soul singer who, to some listeners, was vocally challenged. However, Logiudice made up for any singing deficiencies with a no-holds-barred stage show.

Wayne Logiudice

"He couldn't sing a lick," one Atlanta music fan said of Logiudice, "but he had every single James Brown move down perfect. It was amazing to watch him perform."

The Kommotions had formed in 1964, and its original membership included Emory Gordy Jr., with whom Barry would forge a lifelong friendship based on musical professionalism.

Gordy was originally from Smyrna, Georgia, and had been somewhat of a child prodigy on several musical instruments. He was an alumnus of Middle Georgia College, and, soon after graduating, he became the primary bassist at Bill Lowery's Master Sound Recording Studios. He recalled that his first session was on bass in the summer of 1964, having been invited to the session by producer/singer/songwriter Joe South.

"I guess I became 'house bassist' by default," Emory said. "I owned a bass guitar and amp, and I would show up on time and play in a professional manner."

In addition to accompanying singers and other musicians, Gordy also played on commercials and jingles, summing up his earlier musical career by noting that "commercials, added to phono recordings and live gigs, kept the wolf away from the door."

"Emory was the main 'conduit' for me to meet other musicians, black and white," Barry recalled.

Gordy recounted that while the Kommotions went through various incarnations, the most stable and successful lineup of the band consisted of Ricky Bear on drums, John Ivey on bass, Harry Hagan on trombone, Ray Jarrell on tenor sax (later replaced by Al Sheppard) and Gordy on guitar.

"Somewhere along the way, we picked up a local white 'James Brown–type' singer and performer named Wayne Logiudice," said Gordy. "Wayne was a real showman; did all the microphone tricks, splits, the whole package. The band became very popular and soon became known as Wayne Logiudice and the Kommotions."

Perhaps not surprisingly, the Kommotions would eventually evolve into an integrated band. The overlying civil rights issues of the Sixties didn't necessarily apply to musicians in the area, although there were separate union chapters of the American Federation of Musicians for whites and blacks. Sunday afternoon jam sessions involving white and black musicians were held at an American Legion hall on Auburn Ave. in Atlanta.

"In the early to mid-1960s, segregation of the races was in hostile decline," Emory remembered. "This also applied to music. I didn't realize it at the time, but the Kommotions were breaking color barriers. We were probably the first integrated band in the Atlanta area."

Auburn Ave. was/is an important thoroughfare regarding Atlanta's civil rights history. Ebenezer Baptist Church was one block in one direction from the American Legion hall where the integrated Sunday afternoon jam sessions were held, and the Royal Peacock, a historic black(-owned) nightclub, was one block in the other direction. Gordy recalled that the area was nicknamed "Sweet Auburn," and vividly remembered how he and Barry Bailey first met:

"We were the house band for the Auburn Ave. American Legion Sunday afternoon jam sessions. Many local artists, along with artists and musicians that were booked into the Royal Peacock just up the street, would drop into the Legion. It was the only place in the area that could serve alcohol on Sunday, and 'entertainers' got in free; no cover charge.

"So there were a lot of famous artists and musicians that would be in the audience, like the Isley Brothers—with a young guitar player named 'Jimmy' Hendrix—Fontella Bass, Arthur Conley, and many others.

"One time we had a gig that conflicted with our regular Sunday afternoon American Legion gig. The manager of the Legion club told us if we could find a suitable stand-in, he'd let us off.

"Several bands 'auditioned.' Ricky [Bear] and I were sitting in the back of the club when a group from Decatur High School started playing. They weren't very good—I'm being kind—but when the lead guitarist took a solo, my head went through the roof. It was Barry Bailey. He stuck out like a sore thumb; it was obvious that this guy was great!

"As they were packing up their equipment, I approached Barry, introduced myself, and immediately asked him if he would give me some lessons. Barry was probably sixteen, and by then I was an experienced musician, about twenty-one or twenty-two years old. This caught Barry off guard, but with a slightly embarrassed grin on his face, he said 'Okay.' The next week I drove out to his house in Decatur and picked his brain. It was an eye-opening experience. I consider Barry one of my mentors. The encounter would mark my drift from lead guitar to bass.

"I invited Barry to the next Kommotions rehearsal. It was a no-brainer. When John Ivey had left the group, I had switched to bass, so Barry was hired on electric guitar. But when Wayne performed, I switched to guitar and Barry would play bass. This was because Wayne had a lot of R&B stops and starts in the songs; one song would run head-on into another, etc. It was a 'show' that required a conductor, which was me. So, Barry played electric guitar on three or four instrumentals until Wayne came on."

Bailey: "I met the cream of the crop of local musicians—again, black and white. The Kommotions were my first 'real band'; they were professionals. We played many black venues and a lot of white teen places."

As for the segregated union chapters, Bailey remembered how that barrier came down:

"The white local was #148, and the black local was #462. The combined integrated local became #148-462, not too long after I joined the black local. Three 'associates' from the Kommotions, Emory Gordy, Rick Bear, and John Ivey, were the first white cats to join the black local but had been denied membership at first try, because they were white.

"Eventually, the board did approve them, largely because they were playing many black venues, as I did later on. And the union, of course, wanted to collect work dues. The attraction to the black local—besides that it was considered a little more hip—was that the initiation dues were significantly lower. At the time, I was playing as many black venues as I was white [venues]—maybe more. There were some occasions when I was not just the only white cat in the band sitting in, I was the only white cat in the building. The locals finally merged, with no fanfare or consequences that I was aware of. There was a brief announcement of the merger in the *Podium*, the union periodical, and that was it."

Barry graduated from Decatur High School in 1966. The ongoing musical association and friendship of Bailey and Gordy would result in their playing in another band in the near future, as well as projects as far away as California.

Emory would join another local up-and-coming outfit, St. John and the Cardinals, which featured drummer/vocalist Dennis St. John. Their lead guitarist was a pudgy, bespectacled native of Rome, a city in northwestern Georgia.

••••••

Paul Goddard didn't look like a musician—particularly a rock-and-roll guitarist—and would have been the first to acknowledge such. Perhaps not unexpectedly, he also had an eccentric personality that seemed to validate his non-stereotypical rock musician appearance.

"He was gonna wear his Hush Puppies, his double-knit pants, and his two-pocket shirts, and the hell with what anybody else thought," said J. R. Cobb.

"He may have even had a pocket protector at one point, but that would have gotten in the way of his cigarettes," added Goddard's sister, Nan Jacobs, who was four years younger. "He said 'I want to be considered a rock musician by the way I play; I don't want to have to wear a fancy shirt, and I want to be comfortable.' In today's terms, he would be considered a nerd, but he just was not about 'image'; he would get angry that music was becoming more about 'what you looked like' instead of 'how you could play.'"

A pocket protector (in which a slide rule and pens were usually carried) was a stereotypical item associated with scientists and electrical engineers—and Paul had indeed been the recipient of a scholarship to Georgia Tech University to study electrical engineering. He'd demonstrated an orientation toward such a career field when he was a child in Rome.

"He tinkered with anything that had a cord," his sister recalled, "and I've been told he started doing that when he was around three; he was very inquisitive."

However, Paul didn't create science projects or join science-oriented clubs in high school. He did electrical experiments strictly for his own benefit and knowledge.

"He was his own person," said Jacobs. "He did not participate in any [school] activities if he didn't have to. He was a recluse, but it had to do with the fact that he couldn't see, and our mother always tried to protect him because of his sight problems."

Paul had been diagnosed with glaucoma and cataracts at a very young age and had been in the hospital due to eye surgery when his sister was born. He had multiple surgeries as a child; Jacobs noted that standard surgical anesthesia in those times was ether, "which really messed up his mind in the hospital; he'd have horrible dreams."

He became totally blind in one eye and would have been considered legally blind in the other, had he ever been formally tested. His glasses were so thick that he could start fires on dry leaves by focusing the sun's rays through the lenses.

But Paul loved music.

"Our father listened to classical music," Jacobs recalled, "so there was always music in the house. [Paul's] interest was extremely broad—Wes Montgomery, classical, jazz, probably anything but country, as long as it was musically good. He was a 'sponge,' but he never learned to read music."

Paul's mother tried to make him take clarinet lessons, but he resisted, asserting that he could play music—albeit on another instrument—better than his instructor.

36

His first instrument was a ukulele that an uncle bought for him. He taught himself to play piano better than his sister, who would become a music major in college.

Not surprisingly, Goddard also became an audiophile and would purchase high-end, state-of-the-art gear, creating sophisticated audio systems for his own enjoyment for most of his life.

"He had a wall of equipment," Nan said succinctly. "He loved the full spectrum of sound."

When he was in high school, Paul played lead guitar in a four-piece instrumental band that didn't have a drummer. He graduated from East Rome High School in 1963 and had been named "Most Talented" in the Senior Who's Who.

He began his studies at Georgia Tech but didn't enjoy his higher education, due to his shyness and having to attend huge classes in auditoriums ("If he was sitting in the back, he couldn't see," said Jacobs). He lasted for three years and made good grades, but never graduated.

While there, one of the players who'd been in Paul's band in Rome asked him to play with him in a band at some fraternity parties. Goddard developed his abilities and eventually became the lead guitar player for St. John and the Cardinals. He played on the band's single, "Rampage," which garnered some interest among local fans.

"The first time I met Paul was when he was playing guitar for St. John and the Cardinals," Spencer Kirkpatrick recalled. "I was in the Atlanta Vibrations, and we were opening for them at a club in Marietta called Big Hugh Baby's Loft, which was owned by Hugh Jarrett of the Jordanaires. St. John and the Cardinals were backing a local black artist called the Mighty Hannibal, who had a regional hit called 'Jerkin' the Dog.' Hugh told me the Cardinals didn't have an extra guitarist that night; would I mind playing rhythm with Paul? I told him I'd be happy to, and Paul was a great player."

In 1967, a lot of musical chairs were being shifted around for Barry Bailey. He performed in a trio called Mixed Emotions for the first part of that year and, in a redundant move, followed Emory Gordy Jr. to St. John and the Cardinals in late summer.

Emory recalled that he and Bailey would alternate on guitar and bass, just as they had done when they were in Wayne Logiudice and the Kommotions. Gordy would play other instruments as well.

"Barry and I switched off between bass and guitar," Gordy detailed, "but that guitar would have been subservient to Paul's lead guitar. Switching from one instrument

Earlier incarnation of St. John and the Cardinals. Front: Paul Goddard; back, left to right: Harry Hagan, George Hurst, Dennis St. John, Emory Gordy Jr.

to another was very organic. From song to song, we just played what was comfortable. If there were keyboards there, I would shift over to that, and Barry would play bass. I only played keyboards if they were available; I didn't own any keyboard instruments. I also played trumpet. The entire time that Paul Goddard was with Dennis St. John—and when I was present—Paul played lead guitar."

●●●●●●

At the same time, Bailey, Goddard, Gordy, and other musicians were also involved in another mutual experience as "members" of Jack Martin and the Martiniques, a "for-hire" aggregation of pro musicians that had different lineups for different gigs.

Musician and promoter Jack Martin was a veteran of the Atlanta music scene, having been active since the late 1950s. By the early 1960s, he was working with Bill Lowery's organization in the booking section and later went out on his own. Martin usually played bass, and his band, the Martiniques, could vary in size from a trio backing up a singer to an orchestra with numerous horns.

"Jack booked many 'casuals' [temporary employees]," Gordy recalled. "As such, they were often a thrown-together group of musicians and vocalists, and it was always evolving—whoever was available would be booked for one-nighters."

Among the Martiniques' many assignments were backing gigs for singers on caravan tours. One example of "repeat performances" for the band was a trio of family-owned radio stations—WAPE in Jacksonville, WBAM in Montgomery, and WVOK in Birmingham—that utilized the Martiniques to support singers on more than one tour that had stops in those cities.

The Martiniques backed up Lou Christie, Billy Joe Royal, Joe South, Bobby Sherman, Evie Sands, and others. According to Martin, Christie's favorite backing lineup included Barry, Paul, and drummer Mike Nepote.

"They were the ones that were his first choice," Martin recalled. "He insisted that I try to line them up for him whenever he came to this area."

The Martiniques backstage with one of the popular singers they backed. Left to right: Mike Nepote, Paul Goddard, Barry Bailey, Jack Martin, Lou Christie.

By its very definition, "backing musician" implies that such a player should remain in the background and out of the spotlight, to keep the attention on the singer they were supporting. Martin also appreciated the fact that neither Bailey nor Goddard would show off or perform any kind of self-styled choreography themselves.

"You'd never see Barry or Paul doing any steps together," he said. "They just stood in the back and played their asses off. They did exactly what I asked them to do; they were two peas in a pod."

••••••

Barry's first studio session that produced a hit record happened at Columbia Recording Studios in Nashville on July 12, 1967. The song was Billy Joe Royal's "Hush," written by Joe South.

He recalled that he met the Candymen for the first time in Atlanta two days later, following a Martiniques gig.

"[It was] July 14, 1967, at the Shindig Club in Atlanta, across from Fox Theatre," he remembered. "The Martiniques were backing Rufus and Carla [Thomas].

"I remember that both Thomases were extremely professional and disciplined and were both very well received. In talking to Carla, who appeared to be brilliant, I learned that she was working on her master's degree. After the show, I met some of the Candymen—I'm pretty sure that it was Dean, John Rainey (Adkins), Bill Gilmore, and maybe a roadie—at the infamous Clermont Motor Hotel on Ponce de Leon, where we talked music and got high . . . my pot, of course. John Rainey was excited about a song demo that he possessed, and he played for us. It was Mel Tillis's 'Ruby, Don't Take Your Love to Town,' sung by Bobby Goldsboro; the first time I had heard the song. Obviously, this was before the Kenny Rogers rendition."

The Clermont also housed a legendary lounge / strip joint that vexed Atlanta authorities for decades.

Barry also attended other Candymen performances in the Atlanta area.

••••••

The same year saw Barry jetting out to California to play on an album by Jim "Harpo" Valley, who had been a guitarist with Paul Revere & the Raiders.

"I was hired via Jack and the Martiniques to back up Jim in this area," he recounted. "I'd met Jim when the Raiders had played at some of the caravan shows where we'd backed up singers. He had left the Raiders and was pursuing a solo career. He seemed to appreciate my playing to the point that he invited me to play on his upcoming album recording session.

"He flew me to L.A., where I stayed at his home and recorded with him from December 11 through December 21. Some of L.A.'s best had been hired for the session. He showed me some parts but mostly left me alone to 'do my thing,' for lack of a better phrase."

Barry described his first trip to Los Angeles as "a good bit of culture shock to say the least. David Crosby took it upon himself to be my escort and chauffeur. The first act that I saw live in L.A. was the Nitty Gritty Dirt Band at the Troubadour."

The album by Valley was never released.

"I've no idea why there was no release, and we parted on very good terms," Barry said.

。。。。。。

Barry had begun studies at Dekalb College, a two-year institution.

"I majored in music and was assigned violin, although I had requested upright bass, also known as double bass," he recounted. "But then Roy Orbison called with an offer to go on the road, which was pretty specific, so pursuit of higher education came to a screeching halt. I think I was about to flunk out, anyway."

。。。。。。

Bailey recalled that his first performances with St. John and the Cardinals were in Alabama, backing Orbison, soon followed by recording sessions. Barry appreciatively recounted his experiences with the legendary singer:

"My first shows with Roy—and as part of St. John and the Cardinals—were at the Crazy Horse, a club in Birmingham, in September of 1967. There were some more isolated dates, then May 1 through May 10, 1968, we recorded in Nashville at RCA, first with Roy producing [Atlanta-based singer] Grover Mitchell, then Roy producing Roy, although Wesley Rose and Jim Vienneau are credited.

"Grover's cuts were 'Turned On' and 'Blue over You.' He was among the top two or three vocalists that I worked with through all of my career . . . maybe the best. With Roy, we cut 'Walk On' and 'Heartache.' The last and only extended tour I did with Roy was a series of Canadian dates, February 5 through February 20, in 1969."

One of the "perks" of the Canadian tour for Barry and Paul was the use of powerful British-made Marshall amplifiers, which were fairly new to North America.

"Roy provided two stacks [amplifier head and two speaker cabinets] for Paul and me," Barry detailed. "Part of the 'negotiated' compensation for the tour was that we were to keep one of the stacks each for our personal use. Ironically, I had been using another of Roy's old Marshalls that I received indirectly from John Rainey [Adkins], who had used it at some point in time with the Candymen. It was a 2 x 12 Combo that I used with the Cardinals, Joint Effort, Mixed Emotions, and various other . . . well, combos, including the Martiniques."

As for getting acclimated to his new Marshall stack provided by Orbison, Bailey recalled with a chuckle, "It was mostly a matter of turning the volume control in a clockwise direction. I did learn right away to use the bass channel, since I used the back or 'bridge' pickup on my guitar most of the time. I also learned to position myself to either take advantage of, or avoid, feedback."

。。。。。。

Kitten's Korner was a plush-if-homegrown nightclub located at 842 Peachtree St. in downtown Atlanta. A first impression might have been that it had been modeled after the then-popular Playboy Clubs, but Kitten's Korner didn't require a membership for admittance.

The establishment touted, "35 Beautiful Kittens to entertain and serve you—They Dance—They Sing—They Purr." The Kittens dressed in skimpy tiger-striped outfits and wore cat's-ear headgear. Jack Martin described it as "Atlanta's first disco, with girls dancing in cages."

"Kitten's Korner was not a 'strip joint,'" Emory Gordy Jr. detailed. "I know; [because] I played strip joints in Atlanta. The Korner was not one of them. Strip clubs have very few female patrons; almost totally male. The Korner had gender-mixed clientele. It was almost impossible to get into the place on Friday or Saturday nights. The line to get in stretched down Peachtree for 20 or 30 yards on those nights. The management would turn up the heat and would ask us to play louder, to get a turnover. As I recall, there was a drink minimum, and a cover charge."

While Playboy Clubs were often perceived as featuring jazz combos for live entertainment, "Kitten's Korner was very rock and roll," Emory emphasized. "We'd do a 'cocktail set' from 8 to 9 p.m.—soft ballad stuff with a 'cool jazz' leaning—then go full-rock starting at 9 p.m. and going to 2 a.m."

St. John and the Cardinals often backed up recording artists such as Jerry Butler, the Mighty Hannibal, and others at Kitten's Korner. Other bands that performed at the club included the Roemans from Tampa, the James Gang from Dothan, and the Bushmen from Douglas, Georgia.

Barry recalled that in the latter days of the Cardinals, he concentrated on lead guitar and Paul began playing bass. As for the instrument switch between Paul and himself, Bailey remembered, "It was somewhat of a 'foregone conclusion,' after I had sat in with the Cardinals a few times.

"Maybe it became official when Roy [Orbison] suggested that Paul and I switch, starting on that Canadian tour in early '69. And for the record, there was never any argument or resistance from Paul. He transitioned to bass guitar willingly—actually, enthusiastically—and in a timely fashion. And I think that's when I sold him my [Fender] P-Bass."

Not long after the Orbison tour, Dennis St. John left for California to seek his musical fortune. Jack Martin recalled that St. John returned to Atlanta briefly before making a permanent move to the Left Coast, and that the drummer's last job in Atlanta was with the Martiniques, backing up Billy Preston at Kitten's Korner.

The Atlanta combo in which St. John had played became known simply as the Cardinals, but Emory Gordy Jr. would soon head for California as well, bringing about the demise of that band.

St. John and Gordy ended up playing with Neil Diamond, and Gordy would also become a member of Elvis Presley's TCB Band, as well as a founding member of Emmylou Harris's Hot Band. He later toured with John Denver's band before moving to Nashville and becoming a legendary session player and producer.

••••••

While he had many musical influences, the three major inspirations for Barry were Chet Atkins, Ray Charles, and Jimmy Reed, and around the time Dennis St. John headed to the Golden State, Barry was involved in a one-on-one jam session with Reed at what was supposed to have been a preliminary meeting regarding the possibility of Bailey working with the legendary blues guitarist.

"It would have been during the first half of the year," Barry recalled, "before I started working regularly with or for Buddy Buie. Buddy would have loved some of that action, but I don't remember even discussing the event with him.

"I got a call from someone who was involved with trying to do some sort of Jimmy Reed 'comeback' album. I was invited to meet this person and Jimmy at the notorious Imperial Hotel in Atlanta to jam and discuss participating in whatever this project was. I was a huge Jimmy Reed fan, so this was an invitation that required absolutely no deliberation.

"At about three in the afternoon, I met them both in Jimmy's room, which happened to adjoin John Lee Hooker's. They were doing a double bill at a club in town. After introductions, we just sat around jamming and talking with Jimmy. Needless to say, I was having a ball—as was Jimmy, apparently. While we were jamming, Jimmy got excited to the point that he wanted to get John Lee Hooker up to join in. John Lee passed, as he had been asleep and wanted to continue in repose.

"This went on for at least a couple of hours, when at about five-thirty or so, Jimmy pulled back and announced, 'Well, I've got to go out and get me some medicine.' So after thanking me for coming and bidding me farewell—just for now, I was thinking—Jimmy took off, somewhat hurriedly. There was a little more discussion with the other guy about meeting again, but I never heard anything back, one way or the other. To my knowledge, there was never an attempt at a Jimmy Reed comeback album, and I heard nothing more from or about him until his untimely death, so that experience with him in person turned out to be somewhat surreal."

Bailey came away from the meeting with autographs by Reed and Hooker on a used record album.

●●●●●●

Even as they played onstage together in the Cardinals and the Martiniques, Barry and Paul were seeking other musical options, and they began gigging in a band known as Joint Effort with sax player Charlie DeChant and fellow Martiniques veteran Mike Nepote on drums. That combo jelled even more in the latter half of 1969, following the demise of the Cardinals. Joint Effort concentrated on instrumental jazz / rock music and played what Barry called "freebies" in Piedmont Park, as well as coffee houses/clubs such as the Bottom of the Barrel on Baltimore Place. Positive press about that offshoot band was published in the *Great Speckled Bird*, Atlanta's so-called "underground" newspaper.

It was no surprise when both Barry and Paul began working their way into the local studio scene, usually recording at the Master Sound facility or the LeFevre studio. They also made decent money recording jingles and commercials at smaller studios.

"Some of it was pretty silly, but some of it was pretty challenging, too, because I didn't read [music]," Bailey said. "But fortunately, I could sit down and figure most of it out 'by ear,' anyway."

Clients included the Coca-Cola company, and local automobile dealerships such as D. L. Claborn Buick ("I played sitar on that one," Barry recalled).

"Barry was the go-to guy in town for that kind of stuff," Spencer Kirkpatrick said of the jingle facet of the Atlanta recording scene. "When I was just starting out, he was the 'gold standard'—Barry was everything you wanted to be as a guitar player."

Following one session for the South Central Bell telephone company, Barry was tapped for his first—and only—modeling job, posing on the cover of the Summer 1969 issue of that company's publicity magazine.

central
THE MAGAZINE OF SOUTH CENTRAL BELL   SUMMER 1969

For the
times
they are
a-changin'
STORY ON PAGE 1

CHAPTER 4
Convergence

Slowly but surely, the future members of the Atlanta Rhythm Section began to cross paths with each other in the late 1960s, and one such encounter happened on the other side of the country.

The Classics IV and the Candymen (who were backing up Roy Orbison) found themselves hanging out with each other in Los Angeles, when both bands performed around the same time at the legendary Whisky a Go Go club.

"Dennis (Yost) was still the drummer when we played there," J. R. remembered, "and Roy played on different dates than the ones we did. We went to see him several times because we knew him and the Candymen band very well, and, of course, we loved to visit and raise as much hell as we could. The Whisky was probably in its heyday when we were playing there, and I thoroughly enjoyed those times."

Rodney Justo remembered another encounter between the Candymen and two native Georgia players who were gigging in the Atlanta area:

"Barry came to see the Blues Magoos and us at a place in Marietta. That was when we were really starting to develop our vocals to go along with our musicality. For example, we were doing a song by Little Anthony and the Imperials called 'Hurt So Bad.' I remember Barry commenting on it; he and Paul Goddard were both there."

Members of the Candymen began to migrate to the Atlanta area, but the days of that band were numbered.

"Bill Gilmore was the first one to move to Atlanta," Justo detailed. "Dean and John Rainey were in Dothan. We were good, and we had worked very hard to be good, but around the beginning of '69, John Rainey had a terrible alcohol problem, and he also started becoming habitually late for everything. That's not my style. If you come to see us, it's our obligation to be as professional as we can be.

"One day we were playing in Lansing, Michigan, with Sly and the Family Stone, and when John Rainey got drunk, I'd had enough, and I quit. We worked a couple of more gigs, and it was a very sad thing for me because we'd all put a lot into that band. We were highly regarded, and we had the best management, so maybe the stars weren't completely aligned when it came to us."

Robert Nix would later state that *he* was actually the first to leave the Candymen, since he wanted to concentrate on songwriting, studio work, and producing. He and Bill Gilmore would quickly score a hit when they penned "Cherry Hill Park," a 1969 song performed by Billy Joe Royal.

Dean Daughtry would later join the Classics IV, and Gilmore followed soon afterward. Accordingly, Dean and Bill were members of both of the nationally known bands that beget the Atlanta Rhythm Section, although Gilmore would not become a member of the A.R.S.

Rodney remained in Tampa and assembled a band called Noah's Ark that signed with Buie-Cochran Management and released a single, but that aggregation didn't last long.

••••••

Buddy Buie and J. R. Cobb began their legendary songwriting collaborations soon after the Classics IV relocated to Georgia's capital city. The twosome had polar-opposite personalities—J. R. was a laid-back, talented, and responsible musician, whereas Buddy was more of a free spirit—an imaginative and "hyper" individual who could barely play a guitar.

"I'd usually go over to his house at night, around six-thirty or maybe seven," Cobb detailed, "and a lot of times, we'd be up way past midnight; sometimes it would be three or four o'clock in the morning before we stopped. We'd sit in the living room or den, and it would be me doing the playing on an old acoustic; Buddy knew a few chords but that was about it. It was very informal, but that's the way he liked to work, and I think one of the main reasons was the lack of distractions. We'd try to write several tunes."

The Buie-Cobb collaborations weren't necessarily of the "one person writes the music, the other person writes the lyrics" format. Using his very basic guitar abilities, Buddy attempted to show J. R. what he was envisioning, and Cobb would diligently work out the melody and chords on his guitar.

"Even though he wasn't a musician, he had musical ideas," Cobb explained.

And while both songwriters worked on words, J. R. gave more credit for that facet to Buie.

"I think Buddy was more of a lyricist than I was," the guitarist opined, "because he'd had more practice at it. He'd already had a writing deal, and had been around that part a lot more than me—which means I learned a lot from him about lyrics. And as time went on, we both got more involved in doing both music and lyrics in about an even amount. Sometimes I'd think of the title, sometimes he'd have the title."

Buie and Cobb intentionally focused on writing short, memorable songs that had the potential to be hits. Any songwriting effort that ultimately shaped up like it would run over three and a half minutes or so was less likely to be completed.

Both songwriters would eventually sign on with the Lowery organization, but if Bill Lowery wasn't interested in recording a certain tune they had composed, Buddy would shop it to other producers elsewhere, including Chips Moman in Memphis.

One early tune Buie and Cobb wrote was called "I Take It Back," which was somewhat unusual because it jumped back and forth between two time signatures.

Buie: "It sounds a little dated now, but then, it was a work of art to me. J. R. said to me, 'Are you aware that what you're singing is 4/4 time in the verse and 3/4 time in the chorus? It changes from 4/4 to 3/4!' I said, 'Naw, I didn't notice it, but I like it,' and J. R. said 'I like it, too.'"

Chips Moman took an interest in "I Take It Back" and asked Buie and Cobb to come to Memphis to play it in person. The song was recorded by pop chanteuse Sandy Posey and was a hit.

"It was our first national hit, and our first BMI [Broadcast Music International song licensing] award winner," Buddy said proudly.

※※※※※※

The Classics IV's first recording in Lowery's facility was a single titled "Pollyanna." The session was produced by singer/songwriter Joe South, who had written the tune, but "Pollyanna" ultimately went nowhere in regard to airplay and sales.

Buddy also got his first taste of producing a recording session at Master Sound. Joe South was originally supposed to produce the Classics IV but became ill, according to Buie, "and by default, I was declared [to be] their new producer."

More than one Atlanta music veteran recalled that while the Classics IV would continue as a touring band, studio musicians played most of the music on their recordings. J. R. was reportedly the only member of the band who recorded as well, but the lead vocals were still sung by Dennis Yost.

Recalling both the success of the Classics IV and his songwriting efforts with Buie, J. R. remembered that "the one that really got the ball rolling for us was 'Spooky,' which was a saxophone instrumental that a guy named Mike Shapiro had recorded; his stage name was Mike Sharpe. I told Buddy about it, and he'd already heard it, but he hatched the idea of writing lyrics to it."

The original instrumental version of "Spooky" had been written by Shapiro and keyboard player Harry Middlebrooks.

"It was an unusual collaboration," said Buddy. "Originally a jazz instrumental, and later, J. R. and I wrote lyrics and changed the arrangement to make it more appropriate for a pop song."

"We noted how Mike played the melody on the sax," said J. R., "and we liked the way Harry did that funky little riff on the organ, so we wrote the lyrics using those things to keep the feeling when we added the words. Bill [Lowery] went to Mike and Harry and told them that Buddy and I had written lyrics for that song, and 'are you okay with us putting it out and sharing writing credits?'"

"Back in the day, we found out that instrumentals paid better," said Butch Lowery, who had gone to work at his father's business, concentrating on income and distribution of songwriting royalties. "But having had great success with that song as an instrumental, we got an even bigger hit when Buddy and J. R. wrote lyrics for it."

However, the singer for the Classics IV had initially resisted recording "Spooky."

"Dennis Yost hated the way I wanted him to sing the song," Buddy recalled. "He said, 'It makes me sound like a sissy.' I wanted it to be real seductive and sexy. Dennis went back to Bill Lowery in the office and said, 'Hey, I'm not recording that song that way; it makes me sound weird.' Bill said, 'Hey, man, you do it your way and then do it Buddy's way, and we'll see which one came out best.' It went on to be our first huge record."

The vocal version of "Spooky" was released in October 1967 and charted as high as #3 on US hit song charts.

"When I actually heard that song being played on a big radio station, it was surreal; I got goose bumps," said Cobb. "And 'Spooky' wasn't the only song that had that effect on me if I heard it on the radio for the first time. It took a long time for me to get used to the idea. I was surprised that a lot of them became hits."

J. R. and Buddy also realized that succeeding with a hit song mandated an obligation to put an even more intense effort into writing and recording a follow-up hit.

"I won't say that the record companies in those days 'insisted' on another hit real quick," said J. R, "but they suggested rather strongly that you do something else that was like what you'd done before that was successful," J. R. said. "That makes sense, so we came up with songs like 'Stormy.'"

Almost all the Classics IV's subsequent hit songs were written by Buie and Cobb (including hits such as "Every Day with You Girl") or by Buddy himself. Buddy also got hung up on trying to compose songs with six letters in their respective titles—"Spooky," "Stormy," and "Traces." Succinct monikers, but a magical number of letters for Buie.

Was there ever a song that Buie and Cobb wrote where the twosome thought at a relatively early point in the songwriting process that they might have a hit in the works?

"I think maybe 'Traces' was probably the one that was close to that," said J. R. "There would be times where we'd sit around drinking coffee and talking about what we wanted to accomplish, and we both agreed that we wanted to write a 'standard'—a song that would last longer than us; one that people would re-record. 'Standard' is kind of a dated term now, but we were both really proud of 'Traces,' and it did indeed get recorded by a lot of other people, including the Boston Pops [Orchestra]."

J. R. also cited another—and more personal—reason that "Traces" was important to Buie:

"That song was near and dear to Buddy because it was about Gloria [Seay]."

And Buddy, who had married, would hint that he was still carrying a torch for his high school sweetheart.

"A number of times he would sort of indirectly mention it," J. R. averred, "but he never would talk about it in detail."

"['Traces'] is the thirty-fourth most-performed song in the BMI catalogue," Buie said. "To put that in perspective, Number one is [the Beatles'] 'Yesterday,' and number 49 is [Frank Sinatra's] 'My Way.' ['Traces'] has truly become a 'standard.'"

J. R. also married; he and Bertha "Bert" Absher tied the knot on January 21, 1967. Their son, Justin Travis Cobb, would appear in 1971.

A Buie-Cobb collaboration, "Movies in My Mind," was among the songs would appear on the first album by the Candymen in 1967, and the next year, four songs ("Great Society," "Sentimental Lady," "Crowded Room," and "Goodbye Mama") were credited to that twosome on *The Candymen Bring You Candy Power.*

Summarizing his late 1960s hit-making efforts with Buie, J. R. remembered, "When Buddy and I sat down to write a song, there were two things that we were thinking about—'Can this get on the radio?' and 'Will people like it?' Musicianship and 'how fancy it should be' was never really part of it, because I was never that kind of player, and he wasn't really a musician. A lot of people say, 'Oh, we write for the artistic value';

the Beach Boys' Brian Wilson had an ability to make 'artistic' things that people liked to hear, and while that would also sell records, we had simpler goals."

Obviously, the songwriting abilities of Buddy and J. R. weren't confined to collaborations with each other. Buie would write with other Atlanta musicians, and Cobb's other efforts included working with singer/songwriter Ray Robert Whitley on the Tams' "Be Young, Be Foolish, Be Happy," which J. R. proudly pronounced to be "a beach music anthem!"

Another occurrence that enthralled J. R. was working on sessions at Master Sound with one of his idols, Roy Orbison.

"He came into Bill's to do some demos or some stuff that he never released," Cobb recalled. "I was around him enough to find out he was a very special person. One of the most down-to-earth people I've ever known. Before I ever met Roy, Buddy had told me you could wake Roy up at 4 a.m. and ask him to sing a high A-flat [music note], and he'd hit it every time. He had no limitations; he could sing anything, anytime.

"Roy wouldn't have any chance now in the music business—when he came onstage, he wasn't flashy; he wasn't all that handsome. He stood in one place and sang, and that was it."

The potency of the songwriting by Buie and Cobb would be validated internationally. On the strength of "Traces," "Stormy," and "Every Day with You, Girl," Buddy Buie and J. R. Cobb placed second only to John Lennon and Paul McCartney of the Beatles in 1969 for awards in BMI songwriting. And Buie had also produced the hit versions of those songs by the Classics IV.

••••••

The Classics IV added an additional member following the success of "Spooky." It was decided that Dennis Yost should be out front as the lead singer, and Kim Venable, a former member of the K-Otics, signed on as the band's drummer. The combo's moniker was changed to "Dennis Yost & the Classics IV" to keep the number of members in the band correct.

Cobb recalled that it was thought to be "a better selling point, for some reason, to have somebody's name at the beginning. There was also the possibility that this person might have a longer career than the band had."

But around the time "Spooky" was released, J. R. departed the Classics IV in order to concentrate on songwriting and recording at Master Sound. Obviously, Buddy was enthusiastic about J. R. being more available for songwriting collaborations, and he also wanted Cobb to play on some of the songs he was producing for other artists. However, J. R. would briefly return to the band with which he had first experienced success as a musician and songwriter.

"It took about six months for 'Spooky' to become a hit," J. R. recounted. "Back then deejays could pretty much play what they wanted, and when it started doing really well, the Classics IV asked me to come back and work with them to promote the record, so I went back for about six months, then I left again."

••••••

Barry Bailey met Buddy Buie for the first time at a recording session at Master Sound on July 10, 1969. Emory Gordy Jr. was the individual who urged Buddy to try out Bailey, and recalled Buie's reaction:

"Buie, who hated 'modern' rock guitarists—including [Jimi] Hendrix—complained that all they were doing was using sound effects. He was knocked senseless by Barry's playing. I remember Buddy yelled out, 'I can hear every note he's playing! He's great! And then he complained that I should have introduced Barry to him earlier in his production career."

J. R. would become a studio peer of Barry and Paul Goddard via Buddy Buie.

"I had met Barry when we'd been out on some of those caravan shows, but got to know both Barry and Paul at the Master Sound studio," J. R. recalled. "They both would occasionally work for different artists that were recording there just as I did. The first time I heard Barry play in the studio was on something like a Dennis Yost demo, and [Barry] was phenomenal. Buddy started to use Barry—and later, Paul—on stuff that he was producing there, and we became friends."

As for hearing Paul play guitar, J. R. recalled, "He was a very good guitar player—he played kinda different, the same way he played bass different."

••••••

Buddy had a preference to do his songwriting in an isolated environment, and he began making trips—sometimes by himself, sometimes with another songwriter or two—to Calloway Gardens in western Georgia, near Warm Springs, site of the Little White House, where President Franklin Roosevelt died in 1945. The peaceful setting allowed for less distraction.

Eventually, Buddy's parents placed a small mobile home—which would become known as "the fishing trailer"—on some property that had been purchased for $500 by his sister and brother-in-law in the Thomas Mill Creek area of Lake Eufaula (named after the nearby town) on the Alabama-Georgia border. The lake had been created when Walter George Dam had been built in the early Sixties.

There was no telephone in the mobile home; phone calls had to be made from a nearby store. The fishing trailer's second-hand, window-mounted air conditioner was loud, and its output was anemic and insufficient.

But Buddy (and associates) would hang out in this even more rustic environment for up to two weeks at a time, concentrating on penning new tunes. Occasionally they would take time out for fishing. Buie would stick to this reclusive songwriting ritual for many years.

"That air conditioner made so much noise, we'd have to turn it off to write," J. R. remembered, "but we'd start sweating so much we had to turn it back on."

••••••

Other musicians who arrived in Atlanta with "big-city dreams" in the mid-Sixties were members of the Bushmen, a band from southeastern Georgia. They had formed in Douglas, located near Waycross, in 1962.

"This was 'pre-Beatles,'" said the band's erstwhile bassist, Rodney Mills. "The original idea was that we were going to do this Kingston Trio / folk thing, because the drummer didn't have a set of drums—he had bongos. After a short time, we decided we needed to get the right instruments if we were going to be in a band."

Mills grew up in the Mormon church, as did two other band members, so their first performances were at church socials. Their first moniker was sometimes misunderstood, due to its similarity to a cosmetics brand name.

"At that time, we weren't called the Bushmen, we were called the Revelons," he recounted. "'Revel' means to party or have a good time. We got an artist in Douglas to put our name on the drumhead, but he put the 'Revlons' on the front and painted a picture of a tube of lipstick on it. We didn't have enough money to buy another drumhead, so that was on the drums for a while."

Switching to an electric-instrument lineup, the band played instrumentals by the Ventures, Duane Eddy, and other artists.

"We didn't have anybody who could sing all that well anyway," Mills said. "We ventured out a bit and picked up on some of the black guitar players of the time. There was a music company in Douglas that serviced all the black jukeboxes in nightclubs; we'd buy their out-of-rotation records for twenty cents apiece. We went through stacks of them and found a lot of artists we liked—Jimmy Reed, as well as 'the King family'—B. B., Albert, Freddie."

The fact that the Beach Boys and the Beatles were playing instruments *and* singing *and* writing their own songs made a serious impression on the Revelons (and umpteen other teen bands), particularly when the Beatles appeared on *The Ed Sullivan Show* in February 1964.

"I was not a musician, but I wanted to be a rock star," Mills recalled with a self-deprecating chuckle. "I picked bass because it was only one string at a time. The dream for us as a band was to get to the next level."

The Revelons quickly evolved into the Bushmen, a dynamic show band that played at schools and National Guard armories in more than one state, sporting matching outfits and matching amplifiers ("We only played two bars in our entire career," Mills recalled). On May 4, 1965, they were the opening act for a Rolling Stones concert at Georgia Southern College.

The success of the Bushmen compelled the band members to look in the direction of the Peach State capital, where they would win a battle-of-the-bands event at the

The Bushmen perform at a college date in 1966. Rodney Mills is seen on bass, second from the right among the band members.

Atlanta Merchandise Mart. The competition was headlined by Paul Revere & the Raiders. The grand-prize package included a recording contract with Smash Records.

Their recording session was done at Bill Lowery's Master Sound Recording Studios, and Mills recalled the experience as an epiphany:

"The producer assigned to us was Joe South. I thought, 'This is the coolest thing in the world,'—to be in a studio playing, and when it was played back, it actually sounded good."

The Bushmen's Smash single didn't live up to the label's brand name. Following graduation from high school, members of the band attended junior college then looked to Atlanta again, this time considering a permanent move.

"By 1967, we had gone through all of the schooling we could get down there," Rodney recalled. "Everybody had finally graduated from junior college, and since the Vietnam War was still going on, you had to be in school or you were wide open for the draft. We decided to move to the Atlanta area and get into colleges there. I was supposed to go to Georgia State, and Joey, the drummer, was supposed to go there, too. Two other guys went to Athens.

"We actually leased a little recording studio called Unlimited Sound for six months, thinking we were going to record our own album; we thought we were going to be huge. They had two two-track recorders, so you'd record in stereo, then as you transferred it to the other machine, you could add overdubs. That was my first experience with engineering. We were actually there about eight months instead of six, and whenever I'd get around recording equipment, something inside of me would click."

Rodney never registered at Georgia State. He had been so impressed with his recording experiences with the Bushmen at Master Sound Recording Studios as well as his early learning experience at Unlimited Sound that he visited Meurice LeFevre at the gospel veteran's west Atlanta studio.

"It's the quintessential story about how you get to be a recording engineer," Mills recalled. "I asked him if I could just hang out; I told him I'd do anything he wanted me to do. When I first started out, I'd set microphones for someone who was coming in to record. Their core studio musicians were the Goss Brothers, who played on most of the gospel stuff, so I got to learn their setup and would have it in place when they got there.

"Sometimes if Meurice and I were sitting in the control room, he'd get a phone call, and he'd tell me, 'Doc, watch the console'—he called everybody 'Doc'—and while he was out, I'd do a bit of hands-on [control manipulation] without permanently changing any of the settings. It was way ahead of what I'd worked with at Unlimited Sound. Even then, it wasn't that I wanted to have a career as a recording engineer. I was trading out time that I was helping out for studio time to record the band; they could come in and I would help record them."

The Bushmen were playing only on weekends, and Rodney's enthusiasm, dedication, and prowess at the LeFevre facility led Meurice to offer Mills a job.

••••••

A gigantic Atlanta Pop Festival was staged in Hampton (some distance from the city) in 1969, and a similar event would be held the next year. The first event would be cited by music historians as the national breakout of a loud Michigan hard-rock trio called Grand Funk Railroad. Barry Bailey and his girlfriend Dawn attended the event.

Abetted by the burgeoning interest in "Southern Rock" bands, the pro musicians in Atlanta were endeavoring to garner their fair share of fame and fortune. Hydra was playing the Atlanta Municipal Auditorium so often that one might have thought the members of the band actually resided there.

And as the wild and traumatic 1960s came to a close, most of the musicians who would compose the initial lineup of the Atlanta Rhythm Section were plying their trade, or were headquartered, in the Peach State capital. They were active at more than one studio, were touring with assorted artists, or both.

Barry Bailey and Paul Goddard didn't work strictly at Master Sound; they would also do studio work at LeFevre Sound Studios. They hooked up with drummer Kim Venable and keyboard player Dean Daughtry to record an album with Mylon LeFevre in 1969 called *We Believe*, under the guidance of legendary New Orleans producer/ songwriter Allen Toussaint, with Rodney Mills engineering. Mylon described the recording experience as "just a bunch of friends writing and jamming and having a creative adventure."

We Believe was released in 1970. The record would be cited as one of the earliest "Christian rock" albums and a first "standard"/"mainstream" album from a gospel artist.

"The phrase 'Contemporary Christian Music' had not been coined yet," Mylon said of the early days of religious music being performed on electric guitars, electric basses, and drums. "Everybody called it something like 'Jesus Rock,' but most of the early performers such as Larry Norman were 'folk people' with acoustic guitars. At that time, there had never been a band that really rocked out, trying to minister to people. It was sort of a new thing, and nobody knew what to do with it."

Back-cover photo from Mylon's groundbreaking *We Believe* album, released in 1970. Left to right: Dean "Ox" Daughtry, Barry Bailey, Mylon LeFevre, Paul Goddard, Kim Venable.

Publicity photos showed the quintet of long-haired musicians posing inside and outside a small country church. The list of musicians on the album indicated that "Mylon" was also the name of a band as well.

"I did not start—or have anything to do with starting—the A.R.S.," Mylon remembered, "but when I was putting a band together to do my album, Barry Bailey, Dean Daughtry, and Paul Goddard helped me make the demos and, eventually, the album. And they were professionals—if you're a professional musician, there's no room for an ego in a recording studio."

LeFevre recalled that Barry and Dean backed him at his first performance at the Electric Factory in Philadelphia. Overtures were made to Barry and others about backing Mylon up full time.

"Barry Bailey was a musical prodigy, as far as I'm concerned," said LeFevre. "He made my record really unique."

••••••

When he wasn't busy in the studio or with his own live performances, Barry and his future wife, Dawn, attended numerous concerts in Atlanta. Memorable live shows for the twosome included Cream at Chastain Park (on that band's last concert tour), as well as performances at the Municipal Auditorium by Jimi Hendrix, Donovan, and a Motown review.

••••••

And another 1970 album that included Barry's guitar work was perhaps the most improbable assignment he ever undertook in his entire career.

California again beckoned to Bailey, this time by way of Emory Gordy Jr. and Dennis St. John, who were working with flamboyant pianist Liberace on an upcoming so-called "pop" album, which would be titled *A Brand New Me*.

"I was invited to play on what I guess was Lee's attempt—or his management's attempt—to penetrate the instrumental pop niche," Barry recalled, referring to Liberace by the pianist's nickname. "Ed Cobb, a well-established writer and producer, was in charge of the session and was a pleasure to work with, as was the case with the other musicians, including [Muscle Shoals, Alabama, musician] Spooner Oldham, a noted writer and keyboardist. The arrangements, for the most part, were impromptu and were loosely based on the arrangements from original recordings. Mr. Liberace was never in the studio—at least, while I was there—but he did phone in to thank all of the players, individually, for their participation.

"An exceptional pianist, arranger, and conductor, Lincoln Mayorga, played the scratch tracks that Liberace was to 'mirror.' In my humble opinion, the final product was inferior to what we did with Lincoln in the studio. I guess Lincoln's tracks are now long gone. And, yes, I was quite pleased to have been a part of *A Brand New Me*. It remains the most unusual and attention-getting credit in my résumé."

CHAPTER 5
Preliminaries and the Advent of Studio One

T he beginning of the 1970s saw the future members of the Atlanta Rhythm Section beginning to take an interest in playing with each other of their own volition, if only in jam sessions.

Contrary to what some music fans may believe, however, their initial musical collaborations did not come about due to the construction of a state-of-the-art recording studio in Doraville, Georgia; that is, the A.R.S. didn't germinate as a band at Studio One. Instead, the band and the studio developed in parallel time frames.

J. R. and Buddy contemplate their next composition at Bill Lowery's Master Sound facility.

"Those things happened at the same time," said Barry. "We'd done a lot of sessions at Lefevre and Master Sound, but not necessarily as a 'unit.' But it seemed like two or three of us had been on almost any session in town."

Since Bill Lowery's company was publishing their songs, Buddy Buie and J. R. Cobb were allowed to use Lowery's facility to cut demos at no charge, but, obviously, paying customers had priority. The two songwriters collaborated inside Master Sound at whatever odd hours it was available.

"Two hours here, an hour and a half there," J. R. recalled. "It's understandable why Buddy wanted to have access to a studio on his own terms, so we started looking for places."

After having committed himself to being a record producer as well as a songwriter, Buddy had begun developing his own ideas for a state-of-the-art recording studio that would offer musicians an efficient facility that would be accessible at almost any hour on any day, and that wouldn't be subject to strict adherence to the number of hours that were booked.

And Buddy's aspirations would be hastened due to a falling out with Bob Richardson, one of the recording engineers at Master Sound. Buie then sought to continue his fledgling production career at LeFevre Sound Studios.

"When Buddy came over to LeFevre Sound, he would really get into a creative mode," Rodney Mills remembered, "and as the engineer, I was the one who had to keep track of time. Also, I think Buddy thought it was essential for him to have a studio for not just recording, but also for him to be a creative part of the equation."

Accordingly, Buddy probably looked at his tenure at the LeFevre facility as somewhat temporary.

"Buddy was the catalyst for a lot of stuff back then," J. R. reflected, "partly because he was a talker. He was the guy who could convince people to take big steps, like any good salesman would do."

And future members of the Atlanta Rhythm Section had begun some casual musical interplay in the LeFevre facility as well.

"We'd jam sometimes, but we decided to record several instrumentals at the LeFevre studios in late '69," J. R. remembered. "We were particularly proud of our version of Thunderclap Newman's 'Something in the Air.' In fact, I heard later that Buddy used some of those tapes as demos to try to get the interest of record companies, before we had [Rodney] Justo as the singer. Nobody knows what happened to that music."

"You could tell everybody could play," Dean Daughtry said of the instrumental tracks. "I also played 'One Mint Julep' on the organ, like Ray Charles."

Ox also remembered recording "Mercy, Mercy, Mercy," which had originally been a jazz instrumental written by Joe Zawinul and performed by Cannonball Adderley, followed by a pop version with lyrics that were recorded by the Buckinghams. The version recorded at LeFevre Sound brought the song back to an instrumental format.

Rodney Mills participated in the recording sessions for the LeFevre Sound instrumentals and remembered, "Those sessions were primarily done at the end of a 'legitimate' session. Say, for instance, we were doing tracks for Billy Joe Royal. Once we got the track cut, the players would jam around, and the limitation was how much time we had left on a reel of tape.

"At that time, LeFevre had an eight-track board, and Buddy gave me permission to add to the instrumental stuff. Barry had no effects; he didn't use any gadgets to get his sustain and distortion. He used the amplifier; he never had 'stomp boxes,' and that was the case for his entire career, except for an echo-type device that I found for him in a music store in Atlanta, which he used forever.

"On 'Something in the Air,' J. R. used a wah-wah [pedal], and I found a way to split and overdub Barry's guitar, so you sort of had 'dual echoes' in there. I was trying to be as creative as the band, and with the Rhythm Section, it was always that way."

•••••••

As for the idea that the studio musicians should actually form a legitimate, working band, J. R. recalled, "I believe the idea hatched with Buddy and Bill Lowery. That doesn't surprise me at all, considering their personalities. But at the time, we didn't have a vocalist, and we realized it wasn't going to work without a singer."

•••••••

Buie still yearned for what he termed as "autonomy" ("That was his 'big word' for a while," J. R. recalled with a chuckle), and convinced Paul Cochran, J. R., and Bill Lowery to partner with him in a new facility with state-of-the art equipment and easy accessibility for musicians at all hours. The financial contributions of Buie and Cobb came from songwriting royalties.

Bill Lowery had some reservations, according to his son, Butch. In his position as a sage to area musicians, the elder Lowery insisted that Buddy treat this new venture as a business, not just something to record only bands or singers in which Buie took an interest.

"I told Buddy, 'If you can make money on it, he'll invest in it,'" Butch said of his father.

"Buddy wanted to be the 'alpha dog,'" Buie's brother, Jerry, recalled. "I knew how he wanted the vocals on recordings sung the way *he* would sing them, so I knew that studio was going to be set up the way he wanted."

A building that could be converted to a recording studio was located at the Oakcliff Industrial Park in Doraville, a community that was perceived as primarily rural, northeast of Atlanta. The building was in relatively easy commuting distance from where most of the principals of the business, as well as some of the musicians, were living. It was also fairly close to Lowery's facility and offices.

"It was just a warehouse; a 'shell,'" said J. R. "The owners knew what we were gonna do to renovate it, and they were okay with that. We hired a guy named Shack Jones to renovate the inside and build the control room."

Rodney Mills was hired to design and oversee the construction of the interior.

"I was not part of the initial concept for Studio One," Mills detailed. "I kind of knew that Buddy was going to deal with Lou Bradley, an engineer over at Master Sound, and Lou had been involved with some of the early decision making—like what kind of console they'd have, and maybe some of the other equipment, but they hadn't started building the place."

Bradley, who had engineered the two albums by the Candymen, was indeed Buddy's first choice to be the engineer at the new studio, but Bradley abruptly got a job offer in Nashville, which he accepted.

"So it was like Buddy looked around, and I was the only one in the room," Mills said. "He asked me if I wanted to go to work for him and build the studio. I was twenty-four, and the only thing I'd ever helped to build was a farrowing pen with my daddy for hogs. I didn't hesitate; I said, 'I'm in.'

"I wasn't dissatisfied with working at LeFevre Sound; I'd gotten to record all kinds of music there, and I was working basically seven days a week. But when Buddy had come over to LeFevre, he'd given me a lot of freedom with his own sessions, and I liked his ideas about what the new studio should be. I could do what I wanted to do, under Buddy's oversight. And I continued to work at LeFevre Sound the entire time the new studio was being built; after work, I'd go out to Doraville to check things out."

Buddy called Rodney Justo, who was singing in Noah's Ark in Tampa, to discuss the concept of a rock band composed of elite studio musicians, asserting that he could and would assemble the top musicians in the South for such a band. After Buie cited the lineup he had recruited, Justo accepted the assignment as lead singer.

Rodney headed up from Florida to Atlanta, staying at the Buies' home until his wife and daughters moved up. He actually helped in the construction of the interior of Studio One, as did J. R., Robert Nix, and others.

"We laid carpet, hammered and nailed, installed tile," Justo said. "It was a wonderful experience."

J. R.: "We really didn't know what we were doing in some areas. We built a ten-by-twelve-foot isolation booth with all kinds of padding. We were gonna put drums inside. It was on wheels; you could move it around the studio, and it took four or five people to push it. It never worked for drums because it was way too dead in there; they didn't sound good at all. It wasn't even very good for vox [voice]. We learned about that the hard way and found out pretty quickly that 'completely dead' acoustics wasn't a good thing. We ended up storing guitars in it."

Bill Lowery's Master Sound facility originally had a three-track Ampex recorder. Overdubs were accomplished by bouncing tracks back and forth in a meticulous manner. Studio One had an eight-track recorder from the outset and would upgrade to a sixteen-track recorder about a year after the new studio opened for business.

Offices were upstairs, and a downstairs recreation room contained a ping-pong table. A pool table would be added later.

Studio One opened in early 1970, with an ad touting it as "Atlanta's newest and most advanced recording facility." The ownership was listed as "President, Buddy Buie; Vice Pres., Bill Lowery; Vice Pres., J. R. Cobb; Sec.-Treas., Paul Cochran."

An overhead photo of assorted studio personnel and musicians was part of the ad layout. Among the individuals shown in the picture were Buddy and J. R. out front (and J. R. had strapped on his recently acquired Gibson Les Paul Deluxe "goldtop" guitar), Barry Bailey, Paul Goddard, Rodney Mills, Mike Shapiro, Robert Nix, and Shack Jones.

And Barry was holding his Fender Telecaster guitar upside down, with the back of it facing the camera.

"I flipped the Tele either out of boredom or just being somewhat of a smart-ass—or both," he recalled.

The only female shown in the photo is Dawn Vanderlip, Barry's then fiancé, who's directly in front of the guitarist.

BUILDING ATLANTA

STUDIO ONE

Atlanta's newest and most advanced recording facility

PRESIDENT — BUDDY BUIE
VICE PRES. — BILL LOWERY
VICE PRES. — J.R. COBB
SEC.-TREAS. — PAUL COCHRAN

STUDIO ONE
3864 OAKCLIFF INDUSTRIAL COURT
DORAVILLE, GEORGIA
(404) 451-5129

Grand opening advertisement for Studio One. *C. Rogers*

"I've no idea what she was doing there," Barry said. "She used to go with me to sessions, and she would usually sit in the control room, doing her needlepoint, cross-stitch, or whatever artsy-crafty thing she was into at the time."

••••••

Another legendary music scene that would ultimately define so-called "Southern Rock" was developing about ninety miles down I-75 in Macon, home of Otis Redding, who had died in a plane crash in 1967. Former Redding manager Phil Walden's Capricorn Records featured the Allman Brothers Band as their keystone artists; the sextet's intricate jams were perhaps unfairly stereotyped at times as "blues 'n' boogie," since the Allmans' music often featured unique time signatures and jazz improvisational references.

Nevertheless, the Allmans would generally be considered as being the standard bearers of the "Southern Rock" genre, and the Capricorn label was busy signing up other bands from other southern states.

The Atlanta musicians were generally indifferent to Macon, although the Atlanta Rhythm Section would eventually sign up with Walden's Paragon Agency for concert bookings, and Hydra would sign with Capricorn Records in the early 1970s. However, there was never really a perceived musical rivalry between the two cities.

"There was maybe some 'friendly competition' between Bill Lowery and Phil Walden, as well as between us and some of the guys in Macon," J. R. detailed. "We liked each other. Bill and Phil were quite similar in their approach to their recording artists and songwriters. Buddy never wanted to run a record company, but he was obviously influential in our relationships with record companies."

Barry recalled being too focused on his own music to be concerned about genres or rivalries between bands or music scenes, but he respected the music that the Allmans and some of the other bands were creating.

"Back then, I paid very little attention to labels, and who was signed to them," said Bailey. "The Macon and Atlanta 'scenes' were just two different worlds to me, in spite of what they had in common. Since Buddy already had relationships with major labels, Capricorn was not much, if any, of a consideration."

CHAPTER 6
Salad Days in Doraville

Although Barry Bailey had posed in the photo for Studio One's "Now open for business" ad, his services were still being sought elsewhere. In addition to overtures from Emory Gordy Jr. in California and Mylon LeFevre in west Atlanta, Felix Pappalardi, producer/bassist for a rock band called Mountain ("Mississippi Queen") had recruited Barry for some work in New York City and wanted the Atlanta guitarist for other projects on Windfall Records, Mountain's label. The featured player in Mountain was guitarist/singer Leslie West.

"The recordings took place at Electric Lady [Studios] in New York City," Barry recalled. "The only artist I remember was Maggie Thrett, and as far as I know, the album was never released. I did know Leslie and the others from Mountain, and we jammed on at least one occasion, at LeFevre Studios in Atlanta."

Responding to the reality that Barry was being wooed by other musicians in other locales, Buddy signed Bailey to a separate individual contract as a preemptive move, locking in his business relationship with the guitarist before Bailey signed on with anyone else. Buie had reportedly proclaimed that there had been a "bidding war" between Mylon and himself for Bailey's services.

"I do remember Buddy using the term 'bidding war,'" Barry clarified, "but there was no actual bidding and no war, that I am aware of."

Rodney Justo was already under a similar individual personal-management contract, which he had signed at age seventeen with Paul Cochran, who was now Buddy's partner. Buie would later sign up the other four original Atlanta Rhythm Section members to individual contracts.

"As a group, the Atlanta Rhythm Section never signed a contract with a record company," Rodney Mills confirmed.

Buddy talked with his brother, Jerry, often and let him know about the new band that was in the works.

"He said 'I'm getting a group of studio musicians together; [they're] some of the finest musicians not only in Atlanta, but in the South,'" the younger Buie recalled.

Buddy advised his brother that two names were under consideration—"the Atlanta Rhythm Section" and "Blackbush."

"I told him that 'Blackbush' sounded like a good name for a Southern Rock band," Jerry remembered. "I also said that the first thing that popped in my mind when I heard 'Atlanta Rhythm Section' was an orchestra."

In the spring of 1970, Buddy signed with the A.T.I. public-relations firm to promote his own ventures. The decision regarding a moniker for the band composed of studio musicians had apparently been made when a May 6 press release from that

This publicity photo of Buddy was released in 1970, when he signed with a public-relations company.

P.R. group noted that in addition to representing Buddy, they would also be representing a group of studio musicians "who call themselves 'the Atlanta Rhythm Section featuring Barry Baily [*sic*]."

Obviously, the concept of a bunch of studio musicians becoming a self-contained working band was unprecedented. Other musical environments in other cities—Nashville, Memphis, New York, Los Angeles, even Muscle Shoals, Alabama—had a "usual gang" of first-call players, but those musicians seemed to be content to concentrate on studio work only, eschewing songwriting and touring.

But these upstarts out of Atlanta would be writing their own material (with their producer) and would be playing and singing such songs, striving for a hit just like the artists they'd all backed up in the studio and onstage. They would also be touring to support album releases. While all the members of the Atlanta Rhythm Section had been on tour before, this was a new and first-of-its-kind scenario, and it was intimidating.

"At the time, I was torn between becoming part of that kind of a band," Barry said, "because I was being pursued by Mylon LeFevre to be in his band, and there was also a possibility of moving out to the West Coast and doing studio work with Emory [Gordy Jr.] and Dennis [St. John] in L.A. But because I was about to get married, going on the road or moving to the West Coast weren't good options."

Emory confirmed that he had advised Barry about the opportunities in Los Angeles for a musician of Bailey's caliber.

"I kept in touch as necessary," Gordy said, "and came back to Atlanta to do some work, now and then. I wasn't really 'trying to convince him' to move to L.A. The offer was there, if he wanted it; the A.R.S. was still in development."

Barry and Dawn would marry in October 1970.

••••••

The Atlanta Rhythm Section became an official, working entity in the summer of 1970, with Buddy as their initially unofficial but obvious choice as manager.

As for the ultimate choice of the name, J. R. Cobb credited Buddy Buie and Bill Lowery with choosing the moniker, which accurately described the professional musicians.

"We *were* a rhythm section," he said. "We'd played on other people's records, and that's how they got the idea."

Over time, many local musicians and fans often eliminated the band's first name when conversing about the A.R.S. or its music, referring to the group simply as "the Rhythm Section."

As for the reaction among musicians in Georgia to the formation of an Atlanta band composed of frontline studio musicians, "we knew it was going to be a good band," said Spencer Kirkpatrick, who was now the lead guitarist for Hydra. "My favorite incarnation of the Rhythm Section was the very first one, with Rodney as the singer."

For a long time, Dean continued to reside in Dothan, commuting to Atlanta when necessary (usually on weekends).

J. R. let his hair get long and grew a mustache.

The new band began its slow and methodical work on its first album, but such recordings were secondary to standard studio work, which was already a paying gig.

••••••

July 1970 also witnessed the second and final Atlanta International Pop Festival, held from July 3 to 5 at a raceway in Byron (located even farther from Atlanta than Hampton, site of the 1969 festival).

Over thirty bands and singers performed, including Jimi Hendrix, Mott the Hoople, Rare Earth, Ten Years After, and Spirit. Most of the proceedings were filmed for a proposed documentary, a la the legendary Woodstock movie, which recounted the iconic 1969 festival in upstate New York and had been released in late March 1970.

The second concert would be notable for the rousing return of Grand Funk Railroad, as well as the appearance of two bands from Georgia. The Allman Brothers Band, from nearby Macon, played twice, on July 3 as well as the early morning hours of July 6. Atlanta's Hampton Grease Band, sort of a Southern version of California oddball aggregation the Mothers of Invention, also purveyed their quirky music to hundreds of thousands of music fans.

Barry and Dawn also attended the Byron festival, along with Mylon LeFevre "and a couple of other freaks," according to the guitarist. "Mylon and I were backstage, literally hanging onto the stage during Jimi Hendrix's set, which included one of Jimi's 'Star Spangled Banner' renditions, culminating in setting a Stratocaster [guitar] ablaze. Regrettably, I didn't see either the Allmans or the [Hampton] Grease Band perform at that show."

Selected recordings from the Byron event were combined with music from the Isle of Wight Festival in England (held in late August) for a triple album called *The First Great Rock Festivals of the Seventies*, released in 1971.

Years later, audio and video presentations of Hendrix's performance would be released, as was a recording of both of the Allman Brothers' sets in Byron.

A third Atlanta Pop Festival never happened. The state legislature passed numerous regulatory measures—reportedly at the behest of then governor Lester Maddox—which severely restricted any effort to stage such an event.

••••••

The down-tempo evolution of the Atlanta Rhythm Section meant that the debut performance for the band wouldn't happen until 1971. The brief presentation was a "showcase"—a short, private set for music industry executives and deejays in a rented meeting room / ballroom at the Royal Coach Inn, located at the Howell Mill Road exit of I-75. Mylon LeFevre, his band, and two of his roadies were at the event to lend support, as was Joe South. LeFevre described the performance as the A.R.S.'s "coming-out party."

Paul and J. R. bear down at the Atlanta Rhythm Section's debut showcase performance at the Royal Coach Inn.

The first paying performance for the A.R.S. would be at the downtown Underground Atlanta entertainment/shopping/dining complex, which had become the city's focal point for nightlife, offering numerous clubs and restaurants. The Hampton Grease Band opened those shows.

Dean was upbeat after the Underground Atlanta performance, thinking that this new and different aggregation had something going for it, at least musically.

"We thought maybe we could make some money doing live gigs, in addition to working in the studio," he said.

But for an extended time, not much else happened, so the A.R.S. members continued to focus on their bread-and-butter studio careers. One of the more memorable studio assignments for some of the members around that time was a sixty-second commercial with Billy Joe Royal for Coca-Cola. Studio work also included themes for more than one Atlanta professional sports team.

Moreover, the new band didn't garner any opening slots for tours with bigger-name headliners.

"We had actually started the first Atlanta Rhythm Section album at LeFevre Sound, on an eight-track [mixing board]," said Rodney Mills. "When we went to Studio One, we quickly bought a sixteen-track, and some of that material was transferred to eight tracks on the sixteen-track. We continued to overdub, but we also did some stuff from scratch on the sixteen-track.

"Buddy was the dominant person in the studio, of course. It was treated like 'this is Buddy's toy as well as his working environment.'"

Not surprisingly, Barry became known as the Atlanta Rhythm Section's lead guitarist, but J. R. was no slouch, either. The twosome would sometimes work out

1971: The original lineup of the Atlanta Rhythm Section fine-tunes its music inside Studio One. Clockwise from upper left: Rodney Justo, J. R. Cobb, Barry Bailey, Dean Daughtry, Paul Goddard, Robert Nix.

harmony guitar licks a la the Allman Brothers Band or Wishbone Ash, a respected twin-lead guitar band from London. Moreover, J. R. made a point of being a true rhythm player—locking in with Robert's bass drum and Paul's bass instead of just strumming chords—as well as developing his skills on slide guitar.

"In the very beginning around the studio, it never made a lot of difference 'who played what' to any of us," said Cobb. "If I occasionally wanted to do a solo somewhere, Barry was completely happy to let me do it. But it was understood that he was going to be the soloist because he did it best—no question about that. I knew I'd never be the same kind of lead player that Barry was, but I did have something to offer, and my aim the entire time was to find something that complemented him as well as the rest of the band, and I mean 'style' as well as a model of guitar. I liked a [Fender] Strat better than Gibsons; it had the different sounds I was looking for.

"I didn't want to do anything to impede Barry's playing or get in his way. I only played slide [guitar] because he didn't want to; he probably could have played slide a lot better than me. I really enjoyed playing slide, though; I *loved* Duane Allman's playing. To me, there's nothing worse than hearing two guitar players who are battling onstage; they usually end up stumbling all over each other. You never saw or heard Duane Allman and [Allman Brothers guitarist] Dickie Betts doing that."

"J. R. was not a natural at playing slide guitar," Rodney Mills opined. "He was a guitar player that forced himself to learn a slide part. I'd be in the control room working with him; we often worked on his stuff when nobody else was around. He also played harmonica on some songs and had to force himself to learn harmonica as well. He did well with both slide and harmonica."

••••••

As for the songwriting, J. R. acknowledged the influence of Roy Orbison in new compositions (and it helps to remember that everyone else in the Atlanta Rhythm Section lineup had previously backed up Orbison):

"Roy was one of our idols. It didn't take us long to figure out that lyric-oriented songs were primary; we didn't want to do 'Louie Louie'-type songs—not that we didn't like them. We loved the blues and actually recorded some blues, but couldn't make any money at it."

While there was a Burger Chef fast-food restaurant near the studio, Barry recalled that "the restaurant where we used to drink coffee prior to starting our recordings was a place called the Clock, sort of a fast-food-within-a-diner environment. And if we wanted to get away from the studio for a while, we'd go hang out there."

••••••

On the basis of the strength of "Something in the Air" and other instrumentals recorded at LeFevre Studios, Buddy garnered a record deal for the band with the Decca/MCA company, and *The Atlanta Rhythm Section* was released in January 1972. It garnered a few positive reviews but didn't set the woods on fire. Moreover, J. R. recalled that the band wasn't satisfied with the effort in a musical sense.

"We didn't think we had reached the potential that we were capable of," he said, "but there have been times when I've looked back on 80 to 90 percent of what I've recorded and said—if only to myself—'Boy, you could have done a better job right there.' But maybe years later I'd listen again and say, 'Well, that ain't so bad after all; it's a lot better than I thought it was.'"

If listeners were expecting to hear stereotypical-at-the-time blues-'n'-boogie-based "Southern Rock" on the debut album from the Atlanta Rhythm Section, they probably tilted their heads to one side a la Nipper, the RCA mascot, when they heard perhaps unexpected arrangements and shorter songs, as well as churning acoustic guitars and Dean's quasi-honky-tonk/gospel piano flourishes.

And as if to confirm that the band was taking a different approach, the album's first track, "Love Me Just a Little," was the longest on the record, clocking in at 6:05 (stereotypically in that era, an album's longest track was the final song). The first half of "Love Me Just a Little" contained singing, while the second half featured soloing guitars (both Barry and J. R.).

And the second half of the first song was the closest thing to a jam heard on the debut album. The contents of the record emphasized to listeners that this band was definitely more "song-centric" (to use a term proffered by Rodney Justo).

Another intriguing number was an instrumental called "Earnestine," a rare "non-Buie" composition credited to Nix, Daughtry, Bailey, and Goddard. The likable, semi-shuffle arrangement and foot-patting performance hooked a lot of listeners, coming across like a big-band tune played on rock instruments.

Some tunes such as "Forty Days and Forty Nights" had an almost country-folk approach. There was also the unique time signature of "One More Problem."

Accordingly, the musicianship on the first album had a subtle/subliminal way of serving notice that there was some serious talent in play.

And Goddard's precise and distinct bass sound immediately made its presence known.

"The first thing I noticed when I listened to the album was that bass," Rodney Justo recalled. "The sound he got on that album was beautiful."

"Paul always wanted to get a sound that was not exactly 'compliant' with the music," Rodney Mills clarified. "He wanted it to sound like another band's bass, transposed to the Atlanta Rhythm Section, but that idea, while interesting, didn't necessarily work every single time."

As for the vocals on the debut album, the band's lead singer opined that the performances were in accordance with Buie's production policy, and Justo's recollection validated Jerry Buie's non-musician opinion of why his brother hired him.

"He was like the director of a movie," said Justo. "You were to sing it the way Buddy wished *he* could sing it."

Keyboard player Chuck Leavell began doing studio work at the Capricorn facility in Macon during the early 1970s, but was keenly aware of the efforts of the Atlanta Rhythm Section, particularly since he had idolized the Candymen as a youngster.

"I had followed some of their studio work post-Candymen," he detailed, "and as I was aspiring to become a studio musician, I admired their work ethic and talent. Then somewhere along the line I heard that they were forming a band. Then their first record came out, and I thought it sounded really good. I had always admired Buddy's songwriting. I loved the early song the Candymen did that he wrote, 'Georgia Pines.' But by the time the first A.R.S. record came out, I could tell they had matured as musicians and were starting a fresh new sound."

Leavell also did some Atlanta studio work in those days but never recorded at Studio One.

The cover of the debut album marked the beginning of a decades-long association with artist Mike McCarty, who had also been a native of Dothan, Alabama. Mike's parents were friends with the Buie family, so he was keenly aware of the Candymen, the James Gang, and other local and area bands.

Mike and Jerry Buie were buddies, and McCarty sometimes worked at shows promoted by Jerry's older brother. Mike would take up tickets and perform other concert-related tasks.

"We went all the way back to the days of Bobby Goldsboro, who lived two houses from me," he recalled. "I was a musician wannabe, and I used to go over there and hang out, listening to the Webs rehearse."

Mike and Jerry graduated from high school in 1965. McCarty then garnered a degree in fine arts from Auburn University.

"Auburn had a strong graphic-arts department," he remembered. "I took a lot of design classes, although I was a fine-arts major."

While still a student at Auburn, McCarty began his efforts to work in the design-illustration facet of the music business:

"I hit up Buddy about doing an album cover for the Classics IV, and he told me to work something up. I did, and he sent it into the record company. They turned it down—then hired somebody else to do something almost identical."

Later, Mike created a pen-and-ink illustration that was used on a tour poster for Steppenwolf, a prominent rock band of the time, and he recalled that "when I saw my artwork in print, I got 'the bug.'"

After graduating from Auburn, McCarty moved to Atlanta and began working with a studio called Graphics Group, which also had offices in other large American cities as well as London, England.

The young artist began hanging around Studio One when he wasn't working, and, like his old friend Jerry Buie, he would recall being advised of Buddy's innovative plans for a new band (and its moniker).

"He told me about this concept he had for getting his studio musicians together to record their own material," said McCarty. "Since they had already been playing on a lot of hits, they were going to go for it themselves. At one point, he was trying to come up with a name; he was trying to decide between 'the Atlanta Rhythm Section' or 'Blackbush.'"

The cover of the first A.R.S. album was McCarty's first project for Studio One. However, the artist wasn't particularly satisfied with the way it turned out, since the artwork on the front and back were originally slated to have been on the inside of a fold-open cover.

"It was supposed to have been a gatefold album to start with," he recounted, "but it turned into a single-record jacket, so the intended back became the front, and the intended front became the back. It was a pen-and-ink drawing, but at the same time, somebody had turned me on to using an airbrush, so I tried to airbrush over that pen-and-ink. I overdid it, and it was a total disaster. I was freaking out. I was on a tight schedule, and I did the best I could to save it."

The front-cover illustration shows wispy, ghostlike portraits of the band members on a pinkish-yellow field. The back cover shows modern-day Atlanta burning, as what appear to be Civil War–era characters flee from the conflagration.

While the cover imagery is intriguing, the way the names of the band are listed on the front caused some raised eyebrows as well. The upper-right quadrant features the name of the band, but underneath the listing reads: "Featuring: Rodney Justo, Barry Bailey, with Paul Goddard, J. R. Cobb, Robert Nix, and Dean Daughtry."

The names of Justo and Bailey were noticeably larger than the other four members'. Reportedly, this layout was due to the fact that Rodney and Barry were already signed to individual contracts—Justo with Paul Cochran, Bailey with Buddy Buie—and a larger font on the album cover was apparently one of the perks. Regardless, it would be the only album on which the members' names were cited on the front.

Mike McCarty's early work with the Atlanta Rhythm Section began as a side project—call it moonlighting—but he would eventually quit his full-time job to become a freelance designer-illustrator and artist. He concentrated on the music business but also did illustration work for advertising agencies. McCarty would be considered the "in-house art department" for Studio One but was not an employee; he would be paid for each project individually and was usually able to listen to the upcoming tracks for a new album in advance, in order to get ideas for his own tasks.

"Sometimes Buddy would call me to come out to the studio to hear some things that were in progress," he said, "He'd tell me little stories about the songs, like where they came from. Then we'd go to the Clock and would sit around, drinking coffee and talking about titles and possible concepts. Other times he'd let me know he had a new project in the works and would pick me up for lunch; he'd have a tape of something new in his car."

In the mid-1970s, Mike started his own company, McCarty Graphics, and continued to do contract work as an art director-designer with Buie's business, but he also did work for other companies and other artists, including Bang Records, Album Graphics (Chicago, New York), Kat Family Records, and Mylon LeFevre.

••••••

What could have been interpreted as an ominous occurrence happened at one of the Atlanta Rhythm Section's earliest long-distance gigs, which was in Canada. Although the band arrived as contracted, the equipment was delayed, so the performance was canceled. A smattering of other performances followed for a few months.

Tommy Mann, former lead singer for the K-Otics, saw performances by the original lineup of the Atlanta Rhythm Section more than once in the early 1970s.

"I thought their music was unique," he recalled, "because, considering their name, the music seemed to have a rhythm of its own; it was different and I remember thinking it had to do with the genius of Buddy; I knew he was behind that sound. Paul Goddard was playing some of the best bass you've ever heard; he did stuff that a normal bass player wouldn't do. Rodney was pretty much the only one trying to put on a show, because the others would be concentrating on their music, which they did extremely well."

Studio One's first years as a recording facility were also tough. Potential clients weren't exactly standing in line outside the door to sign up for sessions.

"It was like a boy's club; a plaything," J. R. Cobb said. "We'd go over to write songs and practice on our individual instruments, but a lot of times we'd end up shooting pool or playing ping-pong."

In addition to recording or listening to other sessions at Studio One, J. R. was so enamored with the facility he co-owned that he would simply hang out there for several days at a time.

"I had a cot in my office," he said, "and there were times when I'd go in on Monday and wouldn't go home until Thursday—stay up all night, sleep all day. That didn't make me real popular at home. And when I did go home, a lot of times I'd be so tired from staying up so much at the studio that I'd sleep for a day and a half. I also didn't want to go anywhere, and that also didn't make me real popular at home, either."

Some of the earliest clients who used Studio One were intriguing, such as a rock band from New York State called Elf, featuring lead singer Ronnie James Dio.

Even with the responsibilities of managing a new recording studio, Buddy's songwriting ideas continued to germinate incessantly. He had composed songs with Dean Daughtry, Robert Nix, and J. R. Cobb when they were playing in earlier bands, and continued to work with those musicians; however, he would also work with other songwriters outside the Atlanta Rhythm Section, including other artists who recorded at Studio One.

And Buddy's relationship with his "house band" validated that he did indeed want his studio to figure into the creative process of songwriting, on his terms. Studio One's lack of time restrictions facilitated such a propensity.

"Except for one or two albums, the Atlanta Rhythm Section never rehearsed the songs they were going to record," said Rodney Mills. "Buddy and J. R.—or maybe Buddy, Robert, and Dean—would bring in the song or songs on cassette which they'd done in a songwriting format; most of the time it would be just one musician playing on it. Buddy needed Studio One in order to develop the songs further.

"Buddy called the shots on everything, but 99 percent of the time I was in agreement with him. He would even allow me to disagree with him, if it had to do with the making of a record. I actually had the freedom to argue with him. It was a great relationship, and we never got mad at each other, but sometimes we'd yell. Making a point and standing by it made me realize I could probably go a little further in my career than just engineering."

Not surprisingly, whatever cowriting credits Barry Bailey was able to garner were due to musical contributions rather than lyrics.

Bill Lowery took somewhat of a laissez-faire attitude toward the operation of the facility in Doraville.

"Dad was a publisher and a businessman," said Butch Lowery, "and was not as much of an 'in-studio' person anymore. He let the people that worked there do what they were doing."

As for the recorded material that was coming out of Studio One (including Atlanta Rhythm Section recordings), Bill Lowery was impressed, in spite of the facility's struggles.

"We listened to everything that was recorded there and went through the publishing house," Butch recalled, "and at the time, it was a lot of fun. If Dad heard something he liked, he would jump up and down, yelling that it was a smash. He was a bigger-than-life kind of person when it came to that kind of stuff. You knew you had something if he got that excited about it."

Butch had initially begun working with royalty distribution for his father's company and later became head of the promotion department. He noted that Buddy Buie would continue to head over to Bill Lowery's office on a regular basis for many years, seeking Lowery's advice concerning new songs and new ideas; i.e., their mentor-protégé relationship stayed permanently intact.

••••••

For some veteran rock bands, a certain guitar played by one of the members (usually one of the founders) has become a "trademark" of sorts. For example, Wishbone Ash was founded in England in 1969, and the Gibson Flying V of guitarist Andy Powell soon became an instantly identifiable icon for fans of that particular aggregation.

Buddy and J. R. in an outtake photo from the same session for Studio One's first ad. This image includes a better view of J. R.'s recently acquired Gibson Les Paul Deluxe guitar, which he later sold to Barry. *C. Rogers*

Oftentimes, such guitar enthusiasts or fans were (aspiring or armchair) players themselves, and Wishbone Ash has been perceived as a "player's band" for most of its existence.

And if there's an instrument that Atlanta Rhythm Section fans might consider to be an icon, it's Barry Bailey's Gibson Les Paul Deluxe "goldtop" electric guitar (serial #845552).

The Les Paul was actually purchased new at an Atlanta music store by J. R. Cobb, not Bailey, and was the instrument Cobb was holding in the photo seen in the Studio One debut ad. An outtake image from the same session showed off the guitar even more.

"I wasn't much of a gearhead then, and I had never owned a Les Paul," J. R. said of his former instrument. "I had played a goldtop that had belonged to Joe South which he had left at the studio, and thought I might like to have one of my own."

The construction, finish, and serial number of the guitar indicate that it is a 1969 model, the first year the Les Paul Deluxe was made (and at the time, it was available only with a gold top).

Bailey recalled how he gravitated toward Cobb's new guitar:

"I had been using my Telecaster in the studio, and my Les Paul Jr. in the studio and on live dates, but the Junior was somewhat 'wobbly' regarding its tuning. I started checking out, then borrowing, J. R.'s goldtop. I don't know why I started playing it, but it was like a magnet, so I bought it from him. It was one of better investments I have ever made."

Cobb didn't regret parting with the Deluxe.

"I was playing mostly rhythm and some slide and was looking for a sound that wasn't real close to Barry's," he recounted, "and I found that a [Fender] Strat worked better. The goldtop was and is a great-sounding guitar. It just didn't seem as versatile as a Strat for what I was trying to do. And I still favor a Strat."

The goldtop was nicknamed "Reb" by a member of the A.R.S. road crew. It would become Bailey's primary instrument, onstage and in the studio, for his entire career with the Atlanta Rhythm Section, and artistic images of it would even be seen on more than one album cover in future years.

"Reb" would go through numerous appropriate utilitarian modifications over the decades, including replacement tuners and a Gibson TP-6 fine-tune tailpiece. The guitar also garnered easier-to-grip replacement knobs (and knob replacement happened more than once).

Obviously, such a utility instrument would ultimately display a plethora of wear, but "Reb" would serve Barry and the band well over the decades.

"I'm glad (the goldtop) ended up in the right hands," said J. R.

••••••

As if Buddy Buie didn't have enough irons in the fire, his personal life went topsy-turvy in 1971, when he received a phone call from Gloria, his former high school sweetheart.

Gloria's husband had earned an engineering degree at Alabama and had then acquired a master's degree. He and Gloria moved to Orange, Texas, where he went to work for DuPont. They'd had a son but were divorcing after nine years of marriage.

At the same time, Buddy was going through a divorce himself, and the mothers of the former high school sweethearts made such news known to each other in Dothan.

"My mother had been talking to Grace Buie one day—probably at the café," Gloria recalled, "and she told her I was getting a divorce, and Mrs. Buie told her Buddy was also getting a divorce, and she gave Mother his phone number, and my mother gave it to me."

In an awkward first contact, Gloria called, not knowing that the phone number was the residence where Buddy was still living with his soon-to-be-ex-wife. Buie's stepdaughter answered, thinking the caller was Buddy's sister, who was also named Gloria. She told Buie that "Aunt Gloria" was on the phone.

When Buddy came to the phone and realized who the caller was, he quickly terminated the call, promising to call back, which he did.

"When he called, I didn't know what he had accomplished, but he brought me up to date," Gloria said. "He could not believe I hadn't heard his songs, but I told him I was out in Cajun country, listening to Charlie Pride. I didn't know a thing about songs like 'Spooky' and 'Traces.'"

Reunited: Buddy and Gloria together again, at Mary and Rodney Mills's house, New Year's Eve, 1971–72.

Gloria moved to Atlanta. She and Buddy married in June 1972 at her parents' house in Dothan. The attendees reportedly included members of Grandview Baptist Church as well as barefooted musicians.

••••••

For all of the arduous and meticulous work that the Atlanta Rhythm Section band members, Buddy Buie, and Rodney Mills had put into the band's debut album, the lack of response to it was discouraging.

"We'd worked a long time on that first album," Rodney Mills recounted. "Obviously, the expectations for it were tremendous, so when it didn't happen, most of the musicians probably figured that they could just go back to doing studio work."

Another traumatic problem would erupt when the band experienced its first turnover in personnel— Rodney Justo quit in the spring of 1972.

"I had to do what was best for my family," Justo detailed. "It fell apart in the first week of April, at the beginning of what was going to be an extended tour with Deep Purple. We were in California, and Buddy comes around and says, 'Rodney, what a deal I got signed today! I just came from [cartoon production company] Hanna-Barbera, and I just signed us up to do all of the soundtrack work for a new cartoon series called *Butch Cassidy and the Sundance Kids!*'"

Already frustrated and financially strained, Rodney wondered where he was going to fit into the picture, since soundtracks are almost exclusively instrumental. Buie offered to put Justo on the contracts as a background singer, which didn't sit well with Rodney. He opted to follow up on an offer he'd had to sing in New York as a background/commercial vocalist, which paid much better than a similar job would have paid elsewhere.

"It was not easy," he said of his decision. "I moved to New York, where I worked with singers and songwriters like B. J. Thomas and Barry Mann. Even though I left the band, I stayed friendly with all the guys and Buddy."

The rest of the band understood the reasoning behind Rodney's transition.

"He came up and tried it for maybe a year," J. R. said of Rodney's days as a founding member of the Atlanta Rhythm Section. "We couldn't get anything going, and we didn't work enough for him to support his family. It was a tough time for all of us, but we decided we didn't want it to be the end, and we started looking for a new singer."

Rodney would eventually move back to the South, where he reunited with former Candymen guitarist John Rainey Adkins in a band called Beaverteeth, which also included Adkins's younger brother David. After two albums with that band, Rodney began a successful, decades-long career in the beverage distribution business in the Tampa area.

••••••

Back in Atlanta, Kitten's Korner had evolved into a concert club known as Funochio's, and its nightlife environment had gotten decidedly rougher.

Jeff Carlisi, son of a career US Navy aviator, was an architecture student at the nearby Georgia Institute of Technology (a.k.a. Georgia Tech) in 1972 but had played with bands in Jacksonville, Florida, where he'd graduated from high school. He described Funochio's as "the kind of place where you thought you might have to fight your way out of there."

A raucous band from Jacksonville called Lynyrd Skynyrd was a regular at Funochio's; the hell-raising aggregation would perform there several times in 1972 and 1973.

One night during a Skynyrd tenure at Funochio's, Jeff was in the audience when Barry Bailey sat in with the Jacksonville band. Mylon LeFevre had accompanied Bailey and contributed background vocals.

Ed King, a member of Skynyrd at the time, recalled that Barry played a guitar that was not set up in a standard configuration.

"Bailey showed up and borrowed my Les Paul," King remembered, "which was strung with .011s [guitar strings], and it had slightly higher action for slide. He played it with no problem and just blew me away."

Carlisi: "I already knew about Atlanta bands like Eric Quincy Tate and the Hampton Grease Band, as well as local guys like Barry, but this was the first time I'd heard him play. It was probably just a one-four-five blues jam, and everybody was playing the best blues they could possibly play. And Barry played great."

Jeff would earn his architecture degree but would never put his education to use, opting instead for a career in rock and roll as the founding lead guitarist for 38 Special. The late 1970s would witness that band recording at Studio One.

••••••

The Atlanta Rhythm Section would acquire its new lead singer / frontman soon after Rodney Justo departed in mid-1972. Ronnie Hammond had already been on the premises of Studio One and other local studios, having migrated to Atlanta from Macon, where he had been a singer and guitarist for a locally successful band called the Celtics.

The young vocalist had experienced a tumultuous childhood, having been brought up with numerous siblings and stepsiblings. Both his father and stepfather had alcohol problems. He was close to his brother Steve, who was five years younger.

"My brother had music in his blood his whole life," Steve recalled. "He was very talented and could play almost any instrument."

Ronnie lived with an older sister and her husband for most of his high school years. In those times, he found solace in the Celtics, playing guitar and sharing lead vocals with a bandmate named James Cruz. The band was good enough to record two singles at Unlimited Sound in Atlanta for the Decca label, with Rodney Mills engineering the recording session. They also backed up B. J. Thomas on concert tours in Georgia in the late 1960s.

Following high school, Ronnie made his way to Atlanta, determined to work his way into the music business. He began hanging around local studios, doing odd jobs and

Ronnie Hammond's Macon-based band, the Celtics. Ronnie is seen with a Gretsch guitar, second from the right.

picking up pointers about recording and engineering. He began recording demos and jingles and played all the instruments on one special version of "Happy Birthday."

Hammond had sung a preliminary/"scratch" vocal for "Days of Our Lives," a song on the Atlanta Rhythm Section's first album, while Rodney Justo was out of town on a non-A.R.S.-related recording date. Rodney put down the final vocal when he returned, but thought Ronnie had done a good job on the scratch version.

And when Justo left the band, he recommended Hammond as his replacement.

Steve Hammond believes that Ronnie's multifaceted work around the studio enhanced his recruitment when Justo departed.

"I don't think he ever really auditioned," said Steve.

Rodney Mills: "Even before Rodney Justo left, some of us already knew Ronnie Hammond was talented. His band had recorded at Unlimited Sound before I was at LeFevre, and Ronnie had shown some affinity for rudimentary engineering. And when I was at LeFevre, my friend Don Taylor and I had a small production company, and we heard that Ronnie was thinking about going into the Air Force, but we signed him to a contract; his mother had to cosign.

"He moved to Atlanta and went to work at LeFevre Sound, and he got to meet everyone who ended up in the Rhythm Section. When I left LeFevre, he took over engineering. Later, he started hanging out at Studio One. When Rodney left, Ronnie started filling in doing scratch tracks for Buddy, and when Buddy started looking around to replace Rodney, Ronnie was right there—and Buddy conveniently ignored the contract Don Taylor and I had with Ronnie, but I let that go."

Publicity photo with the A.R.S.'s new singer, Ronnie Hammond, on the right.

"Ronnie Hammond had been coming around the studio, helping out with engineering," J. R. averred, "and we happened to notice that he was a good singer. I was impressed, and I think Buddy was too. But even then, Buddy had some qualms, because Ronnie wasn't a very 'visual' person—nice-looking guy, but he didn't have a lot of charisma, which a frontman would have to have."

Ronnie was several years younger than anyone else in the band, but in spite of any insecurities about suddenly being thrust into a spotlight—not to mention having to replace a veteran singer and showman like Rodney Justo—he resolved to work hard to validate his position as the band's new singer. He even contributed to the songwriting for the band's next album.

Hammond's debut was on the band's sophomore effort, *Back up against the Wall* (also on Decca/MCA), released in February 1973. As for comparisons between his vocals and Rodney Justo's, most listeners would probably have initially opined that Rodney was more of a wailer while Ronnie was more of a crooner, but such a pronouncement would have been an overgeneralization—Ronnie's voice did indeed seem to be a bit more laid back, but he could belt out a tune if called upon to do so.

The band's interplay on their respective instruments seemed to be a bit stronger on *Back up against the Wall*, as exemplified by the churning opener, "Wrong." The ballads "Will I Live On" and "Conversation" showcased Ronnie's plaintive vocals, and that latter tune would become a favorite of many A.R.S. fans.

And an incident chronicled in the title track was based on a true life event in which J. R. had been a participant, years earlier.

"Before the Classics IV got started well," Cobb recalled, "I was in Jacksonville, and a guy who worked at a radio station there told me about a singer named Connie Haines. She'd worked with Frank Sinatra and wanted to do some rock and roll, so me and Joe Wilson went to Las Vegas—that was the first time I'd ever been there—and played with her at the Stardust Inn. We had a bass player and a drummer, and some add-on musicians she lined up.

"Joe and I roomed together, and we'd been there about five days when there was a knock on the door at four o'clock in the morning. It was two men in suits; they didn't show any badges and one of 'em stuck a gun in my face and said, 'Do you have any I.D.?' I did, but to make a long story short, they took us to jail on a Friday night because somebody had committed an armed robbery and we fit the description, as did the kind of car we were driving.

"We stayed in the Clark County jail over the weekend, until some judge let us loose. We were in a big cell; there must have been thirty-five people in there, and Joe and I were the only two white guys. We stayed on our bunks and kept our mouths shut. But I heard one guy saying he was in jail because a man fell over his razor during a fight in a bar, and I never forgot his story. Very few songs I wrote with Buddy were autobiographical, but 'Traces' was, and so was that line about the razor in 'Back up against the Wall.'"

Once again, a gatefold concept figured both into the front and back covers of the new album. Mike McCarty's color drawing envisioned a tapestry showing a fantasy pastoral setting with hills, fields, and flowers—and closer inspection of the illustration revealed marijuana leaves and psilocybin mushrooms. One corner of the tapestry was pulled back, revealing a Confederate Battle Flag and a brick wall underneath.

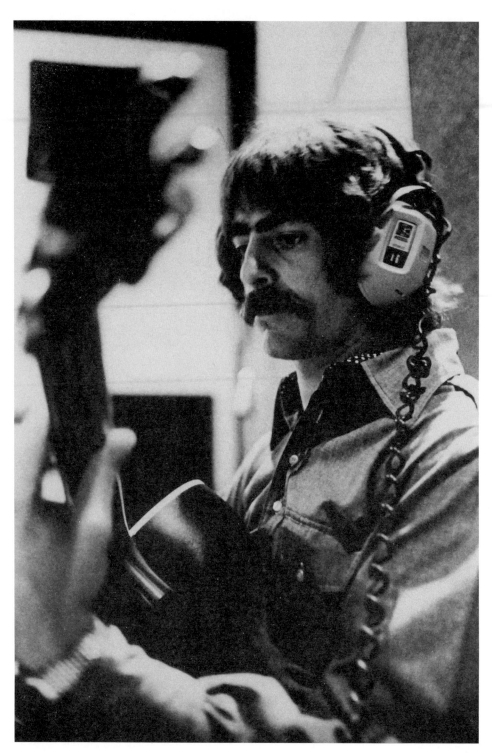
J. R. works on an acoustic riff during a recording session.

Decades later, McCarty would contemplate the display of the Battle Flag as well as the evolution of its symbolism in the public eye since that time, acknowledging that the iconic banner had figured into the marketing of many southern bands in the 1970s.

"It was just an attempt to say 'We are Southern,'" he said. "At the time, the Confederate Battle Flag didn't have the stigma that it has today."

••••••

J. R. thought putting out a follow-up album with a new singer had worked.

"Because of the local success of that album and some national success, we were tickled to death with Ronnie," he said.

Having had his confidence boosted a bit, Ronnie also began writing songs in earnest with Buddy and other members of the band.

"He was very excited about that," Steve Hammond said of his brother's songwriting opportunities. "He used to love going down to Eufaula and writing with Buddy in the trailer. J. R. went on a lot of those trips with them."

••••••

After taking note of the burgeoning "Southern Rock" phenomenon (especially Phil Walden's Capricorn Records), veteran New York musician Al Kooper had moved to Atlanta and had founded a venture called Sound of the South Records, distributed by MCA Records. In the spring of 1973, he would record Lynyrd Skynyrd and Atlanta's Mose Jones at Studio One, essentially leasing the facility from Buddy Buie and associates.

Mose Jones actually had two incarnations, the first of which would be the aggregation recorded by Kooper. Their keyboard player, Steve McRay, was a Vietnam veteran who joined the band soon after he left the Army.

Ultimately, much more attention would be paid to Lynyrd Skynyrd than to Mose Jones by Kooper's record label, even though the latter aggregation was a hometown band. The first incarnation of Mose Jones would record two albums, *Get Right* and *Mose Knows*, under Kooper's aegis, before splitting (for the first time) in 1975.

J. R.: "I remember Al coming around the studio, and people were talking about he'd played with Blood, Sweat & Tears and had done that big *Super Session* album, but now he was producing Lynyrd Skynyrd at our place. Sometimes we'd come in during the day, and they'd come in at night, or vice versa. [Skynyrd singer] Ronnie Van Zant was the taskmaster of that band. He insisted that they rehearse over and over to get their songs as tight as you can imagine."

Former Jacksonville resident Robert Nix played drums on Lynyrd Skynyrd's "Tuesday's Gone," which also included Kooper on Mellotron.

Interestingly, after the contents of what would become the band's debut album (*Pronounced Leh-nerd Skin-nerd*) were completed, the band returned to Studio One and recorded "Sweet Home Alabama" and "Saturday Night Special," which ended up as the leadoff tracks on the band's next two albums.

What's more, Ronnie Van Zant was a fan of Ronnie Hammond's singing, and the two lead vocalists became good friends. Van Zant reportedly commented on Hammond's vocal range, telling the new A.R.S. frontman, "You have the most perfect rock-and-roll voice I've ever heard."

The use of a Fender Stratocaster guitar by another Lynyrd Skynyrd member underlined J. R.'s commitment to concentrate on that brand and model as his primary guitar with the A.R.S.

"When Ed King came into Studio One with Skynyrd, he was the one who really made me want to stick with a Strat," Cobb recalled. "I knew he'd played with the Strawberry Alarm Clock, and he got that 'Strat sound' better than anybody I'd ever heard."

And King himself was a fan of Studio One.

"I loved that place," King recalled. "Very relaxing, and what great sound. I recall Buie coming in during both 'Sweet Home Alabama' and 'Saturday Night Special' [sessions]. He was quite complimentary!"

Listening to some of the studio work by some of the Atlanta Rhythm Section members, King also admired the sound Barry Bailey evoked from his red Telecaster.

Dean Daughtry remembered playing, along with other A.R.S. members, on some of Al Kooper's own material recorded at Studio One, while Robert Nix recalled that Ronnie Van Zant would hang around Studio One when it was occupied by the A.R.S., encouraging the band about taking their sound out on the road.

However, the Rhythm Section continued its live efforts at a measured pace, content to hone its concert chops at numerous venues in Atlanta and the surrounding before seriously considering major touring.

In the first half of the 1970s, Atlanta venues of different sizes would offer concert opportunities for name bands and local up-and-coming aggregations.

Promoter Alex Cooley's Electric Ballroom was exactly what its name said—in a previous incarnation, it had hosted elegant society events as the ballroom of the Georgian Terrace Hotel. That venue would later become known as the Agora Ballroom.

The Great Southeast Music Hall and Richards (the plural of the given names of the two owners) were also viable establishments in that decade. Underground Atlanta would bring in musical acts to entice patrons for its numerous shops, clubs, and restaurants, and the once-grandiose Fox Theatre would experience a comeback by hosting rock-and-roll concerts.

For the bigger artists, there was the outdoor amphitheater in Chastain Park and the Omni Coliseum, which opened in 1972, and was also the home of Atlanta's professional basketball and hockey teams, as well as professional wrestling shows.

••••••

The year 1973 saw the Atlanta Rhythm Section continuing to develop a hometown base of fans by performing at local concert halls and rock clubs.

The band performed more than once at a "Rock at Midnight" series of concerts at the Great Southeast Music Hall to showcase their talent. In mid-March, they tried out covers of Procol Harum's "A Salty Dog" and the Band's "The Weight" at one of the middle-of-the-night shows. A band called Devil's Advocate was the opening act.

One oddball concert booking for the band—perhaps one of the most unusual in the band's entire history—happened on three consecutive nights in early May, when the band performed for the "Rock at Midnight" portion of a "Howdy Doody Revival," featuring Buffalo Bob Smith, the original host of the iconic Saturday morning children's show that was broadcast from 1947 to 1960. While the event ran for six days (and included a few matinees), the "Rock at Midnight" shows were done only on the last three nights of the "revival."

Even more improbable was the placement of gravel-voiced "singer" Tom Waits as an opening act for Buffalo Bob's performances. A local band called Mason opened

for the A.R.S. at the three "Rock at Midnight" performances that were associated with the "Howdy Doody Revival."

July 9 saw the A.R.S. opening for Manfred Mann's Earth Band at Richards. The boys were making steady progress regarding live performances.

••••••

Guitarist Marvin Taylor, former bandmate with Kim Venable and Tommy Mann in the K-Otics in the mid-1960s, had been, in his own words, "scuffling from day to day" as a musician in Atlanta and had done a decent amount of recording work at Studio One. However, Taylor's opinion was that he was in sort of a second-echelon position behind frontline players such as Messrs. Bailey and Cobb.

"It was like I was on the 'B-team,' which was fine," said Taylor. "There wasn't much left to do once Barry or J. R. got through with their parts on a song."

Taylor also recalled a Sound of the South showcase in July at Richards that he attended with members of the A.R.S.

"Me and Robert Nix and Dean Daughtry were at Studio One hanging out," Taylor remembered, "and somebody said that Al Kooper was having a record party at Richards. We kind of said, 'Well, big deal.' There was some band Al brought in from California called Elijah, and Mose Jones, and Lynyrd Skynyrd. We were kind of 'Been there, heard that.'

"Then we were told that the original Old Hickory House [barbecue restaurant] was catering, and we were off to Richards quick! We got three seats right down by the stage and stuffed our faces with barbecue. Elijah was really good; they were like Santana with horns. When Skynyrd came on, they were amazing; maybe the best I ever heard. Ronnie [Van Zant] had on a t-shirt that said 'Sweet Home Alabama'; I'm from Alabama but didn't know where Sweet Home was. It was an incredible show. When Mose Jones played, Al Kooper jammed with them."

••••••

Some musicians, including members of the Atlanta Rhythm Section, have had relationships or marriages that lasted decades. Others have ended up as "recycled singles," sometimes more than once.

Paul Goddard's significant other was a woman named Phyllis Karlip. She was Jewish, and her parents were firm in their desire for her to marry a man of the same faith. Accordingly, she and Paul cohabited for many years. Following the deaths of her parents, they married.

For two A.R.S. members, Studio One would offer other temporary but non-musical use in 1973—at one point, both Ox Daughtry and Ronnie Hammond were actually living inside the facility. Dean had been through a divorce, but Ronnie was just crashing there.

"There was no hot water at Studio One," Dean recalled, "so we took sponge baths by heating water on the 'eye' of the coffee maker. We heated our food in cans the same way. I cooked on that coffee maker many a time."

Daughtry also recounted a near brawl with members of Lynyrd Skynyrd, who were recording there at the time:

"Ronnie [Hammond] and I were staying upstairs, sleeping on cots in Buddy's office. [Skynyrd] came in one morning—they recorded in the daytime, we recorded at night—and they were hollering and cussing; probably still drunk. And anytime

82

you woke Ronnie up, he would be a damn *******, so he opens up the door of the office and yells 'Shut up, you ****in' rednecks!'

"Next thing I know, they're comin' up the stairs after us, so I shut the door and locked it, quick. I even thought about shoving Buddy's desk over to block the door, but didn't."

The two A.R.S. members eventually got an apartment together, in the same complex where Marvin Taylor was sharing an apartment with musicians Jerry McKoon and Paul Day.

And an eccentric songwriter—not a member of the Atlanta Rhythm Section or the staff at Studio One—had taken to sleeping in his car out in the parking lot in front of the studio. One night, he fell asleep in his vehicle while smoking a cigarette and woke up to find the interior on fire. He escaped and smashed in the windows on the front door of the building to get inside, failing to notice a nearby outdoor faucet with a hose attached.

Grabbing two coffee cups, he filled them with water from the small kitchen, ran back outside, and tossed them onto the vehicle, but several repetitions of his insignificant effort were to no avail.

People who might have kept regular business hours at the studio—or even at other businesses in the Oakcliff Industrial Park complex—arrived at work the next morning to find a charred hulk that had originally been an automobile sitting in front of Studio One, and the facility was missing the windows on its front door.

Soon afterward, the same songwriter erected a tent outside Studio One and camped out there. Eventually, the Lowery family reportedly set him up in an apartment.

●●●●●●

A.R.S. members continued to do studio work, of course (even at other studios, since those facilities had been the musicians' original proving grounds). They would look forward to the methodical stability of studio sessions more than many players in other rock bands.

One memorable project for Barry Bailey around this time was his participation in the recording of *High Life*, the second album by Scottish singer-songwriter Frankie Miller, whose vocal stylings had been compared to Otis Redding and Joe Cocker, among others. Once again, iconic producer Allen Toussaint, who had produced Mylon's *We Believe* album, returned to LeFevre Sound Studios for the *High Life* sessions. Toussaint also played keyboards and wrote several songs for the album. Among the other musicians, Joe Wilson, J. R.'s buddy from the Classics IV days, played guitar and slide guitar.

"Frankie was an exceptional singer," Barry recounted. "Most of the material – Frankie's and Allen's songs—was also very good. The sessions were not intensely challenging, but they were not easy either; Allen was pretty particular. Sometimes he would dictate parts, but, as often, he would let us—or at least me—go for ourselves. I couldn't pick any standout tracks, but most memorable, since it's been covered quite a bit, is 'Brickyard Blues.' I still love Frankie's voice, and the comparison to Otis is unavoidable, but that's not a bad thing."

High Life was released in early 1974, and Barry's playing on the album impressed other guitar players elsewhere.

Elliot Easton, who would hit the big time a few years later as the lead guitarist for the Cars, had a habit of paying close attention to session/backing guitarists. He first listened to the *High Life* album because of his admiration of Allen Toussaint, but he quickly came to respect Bailey's non-flashy but appropriate licks and riffs.

"I've always been attracted to tasteful, soulful, and economical players," Easton said of his admiration of Barry's fretwork, "and I always admired many fine session guitarists. I got the same charge out of Cornell Dupree, Reggie Young, or Jesse Ed Davis."

Word was beginning to spread beyond Atlanta about the unique studio-musicians-with-their-own-band concept of the Atlanta Rhythm Section, and the innovative recording ideas proffered by Studio One were garnering some interest as well.

And certain players who would later excel in musical genres that didn't necessarily feature loud guitars were also impressed by some of the sounds that were emanating from Doraville.

"When I started playing bass in 1970, I was listening to everything from straight-ahead jazz to rock, R&B, funk, and pop," said award-winning bassist Mark Egan, who attended the University of Miami's fabled School of Music and would become a founding member of the Pat Metheny Group in the late 1970s.

"I started doing recording sessions in Miami in 1973, at Criteria Studios," Egan remembered. "It was during that time that I was checking out what was being recorded in different parts of the country, and I started hearing the music from Atlanta. I didn't know who the players were, but I really liked the sound and feel.

"My first exposure to the Atlanta Rhythm Section was listening to the entire *Back up against the Wall* album at a friend's house, so 'Wrong' was the first song I ever heard. We used to get together and have listening parties for a wide variety of music, from Miles Davis to Steve Miller, and the A.R.S was part of these listening sessions."

It wasn't any surprise that Egan became disproportionately focused on the playing of Paul Goddard, recalling how the Atlanta Rhythm Section's bassist "drove the band and made it flow. I liked the way that he soloed as well. I've always liked the 'converted guitar players to bassists' approach to playing; it's usually very melodic and so different from the style of someone who has only played bass."

Egan would later record with luminaries such as Sting, Joan Osborne, and the Gil Evans Orchestra. He also continued to listen to the Atlanta Rhythm Section in the ensuing years, noting, "I liked the warmth of the grooves, and the jams that they would get into. I also was fascinated by the compositions and arrangements and uses of odd time meters, and was impressed by their musicianship and unique sound."

••••••

Abetted by strong songwriting as well as precise and appropriate playing and singing, the Atlanta Rhythm Section's second album had indicated that the band was determined to stay in the hunt as a viable musical aggregation.

A series of articles on the "Southern Rock" phenomenon were published in the University of Georgia student newspaper, the *Red and the Black*, in the fall of 1973, and a late September installment profiled the Atlanta Rhythm Section and Studio One.

••••••

Within a few years, Paul Cochran had sold his interests in Low-Sal Music and Studio One. He continued to stay active with other projects in the music field.

CHAPTER 7
Hometown Evolution

n terms of sales, *Back up against the Wall* had performed better than the Rhythm Section's debut album had, but the results were still poor. Moreover, an outright hit song had not been forthcoming from the sophomore effort, so Decca and the A.R.S. parted ways. Efforts at signing with another label soon got underway.

And once the band signed with Polydor Records, they would acquire an important ally in Arnie Geller, who would come to believe in the Atlanta Rhythm Section and their music. Buddy would ultimately refer to Geller as having been the band's "patron saint."

Geller was a native of Detroit and had been the producer of a hit version of "Stand by Me" by Spyder Turner. He had also produced a syndicated "dance party" television show that had started in Detroit on CKLW-TV; the show was technically broadcast from Windsor, Ontario, just across the border, so the station had Canadian call letters. He had also briefly managed a loud and boisterous Motor City rock band known as the MC5.

Arnie was Polydor's director of marketing when he became aware of the Atlanta Rhythm Section.

"I was with MGM [Metro-Goldwyn Mayer] in Los Angeles, which was acquired by Polydor," he detailed. "[Company officials] came out to L.A. to MGM and said they were firing everybody because they were going to consolidate and work everything out of New York, but they asked three of us to stay on, and they asked me to come to New York as 'the MGM expert.' Soon after I got to New York, they gave me the marketing position. At the time, Polydor was partners with Phonogram; Polydor was the German company and Phonogram was the Dutch company, and they became known as Polygram. At the time, they were the largest record company in the world."

Under the aegis of company president Jerry Schoenbaum, Polydor diversified in the 1970s by signing R&B acts such as James Brown, as well as other artists in other genres. Schoenbaum would depart Polydor in the middle of the decade, but not before letting Arnie know about a band from the Deep South that had just been signed.

"He was a great music guy," Geller said of Schoenbaum. "He and I had a close working relationship, and he called me into his office one day and said, 'Arnie, I'm leaving the company,' but he also said, 'I just signed an act by the name of the Atlanta Rhythm Section by way of a guy named Buddy Buie.'

"In big companies, acts can get lost very easily, but he said, 'I really believe in this act. I want to ask you to take on the responsibility for these guys, because I believe they're going to be something, but they're going to need some help.' He felt an obligation; he didn't want to walk out and leave them hanging. So I inherited them from Jerry. I had never heard any of their music."

However, once Arnie listened to some previous A.R.S. material, he became enthusiastic about the band's potential.

"I could hear what Jerry had heard," he recalled. "To me, it hadn't been a question up to that point, because I'd promised Jerry I was going to take care of this band. Once I got into their music, however, I became personally dedicated."

When the Atlanta Rhythm Section recorded its first Polydor album, Geller's marketing acumen motivated him to look forward, not backward—he didn't compare the pending album to previous A.R.S. recordings he'd heard.

"I was in the business of selecting and selling music to the public," he said, "and I would listen to the product that I was going to have to sell."

The unprecedented idea of studio musicians forming their own aggregation to include requisite touring as well as songwriting was intriguing to Arnie, who remembered, "I thought it was pretty cool. I thought about how Glen Campbell had been a studio musician, but this was a whole band of quality musicians who knew what they were doing. And I understood why Jerry Schoenbaum appreciated that, and why he believed in them. They weren't 'just another band'; they had something special."

Arnie contacted Studio One to set up a meeting, and Buddy and Gloria came to New York. At the time, Gloria was pregnant (Benjamin Carlton Buie would be born on February 2, 1974).

"He was totally wrapped up in this project," Geller said of his initial meeting with Buddy, "so it was important for him to get the company to believe in it. I remember that first meeting like it was yesterday—Buddy was trying to explain how he wanted to exploit the phrase 'First-Class Southern Music' for the band instead of 'Southern Rock,' since they were seasoned and respected studio musicians. It was his 'concept'—it wasn't really a 'slogan'—but I used it. It was important because it helped the campaign to show the quality of the musicianship."

As for why an experienced record industry executive from Detroit and a fast-talking producer/songwriter from the Alabama Wiregrass bonded (in New York City), Geller noted with a chuckle, "I have no idea, but we became the best of friends. We were from two different worlds, but there was something that meant we would connect, and that something was mutual respect. It didn't happen the first day, but for me, what started out as an obligation turned into a real belief.

"Buddy was driven to succeed; he was always thinking and always wanted to discuss his ideas. The interesting thing that we had in common was that we didn't always agree with each other, but we complemented each other in our efforts. We developed a lot of ideas together, at all hours. This business isn't a 'job,' it's a lifestyle, and you don't stop doing it at the end of the day and go home."

••••••

Third Annual Pipe Dream's 1974 release gave the Atlanta Rhythm Section and the Buies a hopeful attitude, since the band was on a new label and had a corporate booster in Arnie Geller. However, things were still looking bleak on the horizon, and Buddy's cynical title for the album reflected how such optimism could quickly fade.

"I thought it was very appropriate," Barry said of the title (and the band members still told themselves they could always go back to full-time studio work).

Buddy was listed as producer, but for the first time, Robert Nix and J. R. Cobb were as associate producers, and such a citation would be the case for the next three albums. Even though most of the songs were still relatively brief, the band made it obvious that they were branching out stylistically.

The leadoff track for the new album was "Doraville," a good-ol'-boy salute to the community where the band and studio were located. The whimsical tune would be released as a single and was a song on which Barry Bailey received a rare songwriting credit (in addition to Buddy Buie and Robert Nix). According to Barry and Buddy, the song had resulted from a lack of activity at the studio.

"We had a lot of time to kill," Barry recalled, "and a lot of tape to kill. We were jamming one late afternoon or early evening, and for some reason I started playing this melody, which ended up being the chorus melody in 'Doraville.'"

"One night we went to the Clock," Buddy remembered, "and Robert and I sat down in the booth, working on the melody that Barry had been working with. I just sort of blurted out 'Doraville, touch of country in the city,' and Robert said 'Yeah, that's it.' So we started writing it and almost finished it that night. We went back and showed Barry what we'd done, and Barry played it on the guitar and made some changes."

Paul Goddard's bass had anchored the loping, upbeat tempo of the jam that had been the origin of the song, and the same time signature would be used once "Doraville" began to be developed.

The song's "touch of country in the city" line was on the money, since Doraville was still somewhat rural in the mid-1970s. It left some music fans scratching their heads about the reasons such a song was written.

"When that song came out, it was like 'Doraville? Why would they write a song about *that* place?,'" said one longtime fan. "They still had cow pastures out there!"

Third Annual Pipe Dream had sing-along ballads such as "Get Your Head out of Your Heart," as well as the wistful, down-home "Jesus Hearted People," on which local gospel icons Mylon LeFevre and Hugh Jarrett sang backing vocals. Barry had been the band member who had come up with the original music for the gospel-tinged tune.

"This was a chord progression and melody that I had written on my own," the guitarist explained, "and then presented to Buddy and Robert, who were, for the most part, my 'collaborators' where writing for the band was concerned. It began with me just wanting to write something in an open G tuning, but I was also leaning toward a big gospel kind of feel, as if Eva Mae LeFevre came in banging away—in a good way—on piano in her very identifiable style. I don't remember if I ever told that to Buddy, or if my playing it—over and over—suggested the gospel possibilities. Anyway, it turned out much to my liking and not far from my original concept. The phrase 'Jesus-hearted people' was something Buddy heard an older 'country' sort of lady say at a convenience store in lower Alabama. It was probably something to the effect of, 'Well, they're just Jesus-hearted people—bless their hearts.'"

Obviously, Dean was right at home with his piano introduction on "Jesus Hearted People," and his embellishments throughout the song added to its authenticity in an inimitable manner. Ox recalled that "Jesus Hearted People" "made me feel like I used to feel in church playing gospel songs, and the people where I was raised were the people [cited] in the song."

And Hugh Jarrett inserted an extra bass lyric of "yours and mine" between lines on the final chorus that nailed down the gospel feel of the song.

The semi-jazzy "Angel" garnered a bit of airplay, and Ronnie's plaintive repetition of "You don't love me anymore" in "Close the Door" came across as the most passionate singing he'd done for the band up to that point.

The album's instrumental, "Blues in Maude's Flat," exhibited a lot of upbeat, tasteful guitar playing in a slightly bluesy and very listenable manner. The song, which had an easygoing shuffle tempo, was written by jazz guitarist Grant Green. It cranked off with Barry and J. R. doing harmony licks on twin lead guitars, which was actually somewhat rare for A.R.S. studio work—Barry recalled that he usually double-tracked harmony guitar parts with himself.

The song also showcased Bailey pulling out numerous impressive chord-based riffs and licks, as well as straight-on single-string blues bends.

"I've always been very much of a chord person," he detailed. "In fact, I learned to play off of chords, as opposed to scales. I listened to a lot of players like Grant Green, Kenny Burrell, and Wes Montgomery, when I wasn't listening to blues players like Freddie King, Albert King, and B. B. King. Besides Chet Atkins albums, I used to play along with the Johnny Smith album that included 'Moonlight in Vermont,' which was chords almost straight through."

Paul and Dean also got to solo on "Blues in Maude's Flat," utilizing the melodic number to affirm their own abilities.

"Join the Race" was a flat-out rocker that featured jazz-type chords and riffs. It was written by John Fristoe, who Barry cited as "a very good friend, player, and writer." Once again, Barry and J. R. traded off riffs toward the end of the song.

Another decent rocker was "Help Yourself," propelled by Robert Nix's pounding beat.

And "The War Is Over" was a two-minute, mysterious and ethereal type of interlude (with orchestration) that barely has any lyrics. Considering the timing of the album, it seemed obvious to most listeners that it was a reference to the United States ending its combat role in Vietnam.

Barry was also involved in the songwriting for 'The War Is Over,' recalling that he had created the basic music "quite a while before we recorded *Third Annual Pipe Dream*. I showed it to J. R., and we played it together, mostly for our own entertainment, as we did other pieces, occasionally—some were original, some were copies that we just liked. On more than one occasion, Buddy heard us and eventually suggested we record it for the album. I believe that while we were recording, Buddy, Robert, and Ronnie were sitting out front, listening, and between the three of them came up with the lines and melody: 'The war is over. The fighting done. Let's go home.'

"Obviously, Ronnie's vocal, albeit brief, and the strings—[which were] beautifully arranged, I thought—were added later. When Buddy submitted the song for copyright, we were informed that there weren't enough lyrics to copyright, so no writer's credit would be given to Buddy, Robert, or, Ronnie. This wasn't much of a big deal except to Robert, who wanted credit on anything and everything that he might have had something to do with, and understandably so.

"The observation about Vietnam would be one of a couple of correct interpretations of the theme. Another was simply that the all-night recording session was coming to an end, and the three guys sitting out front who composed those three lines most likely shared that sentiment, individually and collectively."

The album wrapped up with the semi-bluesy, surly yet humorous "Who You Gonna Run to (When You're through Walking on Me)," the title of which explains the message in the song.

The cover illustration for the new release was somewhat similar to *Back up against the Wall*—bucolic setting, hidden/scrutiny-worthy imagery (including a psilocybin mushroom poking up through a cowflop)—but a country lane, a church, and a castle were also seen.

Mike McCarty detailed that the semifantasy setting was created to coordinate with the sentiment of the title of the album.

"I was going through some things in my attic that had come from my mother's side of the family," the artist said, "and found this painting by Charles Craig that was about a hundred years old. I think it was done in Germany; I think that's a German castle and I'd love to find out where it really is. I used that painting as a reference and created my own."

Another curiosity is the phrase "United Brothers," which is seen carved into a rock, along with a mysterious logo. McCarty recalled that words and symbols were added at the behest of Ronnie Hammond.

●●●●●●

In addition to composing a standard press release for *Third Annual Pipe Dream*, Polydor planned an impressive series of events for the Atlanta Rhythm Section's first album on the label, flying numerous journalists into Atlanta in early August. The coming-out party for the new release was enhanced by an overall electrified mood in the city of Atlanta, since Hank Aaron of the Atlanta Braves had just broken Babe Ruth's professional baseball record of 714 home runs.

The day began with a schmooze session with the band and then Georgia governor Jimmy Carter at the state capitol building. Bill Lowery had been instrumental in arranging that meeting, and Carter issued a proclamation supporting the Atlanta Rhythm Section. A picnic followed at Stone Mountain Park.

That evening, the A.R.S. performed at the Electric Ballroom—part of a weeklong booking—and the visiting scribes noted that the boys went down well with the concertgoers. Mylon LeFevre came onstage to sing along on a few songs toward the end of the show.

Buddy (left) and the Atlanta Rhythm Section pose with Georgia governor Jimmy Carter to mark the release of *Third Annual Pipe Dream*.

Band members, Buddy, Polydor officials, and everyone else associated with the Rhythm Section crossed their fingers, hoping that the third album would be the charm.

••••••

And almost imperceptibly, things began to change. "Doraville" became a Top 40 hit, giving the band a bit of breathing room. The song was light hearted enough—it even included a harmonica solo from J. R.—to click with most listeners.

"It became like an anthem," Buddy recalled. "A very 'identifying' song for the Atlanta Rhythm Section; the 'signature' song for the band in the 1974 period. It was very big all over the South. Never made that big of a spot nationally, but it was one of the songs that propelled us forward."

"We were quite surprised when it became a hit," Barry said. "We weren't expecting that at all, but at the time, I didn't really know or care about hits—it was just putting something out there and hoping it got played enough to make somebody buy it. Paul stated that the song was the last thing that he would have thought would become a hit; he was more surprised, and more vocal about being surprised."

"I thought it was neat that they wrote a song that told about what we were going through," said one Atlanta fan. "We were seeing the changes; pastures being replaced by shopping centers."

That same fan, who was also a budding guitarist, remembered differences in the A.R.S. and Capricorn artists:

"The Allman Brothers seemed 'far away'; Duane [Allman] had died, Berry [Oakley] had died. And the Atlanta Rhythm Section had *songs*, which were very hard to play. You couldn't be like Skynyrd; most of us could play Skynyrd licks—'Gimme Three Steps,' 'Call Me the Breeze,' which were A, D, and E [chords]. You had to be a good guitar player to handle the Atlanta Rhythm Section. They made a lot of garage bands better players."

Not only was "Doraville" a hit for the band, it exemplified how band members could contribute ideas—instruments, chord or riff changes, etc.— to improve and embellish the rough melody that the band had already recorded.

"If we did a basic track, we would sit around and listen to it," said J. R. (who *didn't* co-write "Doraville"), "and somebody might say something like 'You know, I can hear a harmonica on this.' That's the way we did everything, and it didn't matter who did what. Buddy was the arbiter as to whether something finally got used or not."

Positive reviews of *Third Annual Pipe Dream* as well as concerts that were well received boosted the band's attitude. More than one article favorably compared the differences in Ronnie's vocals to Gregg Allman's "Southern-Rock"-standard voice, which perked up the young singer tremendously.

However, some "reviewers" apparently weren't paying complete attention to some of the contents of the album.

"I read a review of one of our live shows," J. R. recalled, "and the writer referred to 'Doraville' as 'Doorbell.'"

Another review couldn't get the name of the town right, either. One analysis of a show during the band's weeklong booking at the Electric Ballroom in early August noted "Back up against the Wall" and a cover of Paul McCartney's "Live and Let Die" as standout songs—but the hit single was cited as "Deauville."

••••••

The advent of *Third Annual Pipe Dream* marked the first appearance (but not on the album cover) of a cartoon character that would become permanently associated with the A.R.S.

Mike McCarty had been using his "Funky Fish" image/logo for his own business. It began as a pen-and-ink drawing, and a takeoff on that image would subsequently appear on promotional items for *Third Annual Pipe Dream*, such as a Frisbee. The critter had arms and legs, was wearing a bowler hat and clodhopper shoes, and appeared to be playing an upright bass.

The artist detailed that his creation "was inspired by Paul Goddard and his amazing bass playing. Everybody seemed to like it and the band got some good promo/marketing use from the image."

The Funky Fish was even seen on McCarty's business card of the era.

••••••

Beginning in 1969, Bill Lowery had begun issuing "Gold Clef" awards at an annual ceremony to honor

Buddy and J. R. receive one of many songwriting awards from Bill Lowery at one of his annual "Gold Clef" ceremonies.

songwriters whose compositions had been hits the previous year. Lowery felt strongly that while it was appropriate for singers to be honored for hit songs, the persons who composed those hits should be recognized as well. Winners over the years would include Buddy Buie, J. R. Cobb, Dean Daughtry, Robert Nix, Joe South, Freddy Weller, Ray Robert Whitley, Tommy Roe, Razzy Bailey, and Bruce Blackman, among others.

"Buddy and I went to most if not all of the Golden Clef award affairs and enjoyed them," J. R. detailed. "As I recall, the whole Golden Clef thing lasted only a few years, but I would think that it was probably encouraging to Atlanta songwriters, as it was to us."

••••••

While Hydra's Spencer Kirkpatrick had admired the first album by the Atlanta Rhythm Section with Rodney Justo as the lead singer, "the first time I heard them live was when we played with them in Dothan, at a big livestock building with a dirt floor. We called it the 'Cow Palace.' We did several other shows with them elsewhere. By then, Rodney was long gone, and Ronnie was singing."

Kirkpatrick also recalled what he termed as a prior to the concert "ritual" by Barry Bailey regarding his gear:

"Barry would get a tape measure and calculate the distance from his amplifier to where he was gonna stand. He had discovered a 'sonic sweet spot' there, where he could control everything he wanted to do, including the control of feedback. It was a specific place where everything would become magic."

Paul would create his own onstage setup to improve his performance. Knowing full well that a bass was supposed to stay in sync with a band's kick drum, he would place a cheap, high-impedance microphone inside Robert Nix's bass drum and run it to a small amplifier near his own onstage position as a personal monitoring system.

Dean would display the Georgia state flag on his stacked organ and electric piano. The banner was rectangular shaped and featured a square Confederate Battle Flag on two-thirds of its area, and a blue field with the Georgia state seal on the other third. It was arranged on Dean's setup with the battle flag portion on the front of his keyboard array, and blue-field/state-seal portion wrapped around the right side. It was supposed to have been simply another "Southern" reference with no political advocacy, but some years later the boys would begin to hear that some people were offended by the the Battle Flag portion that was on display.

The band rarely did a sound check onstage as a complete sextet, allowing the roadies/techs to test the sonic viability of the instruments and the mix in the venues where they would soon be performing.

One A.R.S. road crew member recalled that the musicians spent the least amount of time in a venue compared to any other band he'd ever worked with—if the Rhythm Section performed an hour-and-a-half show, they didn't arrive until about thirty minutes before the show and would leave almost immediately after their performance; that is, it would be unusual for them to have spent more than a total of two hours and fifteen minutes at an arena.

Backstage, the band members usually had a fairly quiet wait until the time came for their performances, although one former roadie recalled that if there were separate tune-up and dressing rooms, some of the boys might migrate to where their instruments awaited, and would warm up by playing Beatles tunes.

On the other hand, a musician in another band that occasionally played on the same bill with the A.R.S. reported stopping by their dressing room on more than one occasion to find the band members simply sitting there, pretty much silent.

"It was like I was dealing with the Darlings," the musician chuckled, alluding to the near-catatonic demeanor of the bluegrass band seen (and heard, at least musically) in more than one episode of *The Andy Griffith Show* (the Darlings were portrayed by a bona fide band known as the Dillards).

In addition to engineering the band's studio recordings, Rodney Mills would run the front-of-house ("F.O.H.") soundboard when the band played live.

"That went back to when I was playing in a band myself," Mills detailed. "I had been the guy who hooked up our P.A. [public address] system. Later, I had run the sound for Little Anthony & the Imperials when they'd played at South Georgia College. But I didn't get into front-of-house sound until the Atlanta Rhythm Section got going. Since I'd recorded their stuff, they wanted me to mix them live. If they were in the studio, I was in there with them, so it made sense for me to do the same thing where they were playing live."

Another "Southern" reference by the band that was interpolated by Buddy was the use of a cassette recording of "Tara's Theme" (from the iconic movie *Gone with the Wind*) to accompany the entrance of the band to the stage at the beginning of a show.

As the concert schedule of the A.R.S. began to pick up, Rodney assumed road manager duties in addition to being the soundman at concerts. He described his road manager assignment as being "the guy that settles up with the promoter, that gets the guys up every morning, gets 'em out the door, picks up all the airline tickets every time we were supposed to fly out of town, gets the guys to the airport."

••••••

Some musicians and music critics would complain that the A.R.S. concert experience validated that they had indeed come from a studio environment.

"The public heard the hits," said Spencer Kirkpatrick. "There was an undercurrent among some musicians that their stuff was too polished, too slick, or almost sterile, but that idea would be completely debunked when we listened closely and got to do gigs with them. We realized that they had a great live sound even though it wasn't as loud and bombastic as a lot of rock at the time; they were able to pull out what they'd done on a record, and it was still very valid. I loved 'em; they could do no wrong. Everything would be solid."

"Buddy and J. R. had written songs like 'Spooky' earlier, but those were pop hits; they weren't really rock and roll," Mylon LeFevre opined. "And there's no doubt that the Atlanta Rhythm Section did some pop hits, because that was their writing style. But if you went to see them live, they rocked out. And they helped to create what may be called 'Southern Rock,' but I don't think it's the same genre as the Allman Brothers."

Another potential concert controversy was a lack of animated behavior/ showmanship onstage, with the exception of the lead singer. The other five members of the band tended to concentrate on their music, at the expense of "visuals."

"We were pretty dull," Barry admitted. "We knew we had to work on that, and Buddy tried to 'prod' all of us, for that matter."

"We knew we couldn't just stand still onstage," J. R. said. "We even got somebody to help us wear the right kind of clothes, but how we sounded onstage was always more important than how we looked, and we suffered some criticism for that.

"I always thought that the perfect combination was done by the Who—they played great, but they were also visual. I'm sure we would have benefited if we had done that more."

Some of the performance reticence could obviously be traced back to backup band days, as well as the business-like attitude and duties of studio musicians.

"At an Atlanta Rhythm Section concert, the energy came from the music, not the 'show,'" said one fan, "and if you weren't picking up that energy, it was going to be a boring night."

And one crew member would reference a stage move that had been popularized by Who guitarist Pete Townshend, occasionally teasing Bailey prior to a show with "How 'bout a 'windmill' or two tonight, Barry?' One night he actually threw one of those in, and he looked over at me and grinned."

Paul being Paul, the bassist would often play with his back to the audience to concentrate on his instrument, and he would occasionally quaff inexpensive champagne—usually the André brand—from a cup or glass that was in his personal space onstage.

Rodney Justo had been a more active frontman than Ronnie, but Rodney had also had more experience. Comparisons were inevitable. Nevertheless, Ronnie resolved to overcome his shyness and improve his rapport with audiences.

"He wanted to be like [Free / Bad Company vocalist] Paul Rodgers," one fan opined. "I always thought he felt a 'kinship' because he kind of looked like [Rodgers] at times, and I saw him doing some similar things with the microphone stand. He never looked totally comfortable up onstage, but at least he was focused on the singing. The point is, the band wasn't writing material that was easy to sing; it was very demanding."

"Buddy would work with Ronnie, trying to create more action onstage by getting him to move around a little bit," Gloria Buie acknowledged, "but it wasn't Ronnie's 'natural way.' The true fans, who knew they were listening to great musicians, weren't bothered by what the band did or didn't do onstage."

The A.R.S. vocalist was aware that his task "out front" was more formidable because the band would be concentrating on making music, usually oblivious to any visual facet of a concert.

Rodney Mills: "Singing was a gift for Ronnie, but he was never comfortable with being the frontman—the guy that had to put on a show. Even in the studio, it seemed like the longer we worked on something, he would kind of get into a dark place after a while."

Mills emphasized, however, that Hammond's problems did not cause delays in the recording process.

"Ronnie was a hard worker in the studio," the recording engineer/producer said. "When we were in there working, it was usually a great experience, but some of the songs had to be played in a certain key because of the tunings of the guitars, and they were out of Ronnie's range, so there was sometimes some 'incompatibility' that we had to work through, but we always persevered."

"I'd seen Rodney Justo with the Candymen many times," said Spencer Kirkpatrick. "He'd had a commanding presence and was really engaged with the audience, and he would have carried this over to his time with the Atlanta Rhythm Section.

"Ronnie would definitely try to interact with the crowd, because he knew he was the focal point. But their overall performance was a lot like Hydra's; there wasn't a lot to see, and it was more of a sonic thing instead of a visual thing."

And it helps to remember that Spencer Kirkpatrick was a professional musician, not an average fan.

●●●●●●

As for differences in the "rock star" versus "musician" concept, J. R. opined that Robert Nix was the member of the band who seemed to want to epitomize a rock star stereotype, as had also been the situation when Nix was in the Candymen.

"The rest of us weren't into that," Cobb said. "I couldn't have cared less about it. If I could write some good songs that were successful, that would have suited me fine."

However, Nix's assertiveness served the band well regarding public relations, and the drummer would often be the first one through the door to do a radio interview or other publicity. On the other hand, Paul Goddard would usually be unenthusiastic regarding public-relations work.

The band also didn't necessarily appreciate being labeled as a "Southern Rock" band either.

"We weren't crazy about that term, but we were stuck with it," J. R. said. "Most 'Southern Rock' bands were known for extended jams. We never cared about doing

Robert Nix goes through his paces onstage.

a song for thirty minutes, where everybody plays everything they know three or four times, over and over. It just got redundant. We were more into the "record format"— you play the song like the audience has heard it, do the solo where it's supposed to go—maybe with a few different notes or licks—and that's the end of it. If we had a chance to stretch out, we kinda had to make ourselves do that—but maybe we didn't concentrate on stretching things out, and I won't deny that it was fun a lot of times."

Barry recalled that if he and J. R. got into trading licks back and forth on a stretched-out song, the juncture at which such sonic give and take between the two guitarists began would have been coordinated in advance.

"It was fun," Bailey said, "and we were certainly capable of doing it, although sometimes we felt like we might have gone a little too far regarding improvising. It was nothing particularly spontaneous."

Kirkpatrick: "Every time we played with them, they were in a position where they actually had a little more time to take care of stuff, and they would go at it. Paul would do an aggressive solo; he'd rattle the walls. And whatever Barry and J. R. added was icing on the cake."

"When you went to a stadium show back in those days, the acoustics were horrible," said one Atlanta fan. "You'd get all kinds of echoes and other annoying sounds. But the Atlanta Rhythm Section sounded exactly like they did on a record— often better, if they were able to improvise long instrumental parts. It sounded as pure onstage as it did on an album. And that was the voices *and* the music."

If the boys were in an opening slot at a show, they would be compelled to do their songs in a perfunctory manner because of the time constraint of their set. The same Atlanta fan described such a "preliminary" experience as being "like dropping a needle on one of their records. They weren't able to stretch anything out if they were the opening band. At the times when I saw them when they were the closing act, it was different; those longer songs were magnificent. When they went into a jam, that's when the power of their music came out. They'd take off, and it was almost like a competition between them."

"I saw them at the Electric Ballroom in the mid-Seventies," said another longtime Atlanta fan, "and was blown away by their melodic sound and their guitar playing. They were not the most attractive rock band to emerge, but they made up for it with their music. Their style of playing was very different from Wet Willie, Marshall Tucker, or the Allmans. It seemed they were very much more pop-oriented in the writing but could jam as well as any band."

And the A.R.S. had their fans among other area musicians besides Kirkpatrick.

"I made it a point to go out and hear them, and they were always very tight with excellent sounds," said Chuck Leavell, who became a member of the Allman Brothers Band in 1972. "I saw them as excellent studio guys that had crafted their talents into a band that not only recorded cool songs with great arrangements, but that could bring all of that to the stage and turn on the crowds. They were 'double trouble.' Quite a unique thing, and it was working very well."

••••••

The point could be made that if the Atlanta Rhythm Section's stage presence was visually uninspiring, it was not only a reflection of the workmanlike concentration they had in concert regarding their craft, but also an allusion to their personal lives—band members had separate interests outside Studio One and didn't hang out with each other all that much.

And a comparison to the crew of one of the Apollo moon missions is analogous, since that threesome didn't particularly socialize with each other after working together either.

Whenever he discussed the training facet for the Apollo 14 mission—which was the sixth voyage to the Moon and flew from January 31 to February 9, 1971—Lunar Module Pilot Edgar Mitchell (1930–2016) had often cited his experiences with Commander Alan Shepard (1923–1998) and Command Module Pilot Stuart Roosa (1933–1994) by using a geometric reference.

"If you consider personality types in a 360-degree circle, we were 120 degrees apart from each other," Mitchell said in a 2010 interview. "We represented three totally different styles, which wasn't a surprise. We always thought that but never really discussed it because we *knew* we had different personality profiles. But we had a great respect for each other. We realized that we made up a good crew together; we were very professional, and we treated each other as professionals, but we were not 'buddy-buddy.'"

And the same type of comparison was applicable to the Atlanta Rhythm Section. Heading to a bar to have a beer together after a recording session or carousing with each other after a concert didn't happen too often.

"We'd go to the house after working in the studio," Dean acknowledged. "We didn't hang out."

Outside the studio, band members and their interests and pastimes diverged as well. Barry and Dawn were raising horses. J. R. liked his golf game. Paul was assembling a $15,000 stereo system (in 1970s dollars) in his home. Ronnie liked to go to baseball games. Ox enjoyed working on a couple of classic automobiles he'd acquired.

"Back in those days, my hobby was my LaSalle," Dean remembered proudly. "It was all original; it only had 32,000 miles on it and I only put three thousand miles on it myself. It was in *The Godfather*. And later, I had a '65 Mustang convertible."

J. R. doesn't recall any outside interests for Robert Nix but opined that the drummer's off-duty behavior seemed to be another facet of his would-be rock star attitude.

"Robert embraced the so-called 'rock-and-roll lifestyle' as much as anyone I have ever known," said Cobb, "and he lived it to the fullest. He loved to hang out and party—*hard*—with his pals, and he was good at it. If he had any serious pastimes or hobbies or what have you other than that, I didn't know about them. When we were writing down at the lake, he would fish with us and he loved to stay up late and write, but that was about it."

"They didn't come together at a 'brothers-in-arms' moment in their lives," Rodney Mills said of the band members, "and they never seemed to have a close-knit relationship—not that they disliked each other, but there was a businesslike attitude in a lot of the things they did."

Barry and Paul were also somewhat solitary individuals on the road, usually keeping to themselves during off-days and often dining alone. The guitarist and bassist sometimes roomed together during earlier road work, if doubling up was necessary.

On one trip, Rodney Mills roomed with Goddard, for one night only.

The boys get together briefly following a show. "This band hated having their photos taken," Mike McCarty recalled. "It was like pulling teeth to get them together to do a photo shoot."

"I've never heard such loud snoring in my life!" Mills recalled. "I finally ended up in the bathroom, with the water running to drown out the noise, just so I could get some sleep. I threatened to quit if I had to room with Paul again."

And Paul would let it be known to anyone who would listen that he wasn't particularly a fan of the type of music the members of the Atlanta Rhythm Section were writing and recording. Instead, he was an intense admirer of the "Progressive Rock" genre. The complex arrangements of British bands such as Genesis, Yes, and Emerson, Lake & Palmer fascinated the Georgia bassist, and he would also declare his appreciation for the music of an American progressive-rock band, Kansas.

"He said that the way their music was structured was incredible," Nan Jacobs said of her brother's admiration of Kansas. "I don't think Paul would admit that he was taken with the spirituality of their music, but I do think that was part of it. They were good people, they were great musicians, and they didn't compromise. I think Paul said at one time that their music was as technically perfect as you could get."

As for comparisons of Kansas's original material to British progressive-rock bands, original Kansas bassist Dave Hope noted, "We always had a rock-and-roll base, but the musicianship of the English guys was just off the charts. I think one difference was that while we could play seven-minute songs and change the time signature every thirty seconds, Genesis or Yes couldn't do a rock-and-roll song; it wasn't in their DNA."

"He just thought progressive rock had better musicianship," J. R. said of Paul, "and he kind of looked down on a lot of rock and roll. He definitely didn't like 'Southern boogie'; I don't really know why."

That said, Paul always made it a point to focus on his own musical tasks with his own band in a professional manner. He had been using industry-standard Fender Precision Basses when the Atlanta Rhythm Section germinated, but soon set out to acquire a Rickenbacker bass (preferably in a natural finish), as played by one of his bass heroes, Chris Squire of Yes.

Not surprisingly, stereotypical rock band behavior for the Atlanta Rhythm Section members would include, to varying degrees, indulgence in alcohol, illegal substances, or both. While the boys kept their behavior under control when it was time to work—in the studio or onstage—Ronnie Hammond would struggle with his off-duty abuse problems for many years.

"Ronnie didn't have that much of a problem in the beginning," J. R. recalled, "it sort of 'developed,' and it was at least a couple of years before I noticed it. I don't know if it was insecurity about being the frontman or pressure about being on the road, away from his wife. It got worse as time went on. He was one of those persons—and I've known others—whose personality would change when he reached a certain point in his drinking. It was like Dr. Jekyll and Mr. Hyde. He did things he'd never do when he was sober, and sometimes he did things he didn't even remember later. And of course, he experimented with some other things like we all did, and he went a little further in his experimenting.

"I've always thought that Ronnie was a lot better than he thought he was. We'd give him 'pep talks,' telling him 'you're doin' great.' But his problems seemed to get bigger."

"I knew that Ronnie had issues," said Chuck Leavell. "It was troubling to see some of the things he was going through, and all of us who knew him were worried about his health and his mental state. It was difficult to see some of the things that happened with him, and as friends we were certainly concerned. We hoped he would get things turned around and going in the right direction. He was a very talented guy and always very nice to me when I was around him. But it was obvious that he was making some bad choices and was going down a path that was dark. When that kind of thing happens, it's difficult to watch, but it is up to the individual to turn things around, and Ronnie seemed to have a hard time sorting that out."

••••••

Many musicians, particularly those who were Atlanta-based, paid close attention to the Atlanta Rhythm Section's recording process, which, while businesslike at times, could still get loose thanks to the enthusiasm of Messrs. Buie and Mills.

"I got to hang out a lot at Studio One," said Steve McRay of Mose Jones, "sometimes as a recording musician, but I dropped by many times when the A.R.S. was recording, and sat in the control room, usually just after they had recorded basic tracks or recorded an overdub or vocal tracks.

"It was such a joy to hear those songs in their 'studio form' before they were pressed onto albums, and also to hear what Rodney and Buddy and the guys thought about the recordings. They had fun, they laughed a lot, they experimented with sounds and arrangements.

"It was a total process that they had done many times before in the studio, but it was fresh and it was polished for every song. Every time I got to witness and hear it, I was always amazed about how big, how wonderful, how crafted the sound was. The A.R.S., Buddy, and Rodney were definitely in their element, and I always wished at that moment—and who wouldn't—that I had been in that position to write, record, and produce music in Studio One just like that! It was a powerful time and place to be as a musician."

Around the time of the third album's release, Gloria Buie signed on as the business manager of Studio One. Her initial impressions of the way the facility was run hadn't been positive when she and Buddy had reunited a few years earlier.

"It was a disaster," she said. "It was supposed to make money by being rented out to other people, but Buddy considered it to be a 'nest' or an 'embryo'-type place where he could develop the Atlanta Rhythm Section. He had already had 'singles hits'; now he wanted hit albums.

"And it had turned out to be a play place instead of a moneymaker. It was great from a creative standpoint, but there really wasn't anyone managing it. When they had tried to put someone in to manage it, no one would listen to him. Buddy wanted to do things his way, so I stayed away from it."

Buie admired his wife's organizational abilities and offered her the opportunity to manage the business facet of Studio One. She had already been helping with the Atlanta Rhythm Section's scheduling, logistics, and finances from a home office, so a transition to Studio One itself would be fairly easy to accomplish.

Gloria agreed to go to work at the facility in Oakcliff Industrial Park but—perhaps taking a cue from her own husband—insisted on autonomy:

"I said: 'On one condition—I run the show. If there's something that needs to be done or cleaned up, it needs to be done as soon as possible.'

"It worked. I had offices upstairs and didn't interfere with what was going on downstairs. My secretary would come in before me in the mornings and clean up what I didn't need to see."

"That was a turning point," Rodney Mills said of Gloria's new and formidable responsibilities. "Things were not good, financially, at Studio One. The Rhythm Section was working, but nobody was really making any money off of their records or their concerts. Bill Lowery had been keeping the whole thing afloat. When Gloria took over, everything was done right."

CHAPTER 8
Mid-1970s Buildup

T he year 1975 started off with a positive piece of video exposure for the Atlanta Rhythm Section when they performed on the January 11 edition of *Don Kirshner's Rock Concert*, along with Redbone (a Native American rock band) and Roy Wood's Wizzard. The appearance made numerous other musicians elsewhere sit up and take notice.

"That Doraville sound hit a nerve up here in Kentucky in the 1970s," recalled Greg Martin, lead guitarist for the Kentucky Headhunters. The influence of the band on Martin's own career is exemplary of players from outside the Deep South who admired the sound and musicianship of the A.R.S.

"The first song I heard by the Atlanta Rhythm Section was 'Doraville,' around 1974," he detailed. "After hearing it on WLRS in Louisville and seeing the A.R.S. on *Don Kirshner's Rock Concert*, I went out and bought *Third Annual Pipe Dream*. I was living in Louisville at the time, managing an electronics shop that sold stereo gear and records. Between radio and records, I was pretty much in tune with what was going on musically in those days.

"I knew the A.R.S. was different from most 'Southern Rock' bands, and I think their years of studio work in Doraville gave them an edge over a lot of others. They could switch musical gears and go into different modes easily. I was playing in cover bands, and A.R.S. songs were a part of our set list."

In addition to appreciating the material and approach of the band, Martin also listened carefully to the two A.R.S. guitarists, and how they worked with each other.

"I really loved Barry and J. R.'s guitar work on 'Angel,'" he said. "The interplay was amazing. I was very impressed with Barry's playing and tone. I also loved James Cobb's slide playing; he had a great feel for slide, [and was] a very underrated player, in my opinion."

Coming of age in southern Illinois, guitarist Bruce Brown also thought Atlanta Rhythm Section sounded different from a stereotypical Deep South band.

"I never thought of the A.R.S. as a 'Southern Rock' band," he said. "They had that kind of 'swampy Southern vibe,' but they always seemed more slick and a bit more refined sounding to me, which I liked—a bit more pop, but still a little greasy.

"I always loved Barry Bailey's playing. In my book he had the 'three Ts'—tone, taste, and touch. There was always a sweetness to his playing; very soulful. In an era of long twiddly-twiddly guitar solos, Barry always approached it from the 'less is more' school. His guitar solos were more like 'parts' than just off-the-cuff jamming; they were like compositions inside the song. You could sing along with everything he played."

Brown would move to Nashville in 1980 and, in 1989, joined the Charlie Daniels Band.

••••••

Closer to home, Terry Spackman, who would become a longtime fan of the Atlanta Rhythm Section and the Atlanta music scene ("I lost my virginity to *Third Annual Pipe Dream*"), first heard the band in concert at Dekalb College (which Barry had attended some years earlier).

"It was in between *Third Annual Pipe Dream* and *Dog Days*," he recalled, "because they played songs from *Dog Days* that night, but it hadn't been released yet. I was shocked, because the *Third Annual Pipe Dream* songs sounded just like the album! I'm not saying the vocals were dead-on, but all the guitar parts, all the keyboard parts, all the drums parts were unbelievable. Rodney [Mills] was mixing live shows back then, and he did a great job.

"That's what caught my attention. The fidelity of their music—in concert and on their albums—was so different from Capricorn, ninety miles down the road. It didn't sound like anything in Muscle Shoals, it didn't sound like anything in Memphis, or even like anything coming out of L.A. I was fascinated by how clean, how precise, and how well arranged all of their material was."

Spackman also had a stereotypical opinion about the band's stage presence in the earlier days, including Ronnie's "frontman" endeavors.

"There wasn't anything flamboyant about them whatsoever," he said. "Pretty much anyone who saw their show came to appreciate the music. When I saw them for the first time at Dekalb College, you could tell that Ronnie was working on his 'schtick.'"

A decade and a half after seeing the Atlanta Rhythm Section in concert for the first time, Spackman would sign on as a roadie/tech for the band.

••••••

While he maintained an earnest effort to improve his frontman image and skills, Ronnie would occasionally go over the line. At one show in Florida, he loudly proclaimed to the audience that the Atlanta Rhythm Section and Gregg Allman were the only viable musical acts in Georgia. Not content with just braggadocio, he also badmouthed a less successful but respected band called Grinderswitch that was on the same bill, opining that the members of Grinderswitch ought to go back to working at a car wash.

Grinderswitch guitarist Larry Howard took exception to Hammond's put-down, and a fight ensued. Robert Nix also got involved in the fisticuffs. Recollections varied as to whether the melee happened onstage, offstage, or even outside in a parking lot.

"It was stupid of Ronnie, while on stage, to insult another act," Barry said, "particularly while they were still in the hall."

F.T.U. Student Govt. & Village Center Present A

CONCERT

● WITH *Sugarloaf*

● AND SPECIAL GUESTS *Atlanta Rhythm Section*

● PLUS *Asbury Park*

7:30 P.M.
MONDAY, MAY 26 (Memorial Day Holiday)
Sheraton Towers Convention Center

J. R. wails on harmonica during a performance at Florida Technological University in Orlando. *FuTUre*

"I thought it was a foolish comment to make," J. R. agreed. "Ronnie seemed to think that we were in competition with some of the bands based in Macon, and I don't believe that most of the rest of us felt that way. Anyway, I certainly did not. I seem to remember that Buddy told Ronnie that he didn't appreciate what he had said, but other than that, we just let the matter pass. As I recall, it really wasn't much of a fight anyway."

One concert with a perhaps unexpected aftereffect happened on May 26 (Memorial Day), when the band played at Florida Technological University in Orlando (that institute of higher learning later became known as the University of Central Florida). The Atlanta Rhythm Section was in the middle slot between a band called Asbury Park and headlining band Sugarloaf of "Green-Eyed Lady" fame. In a concert review following the show, the student newspaper, the *FuTUre*, criticized the high volume level at which the A.R.S. played (and the newspaper's awkward moniker was indeed a combination of capital letters—representing the name of the school—and lowercase letters).

The band would get a positive boost in the July 1975 issue of *Crawdaddy* magazine, which had the Rolling Stones on the cover. An extensive article on so-called Southern Rock chronicled—in order—the misfortunes of Mose Jones following Al Kooper's departure from Atlanta to Los Angeles, what was probably intended to be perceived as a typical recording session by the Atlanta Rhythm Section at Studio One, and a Lynyrd Skynyrd concert at the Miami Marina. In the last segment, Ronnie Van Zant opined that the Atlanta Rhythm Section was probably the best band in the South.

Mose Jones split later that year and would regroup in 1977.

An important—and sold out—concert for the Atlanta Rhythm Section and its growing numbers of fans was a July 18, 1975, show with the Atlanta Symphony Orchestra at Chastain Park, as the concluding performance in a "Summer Sounds '75" series. Other summertime presentations featuring the local symphony had included collaborations with noted pianists such as Peter Nero and George Shearing.

The Atlanta Symphony had backed up singer/songwriter Randy Newman the previous year, but the hometown rock band's focused approach (as well as its usual non-blues-and-boogie repertoire) made for a simpatico and exciting presentation for the 6,600 attendees. This event was the first time Arnie Geller saw and heard Polydor's musical protégés live.

A small airplane circled over the outdoor venue, displaying lights that flashed the Atlanta Rhythm Section's moniker in a unique example of airborne advertising. The opening act was pianist Mac Frampton.

The A.R.S. show opened with "Crazy," the leadoff track from the band's upcoming fourth album. One attendee noted that this Chastain Park event was the only occasion where he ever heard that song performed in concert during that era.

Steve Hammond was at that show and described it as "the most beautiful-sounding concert I've ever attended."

Paul's sister Nan also saw the band with the Atlanta Symphony Orchestra in Chastain Park and was delighted.

"I'm a classical musician," she said, "It was like seeing and hearing his world and my world come together. It was magical to me."

The members of the Atlanta Symphony Orchestra were pleased with the concert as well, particularly since they had been allowed to wear blue jeans onstage.

(The A.R.S. had, of course, already played Chastain Park sans symphony, and they would play there numerous times in the future.)

••••••

Two weeks after the collaboration with the Atlanta Symphony in Chastain Park, a performance in Florida turned out to be much more memorable than the Memorial Day show in Orlando. On August 2, the A.R.S. performed at the Gator Bowl in Jacksonville as one of the opening acts for the Rolling Stones during that band's "Tour of the Americas." The other bands in the Gator Bowl lineup were Rufus with Chaka Khan and the J. Geils Band. Barry would describe the opportunity as "much more gratifying than intimidating."

The Stones and the Atlanta Rhythm Section were staying at the same hotel, and on the day before the show, most of the members of the Stones went looking for the hotel bar and wandered into a banquet room where the A.R.S., aware of the importance of the concert, was conducting a rare on-the-road rehearsal.

"A few pleasantries were exchanged," Barry recounted, "and they went on looking for the bar, to which we adjourned upon completion of rehearsal. Some of the Stones were still there, and I spent a little time talking with Charlie Watts, talking mostly about jazz music and jazz players.

"The show went fine, and we and some of our wives attended a very nice dinner at the hotel that night, to which we had been invited along with most of the performers on the show. It was sort of a post-show celebratory thing."

Later that month, the boys played at the Bottom Line club in New York City and commenced what would turn into more than one appearance at the summertime Schaefer / Dr. Pepper Music Festival in New York's Central Park, performing on August 11 at the Wollman skating rink, an outdoor venue.

••••••

Dog Days, released in August 1975, was the most diverse album the Atlanta Rhythm Section had recorded up to that point, and its cover illustration was a straight-on cartoon. Most of its songs were Buie/Nix/Daughtry compositions.

Studio sorcery/experimentation allowed Ronnie's singing to sound somewhat like "unison vocals" on several songs, resulting in a fuller, more confident presentation that was exemplified by "Crazy," which got *Dog Days* off to a rousing start. Dean recalled that Ronnie's vocal abilities had indeed been improving, but a relatively new electronic studio device made by the Eventide Clock Works company was used to enhance the lead singer's vocals. The same item would also be utilized on some of Daughtry's piano tracks.

The second tune, the sardonically titled "Boogie Smoogie," probably grabbed the attention of many listeners who were already fans of the A.R.S. To wit:

A raunchy, tinny-sounding guitar in the right channel serves notice right at the outset that this one's gonna be different. In its first three minutes and twenty-two seconds, "Boogie Smoogie" comes across as a slow-as-molasses, loping and mournful blues tune that is for all intents and purposes a clone of Jimmy Reed's "Baby What You Want Me to Do." Then the song abruptly shifts to an up-tempo, raucous boogie-shuffle that would do John Lee Hooker proud. The entire effort clocks in at over eight minutes.

The Atlanta Rhythm Section may have alluded to the blues a bit on *Third Annual Pipe Dream*, but this time around, the band was assertively purveying a token example of the type of music that it had originally sought to avoid; i.e., the primary reason for the purveyance of "Boogie Smoogie" was simply to demonstrate that they were capable of "playin' de blooz" if they had to.

Other highlights of the album included a string arrangement interpolated into the title track, which was a melancholy reflection on humid, sweaty times in the Deep South (and the song had been written in the sweltering fishing trailer in Eufaula). According to Dean, some of the string players heard on the title track were members of the Atlanta Symphony Orchestra.

"Bless My Soul," written by J. R., was an instrumental scion of "Blues in Maude's Flat" on the previous album, but it still stood on its own. Moreover, "Bless My Soul" was replete with several guitar licks and passages composed of pinch harmonic notes, sometimes referred to as "squeals" (a popular and definitive example of the technique had been proffered two years earlier by Billy F Gibbons of ZZ Top on the latter part of that band's hit "La Grange").

And Barry had begun using pinch harmonics in earnest.

"I just stumbled upon pick-
and-thumb-induced harmonics by accident," he said,
"and I let whatever note was produced stand on its own. Eventually, I learned how
to be more specific about note selection, to the point that some producers and/or
engineers would suggest injecting a particular harmonic here or there on an overdub."

The lush "All Night Rain," the album's closer, would have made a terrific single, but
nothing from the album would garner any serious interest on Top 40 radio stations.

The droopy-from-the-heat hound dog found on the front-cover illustration of
Dog Days was holding a handheld fan with a wooden handle, as found in many older
churches without air conditioning. The pooch was wearing a Confederate kepi with
a Battle Flag emblazoned on it, and a peach with a worm poking out of it hovered
nearby. According to Mike McCarty, the floating fruit was a tongue-in-cheek allusion
to the so-called competition between the Atlanta Rhythm Section and Phil Walden's
Capricorn Records down in Macon.

"How's this, guys?" Mike McCarty (center) shows off his artwork for the cover of *Dog Days* to Buddy and the boys in front of Studio One.

One clever promotional item for *Dog Days* that was distributed in large quantities was a handheld fan, just like the one in the cover illustration, which also appeared on one side of the fan. The item's hype on the flip side touted "A sizzling new album from Polydor to fan the flame."

••••••

Ronnie Hammond's vocal performance on *Dog Days*—if at times electronically embellished—seemed to boost the singer's confidence. Such a trend would continue through subsequent albums, and his brother Steve offered a detailed assessment:

"Ronnie had a lot of talent as a singer and songwriter. His voice progressed to another level with each record presentation, due in no small part of having Buddy as a producer and Rodney Mills as a very skilled engineer. The 'gizmos' definitely enhanced the presentation and brought out what I feel was a desired result of what the particular song wanted to deliver to the listener or consumer of the music, like 'All Night Rain,' with all those layered vocals.

"In short, the gizmos are only as good as the artists, and professionals like Rodney and Buddy that knew how to create the end result. I think that is one of the things that made the A.R.S. so unique and different from the traditional 'southern rock' of the times."

••••••

Dog Days is the favorite Atlanta Rhythm Section album of Atlanta-based blues guitarist Tinsley Ellis, who had first heard the band at the Electric Ballroom prior to the release of *Third Annual Pipe Dream*.

"I was sixteen at the time," the guitarist said of the concert, "and had to borrow someone's driver's license to get in."

As for the fourth release, Ellis opined, "I think they became a great band with that album. All the planets converged with *Dog Days*—playing, singing, and songwriting. Of course, their greatest commercial success came a little later. And it wasn't till years later, in the early 1980s, that I noticed the similarities between Barry Bailey and [blues guitarist] Freddie King. They have the same tone and attack. I'll bet Barry could do a great version of Freddie King's song 'The Stumble'!"

••••••

As the band's fortunes continued to grow, the need for more songwriting increased, as the inventory of ideas and demos that had resulted in recordings began to be depleted. The perpetually prolific Buddy Buie would write with almost anybody and everybody, and J. R. was fine with collaborations between several members of the band and Buddy, even if he wasn't included himself.

"Sometimes Buddy would write with Robert, or sometimes Robert would write with Buddy and me," J. R. detailed. "Dean was pretty active as well. I didn't have a problem with it. When we first starting getting some success, we had a bunch of songs that we'd already written that we thought we could use, but we ran through that material pretty soon, so we needed more songs. It seemed like a lot of our waking hours were spent trying to think up new material. In my opinion, the more people we had to work together—in any combination—the better."

The A.R.S. continued its methodical recording ventures and slowly began to expand its touring schedule, but they were still local favorites, as exemplified by bookings at the Fox Theatre on New Year's Eve for three years in a row, starting in 1975. The opening group for the '75 show was the Steamboat Springs Band, a country-rock aggregation from Athens.

••••••

A year and five days after they had appeared on *Don Kirshner's Rock Concert*, the boys returned to that show, appearing with ABBA, Gary Wright, and Esther Phillips on January 16, 1976.

••••••

Released early the same year, *Red Tape* was an edgier-sounding effort with an assortment of styles, as exemplified by the leadoff track, "Jukin'," which had a vaguely country or western swing vibe and included some rollicking piano from Dean. The track actually segued into Bob Wills's "San Antonio Rose" for a few measures.

The band dabbled in vague allusions to the blues on a couple of tracks, and Barry's guitar tone on "Shanghied" was leaner and meaner. There was also a lush ballad, "Beautiful Dreamers," as well as a unique two-and-a-half-minute workout with unusual time signature shifts called "Oh What a Feeling."

However, *Red Tape*'s reworking of "Another Man's Woman" from the band's first album was worth the price of admission to many listeners. This time, the song clocked in at almost ten minutes in length; the instrumental "outro" was extended, with an initial guitar solo being accompanied by panther-like yowls from Ronnie, followed by an impressive bass solo from Paul that was rapid-fire and resonant. Twin guitars doing raucous solos then kicked in; however, instead of guitars playing their own

MLB 9002-2

respective riffs or harmony licks simultaneously, Barry and J. R. traded licks back and forth, with J. R. playing slide.

While "Jukin'" and "Free Spirit" would be released as singles, they failed to make the Top 100 charts nationally.

The cover illustration for *Red Tape* displays a studio-style reel-to-reel tape recorder with a human torso and arms standing in the middle of flames, playing Barry's Gibson Les Paul Deluxe guitar, as red (recording) tape flies outward in all directions. Mike McCarty would win several awards from art and design magazines for the *Red Tape* cover illustration.

"Buddy was frustrated with the record company," McCarty recounted. "They were trying to tell him what songs to record and how to record them. Basically, he said '**** 'em,' so I came up with the 'red tape' idea about organization, as sort of a protest to Polydor. Buddy gave me the title; I came up with the concept. I don't think Polydor ever realized it was about them."

One interesting item that was part of the album's promotional campaign was a packet of cigarette rolling papers with the *Red Tape* artwork on it. Another was an adhesive tape dispenser loaded with, not surprisingly, red tape.

But sales of *Red Tape* were disappointing, and Polydor was getting antsy.

One bonus from the music on *Red Tape* would be the popularity of the extended version of "Another Man's Woman" in concert. The song would usually close the regular portion of a show (before encores), and Paul's bone-shaking bass solo would immediately win over the audience.

"That [solo] would instantly turn the crowd on," Rodney Mills averred. "Up to then, they didn't want to look at Paul because Paul wasn't a pleasant person to look at, and he usually wasn't looking at them anyway. Then he'd crank that solo, and it was like 'Wow! This is extraordinary!'"

• • • • • •

The boys returned to Central Park in New York on June 23, 1976, for another festival concert at the Wollman skating rink, this time with the Charlie Daniels Band. Having been presented by the Schaefer beer company for a number of years, the festival changed sponsors later that year, becoming the Dr. Pepper Central Park Music Festival.

That summer, the Atlanta Rhythm Section also did a benefit performance for the presidential campaign of Jimmy Carter. During the campaign, Carter's son Chip alluded to a future White House performance for the A.R.S. if his father won the November election.

Other summer shows included a July 5 concert at Lakeside Park in Macon. Southern Illinois University at Edwardsville presented the band for a Mississippi River Festival on July 13, which begat another (and controversial) show at the school's main campus in Carbondale later in the year.

Among the other out-of-state gigs they did that summer was an August 6 performance at the Armadillo World Headquarters in Austin, Texas, headlining over Wet Willie.

The following text is an unedited transcript of a handwritten note from the student government activities council of Southern Illinois University in Carbondale to a college entertainment periodical. It was written following an Atlanta Rhythm Section concert at that school in late 1976:

On Saturday, November 13, Cultural Affairs presented Atlanta Rhythm Section. The concert was a disgrace, starting from when one of the members said, "We have to have something to drink before we can play." A request for alcohol was in the rider. This request was deleted by my advisors in accordance with the no-alcohol policy on campus. The group ended up bringing alcohol in empty guitar cases. While they were performing, they had filled cups on stage. The group ran "out of gas" after less than an hour, drunk, with the volume up too high they continued on. The lead singer got the crowd on its feet and finished the set. The house lights went on because of the fear of destruction on the part of the auditorium manager. The group polished off the

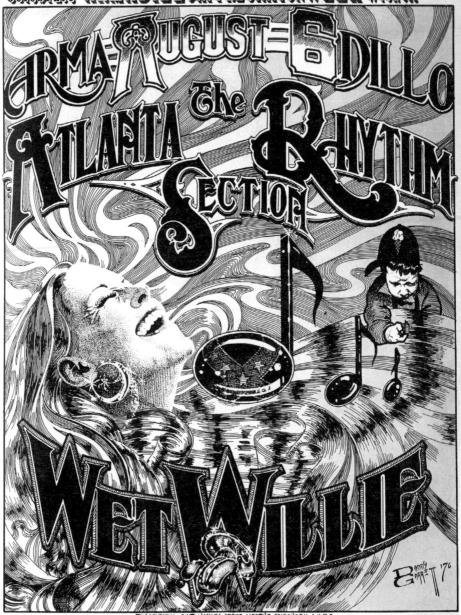

Poster for the August 6 performance in Austin. Variants of this illustration would be used for promoting future events.

remaining alcohol, stumbled back on stage and continued to play. Atlanta Rhythm Section is a disgrace to rock and roll; too immature to play on the college circuit. When they grow up, maybe.

"Working on the road is one of the hardest things you will ever do," Dean reflected, "and I can understand why people get messed up. Mostly, I just drank a lot, but it's a killer out there. I think the most we ever done was maybe twenty days in a row. It'll wear you out quick."

••••••

The A.R.S. finished up the year with a December 30 concert in Macon with the Charlie Daniels Band. They would close out the nation's bicentennial year with their second consecutive New Year's Eve at the Fox Theater; Mother's Finest, an Atlanta-based power-funk band, opened the show.

"It was a great show by both bands; something to be both envious of and proud of," said Spencer Kirkpatrick, who was in attendance.

• • • • • •

Gloria Buie described *A Rock and Roll Alternative*, released in December 1976, as "the breakthrough. If it had not made it, it was going to be the last album."

Interestingly, the album was created in the shortest time period of any Atlanta Rhythm Section album yet recorded. For something that might have had a "make-it-or-break-it" attitude hanging over it, the new effort sounded surprisingly confident. Barry's guitar leads were more passionate and raucous, while acoustic guitars were usually played hard when utilized. Dean's piano integrated itself with songs in a more self-assured manner, and the frequency and quality of harmony/background singing was also on the upswing.

"Sky High" was a strong opening track that may have seemed to be slightly stretched out to some listeners. Abetted by an enthusiastic sing-along chorus, it would ultimately become the band's standard concert opener, as well.

Another example of the more forceful vibe on the album was "Don't Miss the Message," which had an anchor riff that sounded, at first listen, like a slightly mellower version of the Jeff Beck Group's "Rice Pudding," and Barry's guitar break in that song did indeed sound "Beckish."

For many musicians—regardless of their status or respective home states—"Georgia Rhythm" was probably one of the greatest paeans to life on the road ever written. The song had a first-person/autobiographical perspective, but almost any itinerant player in almost any musical genre could identify with its message.

According to Dean, the creation of "So Into You" (written by Buie, Nix, and Daughtry) had been inspired by B. B. King's "The Thrill Is Gone." The song's crisp-and-precise/smooth-and-slinky approach was attractive to a lot of listeners. Released as the first single from the album, "So Into You" would become one of the band's biggest hits ever, peaking at #7 on the Billboard chart.

Even if he didn't always get songwriting credits, J. R. brought his acumen and sonic sensibility to many tunes, and Rodney Mills cited Cobb's playing on "So Into You" as a definitive example.

"Many times, he had a premium part already worked out," Mills said of Cobb, "and his rhythm part contributes so much to that song, from beginning to end. You don't necessarily realize what he's doing, but it shows why J. R. was a master of inversions of chords, changing it up a little bit as it goes along—a different inversion on a different part of the neck. Some bands I've worked with have had a 'rhythm [guitar]' that's just banging and clanging away. I tell them they need to work up a part.

"And J. R. is a piano player who never learned how to play piano. He treats his guitar like a piano; you can do stuff *chordally* and *rhythmically* on a piano, but you can't *strum* a piano."

Bailey recalled his own unique use of "Reb," his frontline Gibson Les Paul Deluxe guitar, on "So Into You."

"I played my Tele on the basic track—a rhythm part—but all of the lead overdubs were done with the Deluxe, including the instrumental 'release' after the first chorus. On this particular section, Rodney Mills, Robert Nix, and I used eight tracks to accommodate all of the parts—harmonies and octaves that I submitted. When Buddy

114

returned from wherever he had been and listened to the finished playback, he thought that it was all done electronically—synthesized—until we corrected him."

The boys also elected to cover "Outside Woman Blues," a Blind Joe Reynolds song covered by Cream on their *Disraeli Gears* album almost a decade earlier.

The penultimate tune, "Everybody Gotta Go," was a bash fest with a unique time signature, and it's easy to imagine the final track, "Neon Nites," being crooned in a smoke-filled, hole-in-the-wall jazz club. Like the introductory song on the album, the last song also meanders a bit before concluding, but "Neon Nites" would actually chart higher as a (third release) single than "Georgia Rhythm," the second single from the album.

The cover photo for *A Rock and Roll Alternative* was a simple onstage performance shot taken by Jim Wiggins, a roadie. The image was hand tinted by Mike McCarty, who recalled that the cover was somewhat no-frills due to a time crunch, which further underlined Polydor's reported demand for another (and better-selling) album, pronto.

However, the front illustration also proffered what would evolve into the Atlanta Rhythm Section logo—three initials with spectrum/rainbowlike stripes and a lightning bolt. It was somewhat of a work in progress when it appeared on the cover of *A Rock and Roll Alternative*, and variants of this look would appear on later albums.

"That actually started off with using that kind-of-metallic lettering on *Red Tape*," said McCarty. "I took the initials from it, and it continued to morph. I was trying to establish a logo to use for merchandising, and, at the time, I was really attracted to art deco designs, so the lettering was sort of a takeoff on art deco, with a contemporary chrome feel to it."

As for the spectrum-like colors, McCarty said, "I think I was a little influenced by that 'rainbow' or 'spectrum' thing on Pink Floyd's *Dark Side of the Moon*."

Once again, McCarty won cover design awards for his artwork on *A Rock and Roll Alternative*.

The Atlanta Rhythm Section logo.

A lighted-sign version of the logo, over twenty feet long, was built by Atlanta's R. A. Roth company to hang behind the band at concerts. At the time, the band was using that firm for lighting at their headlining performances.

"Each individual letter could be turned on and off separately," McCarty detailed, "and the same could be done with each individual 'bar' in the 'rainbow.'"

A review in an Atlanta newspaper speculated that *A Rock and Roll Alternative* might finally be the album that could bust the Atlanta Rhythm Section out of the South, and that prognostication would prove to be on the money. The album topped out at #11 on Billboard's album chart and went gold. The Atlanta Rhythm Section's sixth album had finally vaulted the boys into the big time.

●●●●●●

In January 1977, the A.R.S. hired Atlanta native Jeff Jackson as lighting director, but his duties would expand to include other facets of tour work.

Jeff's roommate was Robert Roth, owner of the lighting company contracted with the A.R.S., and Jackson had already been working on assignments throughout the Southeast at relatively large venues, as well as handling sound and lights for local bands at clubs.

His experiences included numerous R&B shows by artists such as Kool & the Gang and George Clinton's Parliament/Funkadelic. He had mentors (some "passive") in lighting, just like performers had musical mentors.

"I worked for Robert on an 'as-needed basis,'" Jackson said, "going out with a system for one-offs; no tours. We'd take out a lighting system for an arena-type show for bands that weren't traveling with their own production. Most of the time, Robert would be running it, but I'd help set up and would get involved as needed, but I also studied closely, watching Robert and others—'what kind of gels did they have,' 'what colors did they use,' 'what angles did they go with.'"

At the behest of the band, Roth informed Jackson about the new opportunity with the Atlanta Rhythm Section.

"*A Rock and Roll Alternative* had just been released, and 'So Into You' had become their first really big hit. It was obvious that they were going to be doing more headline dates, so the band was looking for a full-time lighting director. Robert bet me I wouldn't last two weeks, and I won the bet. I liked it a lot more than I thought I would."

The new lighting director for the Atlanta Rhythm Section initially thought Roth might win the wager, however.

"I was twenty years old," Jeff detailed, "and I'd never been north of Tennessee in my life. My first three shows were at Rockford, Illinois; Davenport, Iowa; and Stevens Point, Wisconsin, all opening for Styx. I got on the bus one afternoon in Doraville, Georgia, and got off in Rockford; it was twenty [degrees] below zero . . . and I had the flu. It was like, 'What have I gotten myself into?'"

Jackson was not an aspiring musician, nor did he frequent Studio One on a regular basis.

"I never played in a band myself, other than a high school marching band," he remembered. "I would stop by the studio occasionally if [the Atlanta Rhythm Section] was recording, but I found the recording process to be incredibly boring; the live show was my thing."

Jackson was a very observant individual and would become fascinated by the band's musical preparation for an upcoming tour to support a new release, recalling that the band would rehearse for the tour on one day, one time only.

"We'd get a turntable or a cassette," he recalled, "and they'd listen to a song once, then play it through—usually just once—and of course, it would sound like they'd played it a hundred times. It was a rarity if they rehearsed a song more than once.

"There might have been some discussion about what they were going to play before they went out [on tour], but [the set list] didn't change during the whole run. The only show that differed from a set list for a particular tour was when we played a couple of nights at the Bottom Line in New York in '77, right after I was hired. The second night, they played songs that I'd never heard them play before, and I never heard those songs played again. The whole show was totally different, and if you were a true fan, you would've fallen over backwards, because it was flawless."

The new lighting director quickly became friends with Paul Goddard when it was discovered that Jeff was also a fan of progressive rock.

"It made his day when he found out I'd been to a lot of Yes concerts," Jeff recalled, "but when we opened shows for Kansas, it was intimidating to him. He thought Kansas was light years beyond the music that his own band was doing."

Goddard was a hot-natured individual, which compelled Jackson to come up with special lighting for Paul's area of the stage. Jeff also observed Paul's ongoing anti-rock-star sartorial preferences, noting, "He used to kid about keeping J. C. Penney in business."

Like Rodney Mills, Jackson also eventually grew to respect J. R.'s rhythm guitar stylings.

"Not having played in a band, I didn't understand how rhythm guitar worked," he reflected. "I thought 'rhythm guitar' meant you weren't good enough to be the lead guitar player. One thing I learned from J. R. was rock-steady, perfect tempo. He counted off every song, and you could have used him as a metronome. He also did some harmony lead parts with Barry. It wasn't that he *couldn't* play lead, but he wasn't there to do that. There weren't that many players that could do what he did."

Buddy would later promote Jeff to production manager for tours and concerts.

••••••

The Atlanta Rhythm Section's early 1977 booking at the Bottom Line in New York also resulted in the hiring of a primary driver for the band's gear. Journalist Jim Pettigrew, a University of Georgia graduate, was covering the show and was informed by Rodney Mills that the band was looking for a driver. Pettigrew recommended that Mills contact a friend of his named Jerry Coody, a Griffin, Georgia, native who had done roadwork with a regional band called the Strange Bedfellows. That aggregation and the Bushmen, Mills's former band, had worked on the same performance circuit a decade earlier, so Mills soon got in touch.

Coody was a graduate of Georgia Southwestern College in Americus, where he'd majored in history. While in school there, he and three friends had rented a house, and another student who had hung around that residence on a regular basis was Chip Carter, son of Jimmy Carter. The Carter family business was located in nearby Plains.

When Mills called Coody, Jerry was employed at Ft. Gillem, a military warehouse complex in Forest Park. Coody was already an A.R.S. fan, and within a week he was working his first show for the boys at the Roxy, a club on the Sunset Strip in Los Angeles.

The band owned their own small-cube truck, but it had so many mechanical problems that later in the year, management would opt to rent Ryder trucks.

Jay Rampley, who sold t-shirts and other souvenir items at shows, usually accompanied Coody in the equipment truck. Rampley's function was actually set up as a type of independent contractor operation; that is, he was not employed by Atlanta Rhythm Section management.

"If I drove all night, Jay would sleep in the truck," Coody said of a typical haul between performances. "Sometimes it was 150 miles between venues; sometimes it was 300 miles. We'd get to the next hotel, and I'd sleep during the day while Jay took the truck to the venue. I'd get up in the afternoon and take a cab to the gig; I had to be there by five o'clock, and I'd string and tune guitars before the band got there for the show."

Coody also helped with load-out following a show, paying close attention to the band's guitars and classic electronic gear such as Barry's early Marshall amplifiers and cabinets.

"I packed up the guitars myself every night," Coody detailed. "All of the guitars were the same to me; nothing was going to happen to any of them. I'd place them in their cases, then I'd place the cases inside road cases."

• • • • • •

A magazine article that appeared in the February 1977 issue of *Hit Parader* lumped the Atlanta Rhythm Section into the "Southern Rock" category alongside every major Capricorn act. The article was hyped on the front cover as "Rebel Rock—They Ain't Just Whistling 'Dixie.'" For some reason, the Marshall Tucker Band merited two photos. Moreover, the story erroneously cited Al Kooper as having overseen the Atlanta Rhythm Section's early career. Still, it was a profile that came off as positive publicity.

• • • • • •

Two writers on assignment from British music periodicals, *Sounds* and *New Music Express*, traveled with the Atlanta Rhythm Section for a few days in late March, as the band worked in Pennsylvania and Ohio. Bands that were co-billed with the A.R.S. included Kansas and Tom Petty & the Heartbreakers.

Both of the resultant articles attempted to portray the band as being more of a hell-raising aggregation than might be thought, with one of the profiles attempting to divide the members into the raucous-rock-star camp (Nix, Daughtry, Hammond) and the introspective-dudes-on-tour contingent (Bailey, Cobb, Goddard).

Photos accompanying the articles included Robert and Dean flipping middle fingers at the photographer, as well as Ronnie mooning the camera, his bare posterior pressed up against a car window.

One surprising segment of the articles was the talkativeness of Paul, who was plainspoken and detailed about his own personality traits, pronouncing himself to be basically antisocial. He also held forth about the kind of music he preferred and bassists he admired, particularly Dave Hope of Kansas. Perhaps Paul's loquaciousness had something to do with the writers being English, since most of the progressive-rock bands he admired hailed from the United Kingdom. But for whatever reason, such voluminous forthrightness with the press was extremely rare for Goddard.

The growing success of the band prompted Buddy to ask Arnie Geller of Polydor to form a business partnership with him. Geller's move from Polydor would include the creation of a proprietary record label and music-publishing division.

"That was not an easy decision," Arnie recalled. "I remember talking with my wife in a taxi on Third Avenue [in New York City]; I said, 'How'd you like to move to Atlanta?,' and she said 'Over my dead body.'"

Arnie resigned from Polydor in April 1977 (and the Geller marriage would survive). The new venture would become known as the Buie-Geller Organization (BGO).

"Buddy and I became partners on a handshake," Arnie recalled. "And in all our years as partners, we never had a fight."

"Arnie was our liaison to the record labels," said Gloria. "He took the other office upstairs, next door to mine."

Geller quickly got involved with an upcoming mega-concert being planned for Labor Day weekend at Grant Field, the football stadium located on the campus of Georgia Tech in Atlanta. Not surprisingly, the Dog Day Rock Fest had been Buddy's idea. He and Arnie partnered with promoter Rich Floyd (one of the two Richards who had run the now-closed rock music club that had their given names as its moniker).

Buie's original plan was to present the concert at Atlanta Stadium.

Arnie Geller in his office.

"I encouraged Buddy to pursue doing it at Georgia Tech," said Jeff Jackson. "Better sight lines, and you had a bigger capacity. For something like that, straight lines in a football stadium were going to work much better."

The event was to be the first rock concert ever staged at Grant Field, which had been leased from the Georgia Tech Athletic Association.

••••••

In late April, the Atlanta Rhythm Section flew to Amsterdam to the headquarters of Polydor, to be wined and dined by the company, then to English for their debut performance in London at the New Victoria Theatre on April 23. A British band called Meal Ticket opened. Wives accompanied some of the A.R.S. band members on this overseas sojourn.

One review of the New Victoria concert had a generally thumbs-down attitude as it complained about the band pacing their set and working into an extended and rehearsed jam. However, the reviewer then turned around and used almost as many column inches to praise the Atlanta Rhythm Section's Polydor catalog.

Ronnie wails while wearing one of his three-piece, Victorian-style suits.

Other New Vic reviews were positive. One rightly cited the band members' experience as studio musicians as the foundation of their professional performance. Another noted that Ronnie looked like "a real Macon gentleman, dressed as he was in snappy white duds."

The boys also did a lip-synched performance on the legendary *The Old Grey Whistle Test* television program on the BBC (British Broadcasting Corporation), where Ronnie fronted the band wearing the same quasi-Victorian three-piece white suit.

"He also had a tailor-made brown velvet suit," Steve Hammond said of his brother's sartorial preferences onstage during that era. "This was his choice of stage clothes from the mid- to late 1970s. I actually got married in [the brown suit], believe it or not, but as time went on I was no longer slender enough to wear it."

In one British magazine article that *didn't* review the New Vic show, Ronnie waxed eloquent in an extensive interview about what the Atlanta Rhythm Section was trying to accomplish with its music, and he allowed that if he hadn't ended up in music, he would have considered becoming a politician, advocating (US) prison reform, among other personal passions.

••••••

Earlier in the year, Rodney Mills had decided to relinquish his role as tour manager for the Atlanta Rhythm Section to assist in the production of Lynyrd Skynyrd's fifth studio release, *Street Survivors*. Part of the album was recorded at Studio One, and upgrades in recording equipment, including a twenty-four-track mixer and new speakers, had been installed as part of the agreement with the Jacksonville band to return to the studio where their first release had been recorded.

"It was a dream come true that the Rhythm Section was now finally viable," Mills said, "but the studio stuff is what I signed on to do. When I came off the road with the Rhythm Section, I would immediately go into the studio. I quit the road to go back into the studio with Skynyrd."

Mary and Rodney Mills had a one-year-old daughter, so family reasons also figured into his decision. But it also meant a fifty percent cut in his income.

Sammie Ammons, who had been the A.R.S.'s bus driver, would be elevated to tour manager status.

••••••

One unique concert for the boys that year was the "Derby Eve" concert, presented at Freedom Hall in Louisville, Kentucky, on May 6, the night before the Kentucky Derby. Bob Seger & the Silver Bullet Band headlined, and the show was emceed by Wolfman Jack.

••••••

A harbinger for the upcoming Dog Day Rock Fest as well as the next annum's "big concerts" for the Atlanta Rhythm Section was a show on Memorial Day weekend in Oakland, California.

The Left Coast event was part of Bill Graham's Day on the Green concert series, presented at the Oakland-Alameda Coliseum. The other featured performers for the Saturday and Monday shows were the Eagles (who were on tour to support their *Hotel California* album), the Steve Miller Band, Heart, and Foreigner.

BILL GRAHAM PRESENTS

THE EAGLES

THE STEVE MILLER BAND

HEART

ATLANTA RHYTHM SECTION

FOREIGNER

OAKLAND STADIUM

SAT, MAY 28 & MON, MAY 30

Mobile housing was provided for individual bands, where the members could hang out before and after their performances. The sign on the trailer provided for the A.R.S. read "Atlanta Rythem [*sic*] Section," according to Rodney Mills, who kept the misspelled item as a souvenir because nobody else wanted it.

Abetted by the fact that "So Into You" was a current hit, the A.R.S. took the stage in Oakland late in the morning both on Saturday and Monday, following Foreigner's brief and gritty opening sets. The boys played for some forty-five minutes and were warmly received.

The logistics of the California trip were complicated by a booking in Sacramento on Sunday, the in-between day. The boys opened for Gary Wright of "Dream Weaver" fame in the state capital, then returned to Oakland for the Monday show.

Mills was already slated to get off the road to work in the studio with Lynyrd Skynyrd on *Street Survivors,* and the crew was looking for a soundman when the band performed at the Day on the Green shows. Rodney was already aware that Jeff Jackson had done sound work in Atlanta for lesser-known or club bands prior to his employment with the A.R.S., so he offered Jeff the opportunity to mix the sound at the Monday show in Oakland.

"I let Rodney talk me into it because it was a daytime show and there weren't any lights," Jackson recalled. "I did the show, acting like I owned the place, but Rodney was looking over my shoulder. I made it through okay, but I told him I never wanted to do that again. He said, 'Well, you know you could if you had to.' He was pleased with the job I did. My sound career with the Atlanta Rhythm Section lasted one day.

"Fortunately for both of us, we heard about an experienced guy named Greg Quesnel, who we called 'Fernie' or 'Fern.' We tried him out and he was hired. He mixed for the A.R.S. for a long time and ended up working at Studio One as an engineer."

• • • • • •

Greg Quesnel grew up in the southern Dekalb County area of Atlanta. He recalled that his interest in music began through an aunt, who was married to a disc jockey.

"I guess I can trace it back to them," he said. "I used to listen to Wes Montgomery albums, Herbie Mann, a lot of jazz stuff. As I grew up, most of my friends became musicians, and they would practice at my house. As they practiced, I'd say things like 'You're gonna have to change that' or 'You're too loud; you gotta turn down' or 'I can't hear the bass drum; you're going to have to kick a little harder.' So I was 'running the sound' by telling them what to do!"

Like Jeff Jackson, Quesnel never played in a rock band. He had run sound for a number of Atlanta bands, the most noteworthy of which was Motion.

"They were the second- or third-largest rock band on the nightclub circuit," he said. "The other two were Eli and Choice."

Quesnel also ran lights, utilizing a type of lens known as a fresnel, which rhymed with his last name. The drummer for Motion is the individual who came up with the tech's nickname of "Fern" or "Fernie."

"I was also the house soundman at a club called C. W. Shaw's, [located] at Buford Highway at Clairmont Road," Quesnel detailed. "Paul Goddard would come into the club's game room and play pinball all the time. As soundman there, I was in charge of the between-band music. I'm a progressive-rock fan, so the music I'd put together between bands was Gino Vanelli, Genesis, and Yes—artists that Paul loved, so that was the original connection, with Paul. And Jeff Jackson had run lights for one of the bands that played at C. W. Shaw's, but it's my understanding that Paul gave the band my name when Rodney let everyone know he was going to work with Lynyrd Skynyrd on their next album."

When Quesnel got the call about going to work for the A.R.S., he was managing, booking, and running the sound for a band called Terminus.

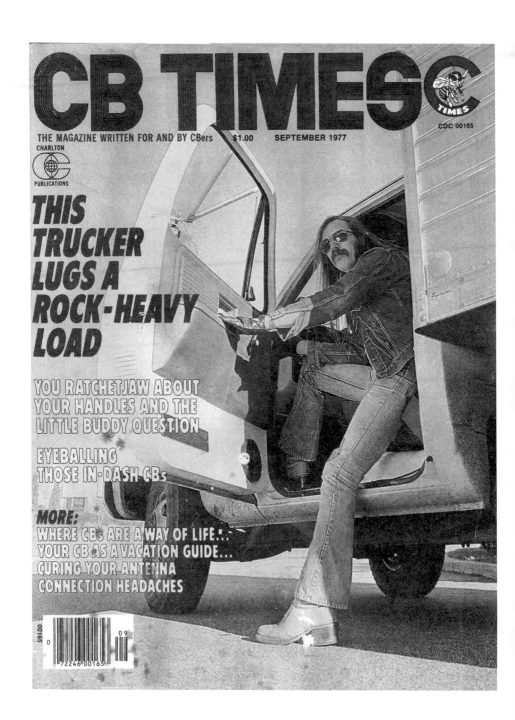

CB TIMES

THE MAGAZINE WRITTEN FOR AND BY CBers $1.00   SEPTEMBER 1977

CDC 00165

CHARLTON PUBLICATIONS

THIS TRUCKER LUGS A ROCK-HEAVY LOAD

YOU RATCHETJAW ABOUT YOUR HANDLES AND THE LITTLE BUDDY QUESTION

EYEBALLING THOSE IN-DASH CBs

MORE:
WHERE CBs ARE A WAY OF LIFE...
YOUR CB AS A VACATION GUIDE...
CURING YOUR ANTENNA
CONNECTION HEADACHES

Greg received a call from lighting company owner Robert Roth at three o'clock one morning; Roth told him that he was going to give Quesnel's phone number to Jeff Jackson of the Atlanta Rhythm Section.

Jackson called some thirty minutes later from California, where the band was playing for the Day on the Green concerts. Quesnel then conversed with Rodney Mills, who wanted him to go to work for the Rhythm Section immediately, but Quesnel said that he had to talk with the Terminus band members. An interview at Studio One with the Buies ultimately happened, and Quesnel began his initial work with Mills less than a week later.

A month after the Day on the Green concerts, Mills was already working with Lynyrd Skynyrd, but he traveled to Denver on a one-shot mixing assignment for the Rhythm Section at the Colorado Sun Day Festival (which featured several Southern bands, Heart, Foreigner, and singer/songwriter Rusty Weir) at Mile High Stadium. A dustup with another band's crew regarding the mixing board proved to be a major hassle for Rodney that he managed to salvage. However, the incident underlined his decision to get off the road and let Fern Quesnel take over the soundboard.

"Fern got to be pretty good at mixing A.R.S. live," Mills opined.

••••••

The year 1977 was a primary one for the citizen's band (CB) radio fad, and less than a year into his tenure with the Atlanta Rhythm Section, truck driver Jerry Coody found himself on the cover of the September issue of *CB Times* magazine. Therein, the long-haired gearjammer discussed the complexities of hauling the band's gear from one locale to another in time for the next load-in, interpolating his CB experiences into his recollections.

Around the same time, word was also out that Studio One was seeking a studio manager, and Coody advised Gloria about his friend Rick Maxwell.

Also a native of Griffin, Maxwell had opportunities to monitor more than one burgeoning music scene in Georgia when he was a teenager, since that city is located about halfway between Atlanta and Macon.

"I met with Gloria and was pretty much hired on the spot," Rick recalled. "It was an unusual situation, because basically, we were not a 'commercial' studio; we were more of a 'project' studio. Buddy, J. R., and Bill Lowery owned the facility, and when the Rhythm Section came in, it wasn't like we were put on a clock. We weren't allotted a certain amount of recording hours per day, per week, whatever. When other folks came in, however, we would bill them accordingly.

"I would set up equipment in the studio for whoever was coming in and would fix anything that was malfunctioning. I'd also order supplies. But if we didn't have a lot going on around the studio, I'd go out on the road with the Rhythm Section, so I kind of got to see both sides."

Maxwell's arrival and his observations from a studio maintenance point of view underlined the ongoing businesslike attitude of the members of the Atlanta Rhythm Section.

"They were not best friends by any stretch of imagination," he said. "They knew what they were there to do, and they made it work better than anybody I've ever seen. They were professionals, and when they got into the studio, they were all focused on the one final goal of making a song that was in the works the absolute best record they could. That was true from the players to Buddy to Rodney, and it would have actually started in the songwriting process. Nobody would accept 'mediocre'; if it was not right, they'd do it over, until they got it right."

Maxwell also underlined the inappropriate pigeonhole in which all too-many writers and music fans tended to place the Atlanta Rhythm Section.

"They were not a 'Southern Rock' band, by any means," he insisted. "Many people tried to put them under the same umbrella as the Allman Brothers and other Capricorn bands. They were about a hundred miles apart geographically, a thousand miles apart musically."

The studio manager also recalled that most of the band's recordings were done at night. Barry or J. R. would occasionally come in during the daylight hours to do overdubs.

●●●●●●

In the mid-1970s, there was actually some recording "overlap," for lack a better term, between Phil Walden's Capricorn conglomerate and Studio One, as a Macon-based band named Stillwater recorded two albums in Doraville for that label. Their debut album was released in 1977, with the sophomore effort, *I Reserve the Right*, following the next year. Moreover, Buddy signed on as producer and, not surprisingly, assisted the band in songwriting for the second album.

Stillwater had also opened for the Atlanta Rhythm Section in concert. The first performance of the two bands on the same bill had been at Lakeside Park in Macon on July 5, 1976.

"Once we were signed, Capricorn set about finding us the right producer," said Stillwater guitarist Rob Walker. "They had considered other producers, including Alan Parsons, for a short time but ended up deciding on Buddy Buie. I believe Buddy was chosen because, in addition to being a producer with a track record, he was a prolific songwriter with many hit songs behind him.

"Sometime in March of 1977, we went to Atlanta to play for Buddy. We set up in a warehouse downtown and played him all the songs we were prepared to record. After hearing the band, Buddy chose the songs he thought would be best for our first record. From there, we left to work on lyrics at a cabin on Lake Lanier near Atlanta. Buddy preferred writing at a lake. While we had written all the music and lyrics for the songs Buddy picked for our first album, we had other music that needed lyrics, and our existing lyrics could benefit from his expertise."

Mike Causey, another Stillwater guitarist, was already a fan of Barry Bailey.

"Barry Bailey was one of my favorite guitarists," Causey said. "From the first time I heard him on the first [Atlanta Rhythm Section] album, I was hooked on his playing. He has such a sense of melody and has such a great touch and control, but he can be what I call 'slippery.' He'll play this great phrase, and at the end of it he just does this really fast slur—something only he can do. I've never heard anyone else play like that. He's someone that a lot of guitar players really respect; he is so smooth! I would try sometimes to emulate him, but there was just no way. He was a big influence on me."

Walker owned a Dean Markley "Voice Box" guitar device (also referred to as a "talk box," or "squawk box") that modified a human voice and a guitar into a buzzing but intriguing sound, as popularized by Peter Frampton on his live double album, released in 1976. Rob had purchased his gizmo at Atlanta's Metro Music ("an impulse buy," he said), and Buie was attracted to its unique application.

At a songwriting session at Lake Lanier, Buddy and Walker came up with "Mind Bender," which would interpolate the Voice Box and would become the only hit for the band.

One-Hit-Wonder status aside, Causey had relished the opportunity of working with a songwriting icon such as Buie.

"If you had a riff and he liked it, he would just start honing in on a melody," said Causey, "and would eventually come up with the song. It was so much fun for us to get the chance to write some with Buddy. He was a very funny man, very smart and very much a businessman. Buddy did not play [instruments] much at all, but he had this uncanny ability to take riffs and make great songs out of them."

Bill Wendt was a tour manager and soundman for Stillwater, as well as an assistant engineer on that band's two albums recorded at Studio One. Wendt would later come onboard with the A.R.S. to run the mixing boards at concerts.

••••••

Preparations for the Dog Day Rock Fest on September 3 proceeded in a methodical manner.

The lease with Georgia Tech gave the promoters "absolute control" of the venue. The artificial Astroturf surface of the football field was covered by a tarp shipped from Canada. Eighty off-duty policemen—thirty from the Georgia Tech Police Department, fifty from the Atlanta Police Department—were hired as extra security personnel.

The Atlanta Rhythm Section got top billing; however, the hometown boys would not be closing the show.

Detroit-based Bob Seger was on a roll with his Silver Bullet Band, as their huge-selling *Night Moves* album, released almost a year earlier, had blasted them into the upper echelon of rock royalty (*Night Moves* would eventually be certified as sextuple platinum in sales).

"I called Punch Andrews, Bob Seger's manager, because we were still looking for acts," said Arnie Geller. "He said 'Well, I don't know . . . ,' but then I told him, 'You and I have known each other for a lot of years. You need to understand that the Atlanta Rhythm Section is to Atlanta what Bob Seger is to Detroit.' He agreed to come."

Considering the prominence of Bob Seger & the Silver Bullet Band at the time, it seemed appropriate for that group to close the event, but there were other reasons for such a maneuver, which, depending on one's point of view, could have been interpreted as clever or surreptitious.

Geller also reached out to other acts and worked with the promotion and marketing of the show, as well as the merchandising.

"In those days, most guys didn't think much about merchandising," he said, "but I had made a deal with Georgia Tech where I got the merchandising rights for the band and BGO. That was in the days before name licensing, and we made a lot of money."

Heart would be making its Atlanta debut at the one-day event. Foreigner's debut album had performed well in 1976, and that English/American sextet was originally slated to play first. However, another aggregation, identified in one periodical as "Cheap Tricks," was added at the last moment. Cheap Trick's second album, *In Color*, would debut that same month and would eventually go platinum.

Some Studio One / A.R.S. / BGO associates took up temporary residence near the stadium.

"I spent a whole week down there getting it ready," said Jeff Jackson. "I didn't even go home; I got a room at the Tech Motel."

South Carolina native Lynn Sinclair was just a few years into his career as a music and program director for radio stations in Georgia and his home state. He had first heard the Atlanta Rhythm Session when they opened for Wet Willie at the Memorial Coliseum in Spartanburg.

"They were on fire that night," Sinclair recalled, "and played the music meticulously and with a lot of spirit."

Sinclair respected the band's approach to their music and would spin any single that the A.R.S. released. He had been invited to the Dog Day Rock Fest as a member of the media.

"I was given an elevator pass by Butch Lowery that gave me access to the press box," he remembered, "which I visited several times throughout the day to escape the heat."

Some 45,000–50,000 music fans (as estimated by a representative of the Georgia Tech Athletic Association) turned out for the event, filling the entire football field in front of the stage as well as most of the seating in the stadium. The show kicked off on time at 3 p.m., with Cheap Trick romping through a brief and energetic set.

"The crowd was ready to go and happy that things had gotten underway," said Sinclair. "Cheap Trick played well and connected well."

Heart makes its Atlanta debut at the Dog Day Rock Fest.
The Technique

The concert ran smoothly and on time. When Heart performed its encore, the band impressed the crowd with a rollicking cover of Led Zeppelin's "Rock and Roll."

And Buddy had shrewdly scheduled the Atlanta Rhythm Section to kick off their set at sundown, which would happen around 8 p.m.

As lighting director, Jeff Jackson wanted the A.R.S. to be the 'first-dark' band; i.e., the first band that needed lighting.

"That, in and of itself, is an effect," Jackson said succinctly.

Accordingly, the first-dark position of the Atlanta Rhythm Section in the lineup was another reason to let Bob Seger & the Silver Bullet Band close. The twilight effect as the hometown boys took the stage was unforgettable to many concertgoers.

"I was running back and forth with all of the radio guys we'd invited," Butch Lowery recalled, "and when the Rhythm Section came on, the sun had just gone down, and it was magic; spectacular. And the crowd was ready."

"The idea was that since they weren't going to close the show, they came on at that time so the lighting would be effective," said Rodney Mills, who was running the sound. "And we had that backdrop sign that lit up, so that was also a pretty dramatic part of the process."

At the same time, many of the attendees lit up cigarette lighters as a salute to the band. Such a collective admiration-by-illumination ritual is usually performed at the *end* of a concert as a sign of approval, and the boys responded with a kick-ass rendition of "Sky High," which had become the band's standard opening tune.

Ronnie reaches out during the Atlanta Rhythm Section's set at the Dog Day Rock Fest.
The Technique

"It was their moment," said Mike McCarty, who was scurrying all over the venue taking photos. "The hometown really came out for them."

Arnie Geller barely got to see the show, due to what he pronounced to have been "a physical altercation with some guys who were selling bootleg merchandise out on the property. I had some off-duty policemen that I hired as security guards. When I saw these guys selling stuff, I went after them. I had to be pulled off of one of them by one of the security guards."

The Atlanta Rhythm Section rocked harder than their fans might have expected, and played "Hitch Hiker's Hero" (from *A Rock and Roll Alternative*) live for the first time. "Angel" was performed for the first time in three years, and Paul, as expected, unleashed a monstrous bass solo on the final tune in the regular set, "Another Man's Woman."

And for all of the previous criticism of the band for their lack of visuals onstage, some concertgoers may have noticed more than one A.R.S. member doing a bug-eyed double take onstage when some female audience members, sitting on the shoulders of their dates, flashed their breasts at the band. Such exposure was part of many 1970s concerts for many bands, and the A.R.S. would have the same visual experiences elsewhere.

The boys were called back for two encores. The first consisted of "Georgia Rhythm" (another first-ever live performance, with Mylon LeFevre joining in on backing vocals) and "Doraville." The second encore proffered "Long Tall Sally" (on which Dean sang lead vocals) and "Boogie Smoogie."

"It was crazy," Mylon said of the Atlanta Rhythm Section's performance. "They were *the* Atlanta band, and 'So Into You' was big at the time. I loved sitting in with those guys, whether it was in the studio or onstage."

Bob Seger & the Silver Bullet Band put on an enthusiastic closing set, which included three songs ("Feel Like a Number," "Brave Strangers," and "The Famous Final Scene") from their yet-to-be-completed next album, *Stranger in Town*. Following the concert, Seger would head to Criteria Studios in Miami to work on more music for the new album. The veteran singer/guitarist made the journey from Atlanta to south Florida by automobile, since he wasn't pressed for time.

"Perhaps traveling by car gave him some 'quiet time' to work on lyrics, etc., as preparation for his recording sessions at Criteria," Lynn Sinclair speculated.

The following day, the local press let it be known that the Atlanta Rhythm Section had ruled the event, which was hailed as being presented in the manner that a rock festival ought to be run. One periodical opined that the performance by the A.R.S. was one of its best ever. The attendees were also cited as being relatively well behaved.

Steve Hammond: "Ronnie told me that at that point in his life, he felt like he had achieved what he'd set out to achieve."

"That one was a shot in the arm for us," J. R. said of the massive show. "Made us realize we might have something going on."

And the stadium's Astroturf field had not been damaged by the crowd. However, a small portion of the artificial surface had been roughed up by forklifts that had been boosting speakers onto the stage during setup.

• • • • • •

Following the successful completion of Lynyrd Skynyrd's *Street Survivors* project, Rodney Mills was unexpectedly given "points" on the album (percentage of sales) as well as a healthy cash bonus by Ronnie Van Zant for his effort. The project had further enhanced his inclination to pursue recording production as a logical step up from engineering.

However, Mills recalled that there wasn't a signed document regarding Van Zant's promise of points from sales, and that accommodation was obliterated on October 29, 1977, when Van Zant and two other band members were killed in the crash of a chartered airplane that was taking Skynyrd from Greenville, South Carolina, to Baton Rouge, Louisiana.

• • • • • •

For all of their mutual musical respect for each other, the members of the Atlanta Rhythm Section and Kansas probably felt a bit of collective awkwardness when a November 4, 1977, performance in Columbia, South Carolina, resulted in a review that slagged the headlining Kansas but praised the boys from Doraville, who had opened. The reviewer complained about Kansas's reliance on high-decibel bombast and special effects. On the other hand, each member of the A.R.S. was noted for his prowess except for J. R., who, for some reason, wasn't named.

• • • • • •

The Atlanta Rhythm Section was among the artists who paid tribute to local musical icon Bill Lowery on November 17, at the Atlanta Civic Center on Piedmont Avenue. The event commemorated twenty-five years of Lowery's multifaceted career in the Peach State capital and was a benefit to establish a Bill Lowery Scholarship at Georgia State University's School of Commercial Music.

Several advance print media articles noted Lowery's decades of music publishing, from Gene Vincent's "Be-Bop-a-Lula" in 1956 to Starbuck's 1976 hit single "Moonlight Feels Right" and the A.R.S.'s then-current hit, "So Into You." Artists such as Tommy Roe and Joe South were interviewed.

Attendees at the event included dignitaries such as Georgia lieutenant governor Zell Miller; Atlanta mayor Maynard Jackson (who proclaimed that day to be "Bill Lowery Day" in Atlanta); Capricorn's Phil Walden; singers William Bell, Mylon LeFevre, and Hamilton Bohannon; and officials from the National Academy of Recording Arts and Sciences.

Performers included Billy Joe Royal, Tommy Roe, Dennis Yost, and Joe South (who was coming out of self-imposed retirement). Lowery became emotional when he introduced Buddy Buie, then the Atlanta Rhythm Section performed—selections included "So Into You" and "Georgia Rhythm"—followed by country singer Sami Jo, with legendary goofus Ray Stevens finishing the gala presentation.

Reflecting on the event, J. R. said, "I remember what an enormous part Bill Lowery played in my professional life and any success that I may have experienced. He took an interest in developing the talents of people like me, and I was extremely fortunate in being able to benefit from his advice and example. I can safely say that most of the endeavors in the music business in which I participated would have never happened without his influence and involvement."

••••••

During the latter half of the 1970s, the Atlanta Rhythm Section would often find itself being booked with an Allman Brothers Band offshoot aggregation called Sea Level. Founded in 1976, the original members included Allman Brothers Band members Chuck Leavell, drummer Jaimoe, and bassist Lamar Williams (but Leavell would leave the Allmans late that year). The Rhythm Section had opened for the Allmans on several occasions, and Sea Level was now opening for the Rhythm Section.

Like the A.R.S., Sea Level took a different path compared to other bands from the Deep South, opting for more jazz-oriented fare. The musicians' impressive individual chops and professional attitudes nurtured a "kindred spirits" vibe between the two bands.

"I suppose there was a similarity between the A.R.S. and Sea Level inasmuch that we were trying to expand beyond 'blues and boogie,'" said Leavell. "The Allman Brothers had elements of jazz in there, as did Sea Level. The Atlanta Rhythm Section had more of a crafted approach—well-written catchy songs, well arranged and recorded. I think we were both 'thinking outside the box.'

"And I do think we shared an audience. The A.R.S. was selling a lot more records than we were with Sea Level, but the fans seemed to gravitate to both of us. We enjoyed each other's company on tour, and there was a strong compatibility. I thought together we made for a really good show, and I always enjoyed being on the bill with them."

• • • • • •

The Atlanta Rhythm Section would close out 1977 with its third-straight New Year's Eve performance at the Fox in Atlanta, supported by Mylon LeFevre. The year had been successful and, in many ways, had been a harbinger/warm-up for the next annum, which would prove to be the most ambitious and hectic in the band's history.

S oon after 1978 began, industry trade publications for the music business formally announced the formation of the Buie/Geller Organization. The blurb in the February 4, 1978, issue of *Record World* pronounced the company to be, "primarily an international management company directing the careers of the Atlanta Rhythm Section and seven other acts currently under its umbrella."

Gloria Buie was cited as being involved in all phases of the new company, and Sharon Lawrence was noted as "director of creative services."

Lawrence had been an independent public relations specialist who would continue in that capacity as an employee for the new company. She would also line up unique promotions, such as a panel discussion at Georgia State University about concert logistics, in which a band member and tour personnel were participants.

BGO Records was a division that would be distributed by Polydor. BGO Music was the new company's publishing division.

Gloria's participation was critical, according to Arnie Geller.

Shown at a Georgia State University panel discussion are, from left, Paul Goddard, Jeff Jackson, and Jerry Coody. The presentation was organized by Sharon Lawrence, far right.

"She handled all the finances," he said, "and I'll say it to this day—she was the only person who could work hands-on with all of the money, and I never had to worry about it. Other employees did a lot of detail work, but they reported to her. Gloria was a gem."

And Arnie also recalled Buddy's propensity to put creativity discussions ahead of housekeeping:

"He had an office, but he didn't like to stay in there. He was always in my office, sitting on the sofa and usually smoking a cigarette, tapping the ashes behind the sofa as we discussed new ideas. When we moved out of there years later, there was a mountain of ashes back there."

BGO would later relocate to its own offices on Northcrest Road near the Embry Hills Shopping Center (still in Doraville, about a mile and a half from Studio One). The new locations had individual offices for Buddy, Arnie, Gloria, and Jeff Jackson and also housed the merchandising division of BGO, run by Peggy Hendricks.

"I wanted to stay near where we lived for quick access to the children and our home," Gloria said. "My office window, on the backside of the building, actually looked out over Kinder Care, where Ben was in daycare. We rented the space and had it redesigned for our purposes. Arnie was responsible for this, and I have to give him full credit for the design. It turned out beautifully and we were very proud of it."

● ● ● ● ● ●

Arnie was also keenly aware of the Atlanta Rhythm Section's lack of stage presence and Ronnie's endeavors to become a viable frontman.

"They were musicians, not showmen," Geller said. "But they got better as they got more experienced. They learned how to work audiences, and Ronnie did a good job with that. But one of the fun things for me was to note the other musicians from other bands and other people in the entertainment business who would be backstage watching and listening.

"And we also talked about not 'hiding' Paul Goddard in the back. He's out there playing his ass off, so we didn't need to make it look like we were embarrassed about him. [We wanted to] put him out there, where he could become a hero to all of the other 'Paul Goddards' in the world."

Issues about the Atlanta Rhythm Section's onstage appearance and demeanor aside, Geller still focused on garnering radio airplay for the band more than any

Paul gets the spotlight onstage in early '78, at the Music Hall in Cleveland, Ohio. *Sue Kastelic*

other presentation format. Concerts or potential appearances on late-night weekend music programs on national television were sublimated in an attempt to get the music of the A.R.S. heard via the airwaves.

"Radio was still about all we had back then," he said, "so we needed that to sell our product."

••••••

Early March saw a prerelease party for the band's next album, *Champagne Jam*, held at Studio One. Some 700 persons attended, including Lynyrd Skynyrd survivors Gary Rossington, Allen Collins, and Artimus Pyle.

When the album was released soon thereafter, the consensus among many music aficionados was that the Atlanta Rhythm Section had outdone itself, fulfilling the potential of *A Rock and Roll Alternative* in spades.

The band's confidence and willingness to diversify was evident right at the outset, as the album kicked off with a roaring tribute to Lynyrd Skynyrd called "Large Time," which was followed by the loping yet insistent "I'm Not Gonna Let It Bother Me Tonight," one of three singles from *Champagne Jam* that would hit the charts.

Buddy would later detail the line of thinking behind the creation of "I'm Not Gonna Let It Bother Me Tonight."

"All my life I've believed you should do—every day—all you can do to achieve your goals," he said. "At the end of a day when I'd done my best, I always said 'I've done all I can do today; I'll worry about it tomorrow.' Well, [co-writers] Robert Nix and Dean Daughtry shared that philosophy."

"Normal Love" is downright lush, replete with gorgeous orchestration and exquisite harmony vocals.

The title track of the album, like "I'm Not Gonna Let It Bother Me Tonight," is a loose and laid-back tune that fits Ronnie's voice perfectly.

On the other hand, "Imaginary Lover" is a brooding composition that hooks a listener with its mysterious, slightly reverberating mix.

However, the band doesn't get mired in any perceived easy-listening format, since "The Ballad of Lois Malone" is a honking stomp with lyrics that would probably be considered politically incorrect in the ensuing decades.

Moreover, "The Great Escape" is an indictment of drug use, and some listeners may have speculated if anyone in particular had inspired that Bailey-Buie-Nix composition. However, the afflatus for the lyrics was actually a "composite character," according to Barry, whose angry-sounding guitar is noticeable on that song, as well as on the one that follows it, "Evileen."

Buddy Buie and Robert Nix were listed in the album credits for *Champagne Jam* as "producers." No associate producers were cited.

Mike McCarty's "Funky Fish" character was updated in full color for an appearance on the album cover of *Champagne Jam*. This time around, the critter was sporting a "gimme" cap with "ARS" emblazoned on it, and was cradling a glass of bubbly along with its bass, which now appeared to be an electric hollow-body instrument.

"I received several more awards from commercial advertising art and design magazines for that piece during that era," the artist recalled.

●●●●●●

The publicity campaign for the album interpolated the phrase "The Toast of Rock and Roll," and advertising was seen on billboards and in magazines.

One of the publicity photo shoots was done inside a liquor warehouse, where the band posed among assorted cases of champagne. Given his preference for that beverage, the typically reticent Paul seemed to be right at home, and he even posed for goofy solo photos with his bass.

Billboard in Hollywood, California, promoting *Champagne Jam.*

Bubbly fun: Paul poses with cases of champagne in a publicity shot.

Album reviews that appeared in March and April were mixed—*Crawdaddy* and the *Beaver County Times* (Pennsylvania) decried the record's contents as bland and unimaginative, but the *New York Times* and the *Chicago Sun-Times* praised the new disc.

A profile of Dean in a Richmond, Virginia, newspaper preceded a concert with English singer Robert Palmer and American progressive rock band Crack the Sky in that city. Therein, Ox noted that the Georgia state flag—two-thirds of which was the Confederate Battle Flag—would not be displayed due to his recent acquisition of a Yamaha baby electric grand piano, which had a more elegant-looking curved front. The lack of a boxy instrument setup made it impossible to display the banner.

Reviewing the Richmond performance several days later, the same reporter opined that the Atlanta Rhythm Section deserved to be compared to the Band and Little Feat regarding strong individual players who performed as a team.

Some reviewers may have preferred earlier albums over the new release, but *Champagne Jam* would become the Atlanta Rhythm Section's only platinum-selling album, and many fans would opine in the ensuing years and decades that the 1978 release was indeed the band's best.

Ox gets into the ozone onstage.

The hit singles on the album (and their respective highest Billboard rankings) were "Champagne Jam" (#43), "I'm Not Gonna Let It Bother Me Tonight" (#14), and "Imaginary Lover" (#7).

And while there aren't any statistics to cite, "Imaginary Lover" would probably also have a high ranking in the pantheon of rock music in a listing of songs that were intentionally played at the wrong speed by some fans.

••••••

While "Imaginary Lover" might have owed a possible tip of the headstock to ethereal Fleetwood Mac ballads such as "Rhiannon" and "Dreams," the legend about a cover version of the Atlanta Rhythm Section song actually being recorded by the mighty Mac began when a radio deejay accidentally played the A.R.S. hit at a faster speed than specified. However, listeners called in to express their approval of the tune, thinking it was a version of the song that had indeed been recorded by Fleetwood Mac. The song sounded peppier, and the vocals sounded like chanteuse Stevie Nicks fronting the band she was currently a member of.

Nicks herself heard about the musical incongruity and purchased her own copy of the A.R.S. song. Playing the disc at a faster speed, she dubbed "Imaginary Lover" onto cassette and submitted it (as a gag) to bandmate Christine McVie; the speeded-up tune was supposedly a demo for Fleetwood Mac's future consideration. McVie was said to have been impressed by what she thought were Nicks's vocals and the "arrangement" of the Atlanta Rhythm Section tune.

••••••

As the buzz about *Champagne Jam* continued to grow, Buddy and Arnie implemented a brilliant marketing plan to garner wider interest in the band and the album, abetted by a brand of chewing gum.

The redoubtable Carefree Sugarless Gum Tour was organized by creating twelve contests by twelve Top 40 radio stations in twelve markets. The high school, junior high, or middle school that collected the most gum wrappers would get a free concert in the school gym by the Atlanta Rhythm Section, and the school's Parent-Teacher Association (PTA) would receive a sizeable donation.

However, Buie and Geller picked the twelve markets, all which weren't particularly strong for the A.R.S., and made sure the radio stations sponsoring the local shows had a Top 40 format instead of an album-oriented rock (AOR) format. The band even recorded radio spots for the stations.

One rule of the competition mandated that a school that was competing had to be able to pick up the signal of the radio station that was sponsoring the contest. Such a strategy meant that the then-current single, "Imaginary Lover," would receive a lot of airplay in those markets, and the band would probably get a decent share of airplay on AOR stations, as well.

Moreover, the initiative was a "per capita" contest (i.e., how many gum wrappers per student). The list of winners indicated that smaller schools and Catholic schools won a disproportionate number of the competitions in their markets.

The airplay of "Imaginary Lover" for the Carefree Sugarless Gum contest would ultimately break out both the single and the album in markets where the band had never had previous success.

Most of the shows were presented that spring, and, somewhat conveniently, several of the schools were located in the heartland of the United States.

The band veered off the chewing-gum trail to play a "Grad Nite" event at Disney World on May 12–13. The park was open all night for graduating seniors, and the other acts were Sea Level, Hot, High Energy, Con Funk Shun, and Solar Wind. After the Disney World performance, they completed the remainder of the Carefree Sugarless Gum concerts.

Recollections from the contest and tour included having to contend with a hostile principal in San Antonio, Texas, who read Jeff Jackson the riot act about his adamant opposition to the show during an initial phone call to set up the concert. When the band showed up to perform, law enforcement officers were swarming all over the school's campus.

Other schools had wanted the band to perform as early as 8:30 a.m. for a morning school assembly event, but it was quickly established that no shows would be presented before noon.

In addition to San Antonio, the locales where concerts were performed included Chickasha, Oklahoma (thirty miles south of Oklahoma City, where the radio station was located), Tahlequah, Oklahoma (Tulsa radio station), Leavenworth, Kansas (Kansas City station), Omaha, Nebraska (local station; the winner was an all-girl Catholic junior high school), Pacific, Missouri (St. Louis station), Belmont, North Carolina (Charlotte station), Dobson, North Carolina (Greensboro station), Marysville, Ohio (Columbus station), and Birmingham, Alabama.

But a show presented in rural Arkansas was probably the most memorable for band members and crew.

Dell, Arkansas, was ninety-two miles from Memphis, where the sponsoring radio station was located, and the winning school had 200 students from kindergarten through twelfth grade. It was determined ahead of time that the electricity at the school was woefully inadequate for the band's gear, so local officials ran a power line some two miles to the gymnasium.

The A.R.S. buses and equipment truck turned off a main highway and drove for over a mile on a dirt road to get to the school. Jay Rampley set up his usual booth in the gym to sell t-shirts and other concert souvenir items, but he didn't expect to do much business.

When school was dismissed that afternoon, students entered the gymnasium by class.

The kindergarteners were placed in the front row. Concerned about volume, the band toned down their performance, but the reception to their music was ecstatic.

And Jay Rampley sold out of merchandise.

"This was the biggest event that these people had ever experienced in their lives," Jeff Jackson explained. "Even the kindergarteners were pulling out hundred-dollar bills, and they had shopping lists from parents about sizes of t-shirts to buy. Jay did the highest per-head sales of merchandise for the entire time he worked for the Atlanta Rhythm Section. He sold as much as he would have sold in an arena!"

When the load-out was completed, the equipment truck became stuck in the mud and had to be pulled out.

••••••

That spring, the Atlanta Rhythm Section somehow also found the time and the wherewithal to field its own charity softball team. Participants included musicians, roadies, studio personnel, and others.

In June, the team played a game against 96 Rock, a local radio station, benefiting the American Cancer Society, at Atlanta–Fulton County Stadium prior to a Braves game. The A.R.S. team was supported at the game by cheerleaders from the Atlanta Hawks professional basketball team. Chief Noc-A-Homa, then "mascot" of the Atlanta Braves, was also a fan. When the game was played, "Imaginary Lover" was still in the Top 10 on Billboard's singles chart, giving the event and the band an extra boost.

"I got drafted to umpire second base and got yelled at a lot," Jeff Jackson recalled. "96 Rock won."

••••••

Ronnie had begun an interesting approach to the band's encores. The band would usually finish with an extended version of "Another Man's Woman" and would exit the stage, then return. The encore segment usually opened with "Georgia Rhythm" (on which Ronnie played acoustic guitar), but one night he began noodling around with an acoustic interpretation of the Beatles' "Rocky Raccoon" as Barry and J. R. were still tuning. Stationed at the soundboard out in the audience, Jeff Jackson and Fern Quesnel were dumbstruck.

The Atlanta Rhythm Section softball team poses with Chief Noc-A-Homa (back row, left) at Atlanta–Fulton County Stadium.

"Fernie and I looked at each other," Jackson remembered, "and we were both thinking 'What in the *hell* is he doing?' He even expanded it, adding verses to it night after night. But then it got to where the band liked it, and they'd join in after the first verse. There was never a rehearsed ending for it, because you never knew how long Ronnie was going to go. It was always a train wreck at the end—either he'd stop and they'd keep going, or vice versa."

One line in "Rocky Raccoon" cites a Gideon Bible, and at one memorable show, truck driver Jerry Coody brought one of those books from his own motel room and placed it by Ronnie's acoustic guitar.

"I thought Ronnie would get the joke immediately," Coody recalled, "but when he walked out and saw the Bible, he picked it up, walked over to a microphone, and started reading out of it to the audience. Well, that didn't last long; the only people who thought it was funny were me and Ronnie."

As a (legitimate) encore song, "Georgia Rhythm" would usually go over well. When Ronnie bellowed "One more time!" and the band repeated the chorus, Jackson would turn up the house lights so the entire audience was illuminated for a gigantic sing-along.

* * * * * *

Many of the 1978 concert events at which the A.R.S. performed were humongous, to say the least.

In late June, the Atlanta Rhythm Section performed at the annual Knebworth festival/ megaconcert in London. The gigantic 1978 edition was billed as "A Midsummer Night's Dream" and also included Genesis, Tom Petty & the Heartbreakers, Jefferson Starship, Devo, and Brand X (an English jazz-rock ensemble). Roy Harper was a late addition whose name didn't appear on posters promoting the event, which was slated to run from 11 a.m. to 11 p.m. on June 24.

"There was an unbelievable amount of people," J. R. remembered. "There was a big chain-link fence down in front with people hanging off of it. We did okay, and considering the number of acts, it ran pretty well. I don't recall any major problems, but the catering wasn't great."

More than one American aggregation performed under stressful circumstances.

The Jefferson Starship performed with borrowed amplification, and without their female lead singer, Grace Slick. Several days earlier, their gear—including numerous vintage Fender amplifiers owned by guitarist Craig Chaquico—had been destroyed onstage at a rock festival in Germany, when the audience had rioted following the abrupt cancellation of that band's concert due to Slick's so-called illness.

Devo was apparently out of its element at Knebworth, since some members of the crowd didn't seem to understand their quirky "New Wave" music, as well as stage outfits that made the band look like rejects from a Roller Derby team. Soon after they began their performance, they began to be pelted with beer bottles and other trash.

Ronnie and Robert onstage at Knebworth, June 24, 1978. *Paul Bednall*

Numerous concertgoers also proffered a surprise—albeit positive—for the Atlanta Rhythm Section when the boys began their own set.

"When the band started playing, Confederate Battle Flags 'sprouted' all over the audience," Jerry Coody remembered. "I remember thinking, 'Where are you gonna find Confederate Battle Flags in London?' It had nothing to do with politics; it was because of the band—a 'we love you this much' kind of a thing, and that's *all* it was."

"I wasn't surprised," Ox Daughtry said of the appearance of Battle Flags out in the crowd. "Skynyrd had played Knebworth a couple of years before us, and the same thing happened to them."

One large Battle Flag was offered to J. R. by a member of the audience, and the A.R.S. guitarist waved it around a bit.

From his perch at the mixing-board tower out in the audience, Fern Quesnel encountered a critical audio problem right at the outset of the A.R.S. set.

"There were, of course, speakers on each side of the stage," he remembered. "I got up into the tower, and when the band started up, one entire side of the P.A. (public address system) was out of phase with the other, so they were canceling each other out. It had to be fixed while the band was playing."

Jerry Coody also recalled that Craig Chaquico of the Starship sidled up to the side of the stage during the Atlanta Rhythm Section set to watch Barry play.

"He wasn't the first person to do that," Jerry said.

"I first became aware of them through word of mouth," Chaquico said of the A.R.S. "Back then you couldn't really even pass along a cassette yet; you had to get your hands on an album and sit down and listen to it, or catch them in concert. I had only a fleeting chance to hear of them before we shared the stage but was already becoming a fan."

And Chaquico also praised the mix of artists at Knebworth, remembering, "They all had their own styles from [Genesis's] huge grand English keyboard synthesizers and Phil Collins on vocals and drums, to Tom Petty and his amazing band in all those arrangements with Mike Campbell on guitar—who I've always thought knew how to play the right parts with all the right sounds for all the right songs—and the Atlanta Rhythm Section's soulful masterpieces that have all withstood the test of time and quality. Devo was brand new and many people didn't know what to make of them but [they were] another classic band at a crossroad."

One reviewer opined that the crowd was "curiously unmoved" by the A.R.S. set and "bored" by the Brand X performance, but the efforts of Tom Petty & The Heartbreakers and the headlining Genesis were praised.

And Paul Goddard couldn't have cared less about a concert review anyway—it was a highlight of his career to have played on the same stage on which Genesis would tread later in the day.

● ● ● ● ● ●

A week after Knebworth, a huge and enthusiastic crowd filled up the Cotton Bowl in Dallas on July 1, 1978, for the first annual Texxas Jam. The attendance was estimated at 80,000, including approximately 20,000 fans who had reportedly camped outside the gigantic venue the night before.

Other performers included Aerosmith, Ted Nugent, Frank Marino and Mahogany Rush, Heart, Journey, California upstarts Van Halen (their second appearance in

Texas), Cheech and Chong (who did dope-oriented schtick between acts), Head East, Eddie Money, and Walter Egan.

"There was a massive crowd, and it was hot," Jeff Jackson remembered. "It was rare for me to be onstage, but [the event staff] had their own lights, so I was helping with changeovers with band equipment."

Concert staff members monitored the temperature down on the packed football field, recording that it consistently registered at over 120 degrees. The heat was so rough that fire hoses were turned on the attendees to cool them down. Ice was a premium commodity, and some heat victims had to be placed in tubs of ice and alcohol to revive them.

Once again, Fern Quesnel was out in the audience, running the mixing board from a temporary tower some ten feet high. But he'd had to work his way through the crowd to get to his post, and the minor elevation of the tower did not provide any real relief from the excruciating heat.

"I'd never experienced anything like that," said Quesnel.

"Buie never did like for me to drink onstage," Dean recalled, "but it was 126 degrees, and he brought me two beers and put 'em on the piano. And Paul Goddard kept on rockin' in that heat! I think the straw hat he was wearing belonged to [tour manager] Sammie Ammons."

The Atlanta Rhythm Section played during the day (Ronnie took his shirt off), but it was still so hot that night that Ted Nugent passed out onstage due to hyperventilation. He would return to the stage later to jam with Aerosmith (a first occurrence).

Humongous crowd, high temperatures: onstage at the Texxas Jam at the Cotton Bowl, July 1, 1978.

Greg Quesnel rarely watched other acts at shows where the Atlanta Rhythm Section performed, and, for that matter, rarely watched the A.R.S. onstage, since he was focused on his soundboard. One exception to such a personal guideline occurred at the Texxas Jam.

"That was my very first introduction to Journey," he recounted. "I knew nothing about them; I had never really even heard the name. But Jeff was telling me that this Steve Perry guy was one of the finest singers he'd ever heard. So I was on the side of the stage listening to them at the Texxas Jam."

······

Three days after roasting in Dallas, the boys performed in Buffalo, New York. The bill was headlined by the Rolling Stones and also included Journey and April Wine. The entire show was a daytime presentation at Rich Stadium (home of the Buffalo Bills).

That particular venue would seat 80,000 fans for rock concerts. As was the case with many shows, performing bands received a bonus if the venue sold out. Buddy had negotiated a bonus "bump" for the Atlanta Rhythm Section if the attendance for that particular show hit 72,000. The show was not sold out, but 73,000 tickets were sold.

"Buddy was really proud of himself," Jeff Jackson recalled. "He strutted a good bit after that show."

Eight days later, the boys played another show at the Dr. Pepper Festival at the Wollman skating rink in New York's Central Park. This time, they were supported by Aztec Two-Step. The performance garnered an important, positive review by veteran journalist Robert Palmer in the *New York Times*, in which each member was praised individually, including "J. R. Codd" [*sic*].

Jackson recounted that the Atlanta Rhythm Section's show in early August at the gargantuan ChicagoFest music festival in the Windy City was "a huge show for the band." The two-week event, which debuted that year, would ultimately be pronounced to have been the largest event of its type in the world.

The outdoor venue was on the city's recently renovated Navy Pier, and the size of the crowd for the A.R.S. concert was estimated at 20,000–25,000 people.

The band played in Dothan, Alabama, on August 18, at the Dothan Civic Center, with Rick Derringer and Frank Carillo opening. The back-in-ol'-familiar-territory booking seemed like the antithesis of the megaconcerts they'd been playing.

However, there would be more of the giant shows coming up very soon. The band quickly headed down the Gulf Coast of Florida to perform at Tampa Jam 1 the day after the Dothan concert. Among the other artists at the festival were Joe Cocker, Wet Willie, Alvin Lee and Ten Years After, Seals and Crofts, and the Cooper Brothers, a late addition to the then-struggling Capricorn label.

Bowmanville, Ontario, Canada (located near Toronto), hosted the Canada Jam music festival at a local racetrack on August 26. The Atlanta Rhythm Section was quite popular with Canadian music fans—*A Rock and Roll Alternative* and *Champagne Jam* would go gold in that country—and the boys would also play the Calgary Stampede more than once during the 1970s ("The fans and the venues were always great," J. R. recalled).

"A helicopter picked us up at the Holiday Inn," Dean said of the Canada Jam event, "and I loved the goose liver pate in our dressing room."

Performers in Bowmanville also included the Ozark Mountain Daredevils, the Doobie Brothers, the Village People, Dave Mason, Wha-Koo, Prism, the Commodores, Kansas, and Triumph. The attendance was estimated at 110,000. The presentation lasted some eighteen hours.

The gig also provided some members of the A.R.S. road crew with a memorable sight backstage—as they were loading up the band's gear following their performance, they noticed what appeared to be a policeman, an Indian, a construction worker, et al., on the steps by the stage. One member of the crew was thinking that "there must be some kind of weird emergency," but they were then informed they were looking at the next act, the Village

People. The techs had never heard of the New York–based disco group.

Inspired by the results of the previous year's Dog Day Rock Fest, Buddy and Arnie teamed with promoter Alex Cooley to present the one-day Champagne Jam, to be held once again at Grant Field, one day short of a year after the Dog Day Rock Fest had been staged.

"The *Champagne Jam* album was a big hit," said Arnie, "and became the obvious name for our concert tour and subsequent promotional activities. And for Atlanta, 'Champagne Jam' was now more than just an album title; we envisioned it to be an entire concept that could translate into an annual celebration with a built-in marketing theme. Buddy and I developed the event together and then met with Alex Cooley, who loved it."

The 1978 lineup included the Atlanta Rhythm Section, Santana, the Doobie Brothers, Eddie Money, Mother's Finest, and a revitalized Mose Jones, for whom Buddy had recently garnered an RCA recording contract.

Marvin Taylor was now Mose Jones's guitarist, and he recalled that the band had attracted the interest of two RCA executives that Buie was shepherding around Atlanta. The company representatives were actually in town to check out another band, but happened to be in a club with Buie where Mose Jones was playing, and had been impressed. Taylor recalled that Buddy had been stuttering excitedly when he had informed the band members that RCA wanted to sign Mose Jones.

Perhaps not surprisingly, many if not most of the songs for the new Mose Jones album (*Blackbird*) were written in the fishing trailer on Lake Eufaula, and Buddy produced the recording sessions. The album was released in 1978, and the Champagne Jam festival would be a formidable opportunity for the hometown band, since it was to be the first performance of an extended tour to support *Blackbird*.

Once again, the Atlanta Rhythm Section would be headlining but would not close the show. This time, however, the Doobie Brothers, who were originally slated to be the final act, balked at finishing the daylong event.

One potential disadvantage for show-closing performers is that an audience might be so satiated or worn out after a full day of music that its ranks might start thinning out toward the end of the event. The Doobies were aware of such a possibility and declined to be the last group to play. They would actually play third from last (without lights), followed by the Atlanta Rhythm Section (once again as the "first-dark" band), with Santana finishing the day's music.

The upgraded/updated image of the Funky Fish creature seen on the cover of the *Champagne Jam* album also appeared on official laminated passes for the event.

Bird's-eye view of the stage and part of the audience at 1978 Champagne Jam concert. *Earl Wilkins, The Technique*

The attendance was estimated at 60,000. Mose Jones cranked off the proceedings right on time at 2 p.m., and the show ran like a fine-tuned machine, with short intermissions between acts until the 11:30 p.m. closing time mandated by Georgia Tech officials. Like the Texxas Jam, the heat factor resulted in the audience being drenched with water from fire hoses.

"It got so hot out there that they had to hose the crowd down," Tinsley Ellis averred (the aspiring blues guitarist was out in the throng himself). "I think it was the worst sunburn I've ever had. And the music was even hotter!"

Mose Jones keyboard player Steve McRay had his own enthusiast recollection/review of the rest of the event:

"It was a great show, great lineup, and the crowd was very much into it—it was hot, and people were crammed in down front. I do remember the water hoses shooting out to the crowd at times. We were all hanging backstage and at different times we'd run into the different performers.

"Mother's Finest sounded great, as usual—the original band, and they were firing on all cylinders. The Doobies sounded great, too. With their old and new songs sung by Michael McDonald, they killed it. And the crowd sang along.

Mose Jones kicks off Champagne Jam '78. Band members are, left to right, Randy Lewis, Marvin Taylor, Steve McRay, Chris Seymour. Note the performance schedule and clock on the side of the stage, seen just above keyboardist McRay's head. Clad in the dark shirt and sunglasses, Arnie Geller is seen directly beneath the clock, surveying the crowd. The shirtless roadie checking on drummer Seymour is Chuck Fowler. *www.java-monkey.com*

"I wasn't a big fan of Eddie Money, but he sounded good, and as I recall he cut up and talked to the fans more than anyone else.

"The A.R.S. played next to last, and the crowd was ready for them. They were at their peak and knocked it out of the park, I thought. Just great musicians playing great Southern music!

"By the time Santana came on—and I really wanted to see them—it had been a long hot day, and I hate to say it, but we left early. So I remember hearing Carlos's soaring guitar as we were leaving Grant Field. Lots of rhythms and lots of notes; it was really sounding good, but by then my ears needed a rest."

McRay's bandmate Marvin Taylor was also fascinated by the music and the crowd.

"It was hot as Hades," the guitarist recounted, "and I remember seeing [Doobie Brothers guitarist] 'Skunk' Baxter throwing my little boy, who was three or four, up in the air backstage. When it was time to go play, I didn't have time to get scared. We were really psyched up, and it felt like we played everything at twice the normal speed.

"Eddie Money was wearing a white towel around his neck and occasionally looking way out at the back of the stadium, taking it off and swinging it around overhead, and the people way out at the back of Grant Field would scream and holler. He found a way to totally reach them."

The set by Mother's Finest was also one of the rare occasions where Fern Quesnel took the time to watch a performance.

"I was a big Mother's Finest fan," he recalled, "so I watched, and everybody responded very enthusiastically to them. And tell me what genre that band is—are they funk, are they R & B, are they rock? I still don't know to this day!"

The Atlanta Rhythm Section would take the stage at sundown, and the timing made for an effect that worked perfectly yet again. Members of the press noted the juxtaposition of the setting sun and the kickoff of the hometown boys' performance.

"Barry's work on 'Angel' was unbelievably eloquent," said one fan. "Best version of that song I've ever heard."

Mylon LeFevre sat in on supplemental vocals once again, as did JoJo Billingsley, who had been a member of the Honkettes, Lynyrd Skynyrd's trio of female backing singers. Billingsley had also provided background vocals on the *Champagne Jam* album.

Santana played the final set of the day to a crowd that had dwindled to an estimated 10,000.

Concertgoers, media, and road crew members noted that the show ran smoothly, and no major problems occurred. There had been just one arrest.

●●●●●●

Following their triumphant repeat performance at Grant Field, the A.R.S. made a quick hop to Germany, where Ronnie was involved in a brief brouhaha with authorities because he did not have his passport on his person, having packed it in his suitcase. Robert Nix also got into a minor scuffle with German airport security officials, but everyone in the band was allowed to enter the country.

Interestingly, the Atlanta Rhythm Section was the only American band to appear at a daylong outdoor concert in Pforzheim. The numerous British artists to appear at the "Open Air Festival '78" on September 9, included Status Quo, Wishbone Ash, Uriah Heep, the Climax Blues Band, David Coverdale, and No Dice. A German progressive rock band called Jane also performed. The A.R.S. was hyped on the promotional poster as "Special guest from USA."

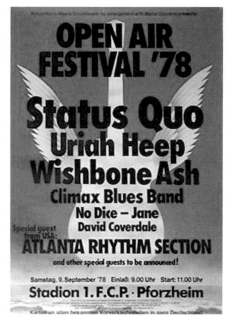

In mid-September, the boys performed in Pensacola and Port St. Lucie, Florida, with Louisiana's LeRoux ("New Orleans Ladies") opening. The A.R.S. then went out on a tour that concentrated on colleges, including performances at Grove City College in Pennsylvania on Saturday, September 23, followed by a concert at Lehigh College in the same state the next day.

The band then set its sights on Washington, DC, for what most fans would probably consider to have been the most prestigious performance in the band's history.

History would note that the Atlanta Rhythm Section was the first rock band to play on the south lawn of the White House, the official residence of the president of the United States, on September 25, 1978.

Georgia native Jimmy Carter had been the nation's chief executive for over a year and a half and had been cloistered at the presidential retreat known as Camp David starting on September 5, during intense negotiations between Israel and Egypt regarding a peace treaty. The talks would last for thirteen days. During that time, Willie Nelson performed outdoors at the White House for an event that saluted the NASCAR stock car racing organization and its drivers, but the president did not attend, remaining sequestered at Camp David.

Initial agreements between Egypt and Israel were signed on September 17 and were known as the Camp David Accords.

Eight days later, the president and his family sponsored a barbecue and concert at the White House, featuring the Atlanta Rhythm Section as entertainment. Chip Carter had followed through on his promise to the band during the 1976 presidential campaign and had made arrangements for the band to perform.

"I was working with the logistics," Gloria said of the preparations, "and the White House had to do a lot of background checks. It was going to be a picnic on the lawn, and we were going to take a lot of people who had been helpful along the way—our travel agent, our banker, others. The White House staff had their own staging requirements, so we had to work with them on that, but they pretty much let us do what we wanted to do."

Arnie arranged for some fifty important radio program directors from all over the country to attend the unique event.

"Part of their job to say 'Thank you' afterwards would be to play the next Atlanta Rhythm Section record when it came out," Geller said of the program directors.

Band support personnel who weren't out on the road began flying into Washington from Atlanta as early as September 21. They began coordination with White House staff members as well as the Secret Service as to how many vehicles were coming, what kind of power supply was needed, etc. Backup plans were formulated for an indoor show in case of rain, the A.R.S. representatives were advised that the volume would have to be dialed down considerably if that scenario transpired.

A decision had to be made as to whether the event would be a private party or open to the White House press corps. If the event was private, the band would provide power and staging per the requirements to White House staff and would use their own lights and sound equipment. If the press corps was to be admitted, A.R.S. lighting would be left in their equipment trucks, and bright white "media lights" would be used. Risers would be built to allow the press to take in the show and to give them good camera angles.

Considering the huge amount of potential publicity involved, the media were admitted, and Jeff Jackson took the night off from his lighting duties, assisting Fern Quesnel at the soundboard.

Someone informed a member of the crew that the "sniffer" dogs that were going to be escorted through the tour buses and equipment trucks were trained to find explosive material, not drugs.

The Atlanta Rhythm Section meets the President of the United States, who is wearing the tour jacket that the band presented him.

That said, ghostlike/"iffy" legends exist about who might have ingested what illegal substances, and where—not just in tour buses, but on the premises of the White House itself.

The invited guests were "friends and workers" from the 1976 presidential campaign, according to a press release. Also attending were numerous offspring of legislators, cabinet members, and White House aides. Prior to the show, the president met with the band members and was presented with a tour jacket.

"He was a pretty cool guy to talk to," said J. R. "Some of us weren't in tune with his politics, but that day, it didn't matter."

Fern and Jeff had been forewarned that President Carter was an audiophile, and that there was a chance he might stop by the soundboard to examine the equipment.

And when the president came striding out of the White House to the strains of "Hail to the Chief," he did indeed go by Fern and Jeff's station for a brief chat about the gear they were using. Video from the president's stop at the mixing board was shown the next morning as part of the overnight news segment on ABC's *Good Morning America*.

The recording of "Tara's Theme" would not be heard over the P.A. at the White House performance. The band was already onstage as President Carter approached the microphone to speak, and Buddy came running up to Fern at the mixing board, instructing Quesnel to record Carter's remarks.

The only cassette that was available had the recording of "Tara's Theme" on it, so the music on that particular item was recorded over by the president's brief speech.

President Carter's introduction of the Atlanta Rhythm Section to the crowd included a familial anecdote.

"My son Chip said I was too old for this," Carter said, "but Chip said if I let him use my backyard, I could come . . . I think I have a lot in common with the Atlanta Rhythm Section. I remember when they first started, critics and commentators said they didn't have a chance. They said the same thing about me."

When the performance began, the president listened to a few songs with his grandson sitting on his lap, then he left the proceedings to the younger attendees.

Dean's recollections of the event included the politeness of the security officers, plenty of beer, and Ronnie urinating on the White House lawn because the tour bus was locked; restrooms in the White House itself were too far away.

Following the show, Jerry Coody and Jay Rampley went into the White House with Chip Carter to shoot pool; the table had reportedly been left on the premises by Richard Nixon.

"I left the Ryder truck running right there on the White House lawn," Coody recalled. "We shot pool and drank scotch for three hours and got hammered."

When Coody and Rampley finally left the White House in the wee hours of the morning, their truck was quickly pulled over by DC police on Pennsylvania Avenue, a street that did not allow commercial traffic.

"If they'd stuck their head in the cab, we would've gone to jail," Coody remembered, "so I jumped out of the truck before the police got out of their car. I walked up to the police car and told them, 'Look, I know I'm on the wrong street; we just left the White House, and I'm trying to get to my hotel.' The police bought my story—I mean, if some longhair walked up to you and said he'd just left the White House at 3 a.m., would you believe him? Maybe the cop thought nobody was dumb enough to lie about that. He told me to take a right, and I got back in the truck and drove off."

The two crew members lurched back to their hotel (the Marriott in Crystal City, Virginia) and parked in front.

"The next day, I looked out my hotel window," said Coody, "and I'd parked in the middle of a cab stand, about eight feet from the curb. There were taxicabs on all four sides of the truck."

Following the White House performance, the A.R.S. continued on its longer-than-average tour, still playing mostly at colleges, including the University of Akron, Illinois State University, the University of Wisconsin, and the University of Minnesota.

President Carter sent out individual notes to band members, thanking them for playing the White House barbecue. Paul was not a Carter fan, and, considering the bassist's personality, his reaction to receiving the letter was not surprising.

"Paul was a very private person," Gloria detailed, "and he was irate that we had given his address to the president."

••••••

The Atlanta Rhythm Section continued to be a hot act through the fall of the year, and the band participated in another facet of show business in mid-November, when they hosted an episode of *The Midnight Special*, a concert program on NBC.

The advance script noted that the musical guests were to be Sea Level, 10cc, and the Cars. Ronnie would be making introductions of other acts, even some who were not slated to perform at the same taping session.

The show was to be taped on three soundstages in front of a live audience in Los Angeles on October 30. The boys had to submit to makeup and hair styling before they got in front of the TV cameras, and such cosmetic procedures didn't sit too well with J. R.

Permanent host Wolfman Jack was not on the premises, nor were the Cars. The Wolfman's introductions would be dropped in, and the Cars' segment had already been recorded.

Confusion ensued when 10cc, already set up on one of the soundstages, was not allowed to use their own stage monitors, so that band walked off the set. Musical segments with Crystal Gayle and Paul Davis would be added to replace the time allotted for 10cc.

The A.R.S. performed "Champagne Jam," "Imaginary Lover," "So Into You," and "I'm Not Gonna Let It Bother Me Tonight." Footage from the White House concert a little over a month earlier was also interpolated, and the boys jammed with Sea Level on "Long Tall Sally."

Ronnie wasn't comfortable in his new role as an announcer. He botched some of his introductions, which required several takes, but he eventually got the job done.

The show was broadcast on November 17, and included segments by Van Morrison and Ambrosia. While the final presentation seemed to have been put together well (and the broadcast mix of the A.R.S. performance sounded good), the overall attitude of the band was that the undertaking had been a pretentious experience.

"It was very interesting," J. R. said sarcastically. "One of the things that struck me was that you learn very quickly in television that they're concerned about 'how it looks.' They don't really care too much about 'how it sounds,' and sometimes, the sound would suffer, quite a bit."

And of course, the Atlanta Rhythm Section wasn't a "how-it-looks" band. They would never make a so-called "serious" or "artistic" music video, opting only for a few experiments with performance videos. Moreover, J. R. would later consider the debut of MTV in 1981 to have been "the turning point where people that stood flatfooted but sang great—like Roy Orbison—were no longer needed."

••••••

Late that year, Steve Hammond signed on to be his brother's personal assistant; the younger sibling described the position as being a type of valet, and the assignment would last for several years.

Perhaps not surprisingly, it seemed like the farther away from the South the band performed, the more they were expected to come across like a stereotypical "Southern Rock" outfit. An October 28 booking at the Shrine Auditorium in Los Angeles—with Sea Level opening—elicited a positive review in the *Los Angeles Times* that appropriately detailed why both bands didn't seem to be representative of the genre in which they would typically be pigeonholed.

Early November performances included a trip to Vancouver, British Columbia, Canada, followed by several dates opening for the Allman Brothers in a run through the Southeast in late November. That brief tour proffered a decent income but wasn't particularly popular with the band and crew, since it happened around Thanksgiving and no one wanted to be on the road, away from their families. Moreover, the venues were older halls that weren't in good condition. Consequently, the performances of both bands were somewhat lackluster—and they even had to perform in Charlotte on Thanksgiving Day itself.

The band made a quick trip to New Jersey in early December as part of a lineup at the Capitol Theater in Passaic. Cheap Trick and English rockers UFO performed on Friday, December 8, while the A.R.S. and Eddie Money performed the next evening. In late December, the boys played at the Boutwell Auditorium in Birmingham (where Nat King Cole had been attacked onstage by white racists in August 1956).

The opening band was the Dixie Dregs, a unique member of the Capricorn label's roster. The Dregs proffered a complex hybrid of rock and jazz-fusion music, and their rapid-fire arrangements and the impressive playing of lead guitarist Steve Morse amazed Barry.

Four days later, the A.R.S. concluded the most active year in its history by ringing in 1979 at the West Palm Beach Auditorium with the Guess Who.

"We knew this had been a good run," said Rick Maxwell. "We knew we were making some hay."

••••••

Another BGO artist in another genre had scored a huge hit in 1978. "I Love the Nightlife," by Atlanta singer Alicia Bridges, was reportedly supposed to have been marketed as an R & B single. However, a thumping kick drum added to the song as an afterthought meant that it would go all the way to number 2 on Billboard's disco music chart, having been picked up for distribution on the Polydor label.

"I worked that one hard," said Arnie Geller. "It was on the singles charts for thirty-four weeks."

••••••

One interesting "migration" in the rock music world happened in the mid-1970s, when all of the original members of Kansas (except violinist Robby Steinhardt) and their road crew relocated to Atlanta. Guitarist Richard Williams, who moved to the Peach State capital in 1978, recounted how he first heard Atlanta Rhythm Section recordings, and how the members of Kansas got to know the hometown band:

"Topeka was not the musical mecca of the world. Atlanta had a very vibrant music scene going on, and after several stints at Alex Cooley's Electric Ballroom, we fell in love with Atlanta . . . and the women.

"I was the last to make the move. Since I was still living in Kansas, I wasn't aware of [the Atlanta Rhythm Section's] Southern following, and I believe the first song that had caught my ear was 'So Into You' from *A Rock and Roll Alternative*. It had a nice laid-back groove; [it was] a well-crafted tune, but the guitar theme and solo was what I really noticed. Smooth and tasty, with the absolutely perfect 'singing' tone.

"By the time we toured together, I was much more familiar with the material but knew little about the band other than rumor. Through the grapevine, I had heard they were a hard-partying bunch, [they] had a bit of an attitude, and they were no one to **** with. While they did have their share of fun—as a lot of us did in those days—they were professional and all business on stage, and really good guys to work with. It was a good combination—two good bands, different styles, but a great contrast."

Eventually, Paul Goddard would be offered a once-in-a-lifetime opportunity during a Kansas / Atlanta Rhythm Section double bill that he would never forget.

"Paul played 'Carry On, Wayward Son' with us on one of the last nights of a tour," Williams remembered. "He was noticeably excited and nervous. I think it caught him a bit off guard, but he played it flawlessly. Paul was a Kansas fan, and he knew every note. I loved it!"

"It was like Paul had died and gone to heaven," Barry confirmed.

As for the place of the Atlanta Rhythm Section in the lineup of so-called Southern Rock bands, the Kansas guitarist noted, "There is an aspect to the Southern Rock sound that is identifiable; thus, it became a genre. The A.R.S. was more on the periphery of it—a similar alternative with a twist, and therefore a very original 'one of a kind' band within that musical style."

CHAPTER 10
1979: Turnover and Less Touring

s the 1970s wound down, it wasn't surprising to some band members and other persons within the Atlanta Rhythm Section organization that Robert Nix was beginning to get alienated about the musical direction of the band.

"Robert let it be known that he wanted to pursue other things," Butch Lowery said diplomatically. "He wanted to do other songwriting with other people, as well as producing, but there had been clashes with other band members, too."

"He wanted some production credits that Buddy didn't think he deserved," said J. R., "but I wasn't around when they were doing things like mixing, so I don't know how much credit he should have gotten. He said he didn't like the direction the music was going, but he was having some substance abuse problems of his own, and he had gotten hard to work with. There was a lot of friction between him and some of the rest of us."

"In my opinion, Robert was the one that wanted to be a rocker," said Jerry Coody. "He wanted to play rock and roll; he didn't want to play love songs or ballads. He never told me that, but I could tell from the way he played on certain songs."

It didn't help that Nix suffered from chronic episodes of gout, which were getting worse. A November 1978 performance in Houston had been canceled at the venue, even though Stillwater, the opening band, had already played. The band considered letting a member of the crew play drums, but that was quickly shot down by a unanimous vote of the healthy musicians.

"The show was canceled at 9:30 p.m.," Jeff Jackson recounted. "A crowd of about 10,000 started throwing stuff at me when I made the announcement from the stage. Lesson learned—don't give people bad news from center stage; go behind the P.A."

While Nix and Buie had collaborated on some classic songs, their similar personalities would frequently clash. Dean often found himself caught in the middle, having to listen to phone calls and complaints both from Robert and Buddy, each badmouthing about the other.

Different individuals had different recollections about whether Nix quit or was fired, but one confrontation between Nix and Buie at the BGO offices actually became physical and finalized the original drummer's exit from the Atlanta Rhythm Section.

"Buddy had loved writing with Robert, just like he loved writing with J. R.," said Gloria. "It broke Buddy's heart."

Local drummer Roy Yeager, who had done session work and had toured with pop singer Lobo, was recruited to replace Nix.

"I could tell the differences between Roy's technique versus Robert's technique, because I was so close to it," said Rick Maxwell. "Robert was more straight ahead, or more of a 'metronome' type, and Roy was a bit more flashy [and had] more attack. There was a distinct difference in their approaches to the songs."

• • • • • •

Many—if not most—fans of the Atlanta Rhythm Section probably considered 1979's *Underdog* to be not just "diverse," but perhaps a type of "experimental" album as well, since the band presented songs with different sounds, arrangements, and styles than might not have been heard in earlier times.

And such an off-the-beaten-path propensity is evident right at the outset. Instead of kicking off the proceedings with an up-tempo rocker like "Sky High" or "Large Time," or a country-influenced tune like "Jukin'," the mellow and plaintive "Do It or Die" sounds like something that was culled from a James Taylor songbook. However, the tune stands on its own, and its viability was validated when it became a Top 20 hit.

String arrangements were heard on more than one song, with the perky, melodic presentation of "Born Ready" sounding like a definitive Top 40 / radio-ready song (but it wasn't released as such). "Indigo Passion," also lush with strings, had an interesting "waltz"-like time signature.

"When we wrote 'Indigo Passion,' it sort of demanded a three-quarter tempo," J. R. explained.

"I Hate the Blues" comes off as a complaint about having to play that particular musical genre (as opposed to being a commentary regarding the "state of mind" definition of the blues).

"I'd written a song phonetically called 'Boodle Dy,'" Dean recalled. "We were just kidding around, but it later became 'I Hate the Blues.'"

Improbably, "I Hate the Blues" segues into "Let's Go Get Stoned," a cover of a classic #1 R & B hit for Ray Charles in 1966 (it had been originally recorded the previous year by the Coasters). The medley includes some blistering slide work by J. R.

Robert Nix's last cowriting effort for the band was the intricate "While Time Is Left," which featured an artsy arrangement with strings as well as sarcastic lyrics penned by Buddy.

The album did have its moments of commendable up-tempo music, however. "It's Only Music" had an insistent beat, with the tone of Barry's guitar and Paul's bass particularly noticeable in the mix. The band's redo of "Spooky" was more assertive than its predecessor and features jazzlike guitar riffs from Barry and a bouncy piano solo from Dean. Released as a single, "Spooky" also broke into the Top 20. Both "Do It or Die" and "Spooky" were also getting airplay in the up-and-coming adult contemporary radio format.

Ronnie was getting more involved with songwriting, and his plaintive "My Song"—the last song on the album, cowritten with Buddy—didn't even have drums. Working with acoustic guitars and yet another string arrangement, it was a sweet, quiet, and heartfelt rumination on a working musician's desire to occasionally play something for his own enjoyment.

The cover of *Underdog* displayed members of the band, er, walking the dog. Robert Nix was shown, along with Ronnie Hammond, in the forefront of the sextet. Nix had played on all the songs on the album except "Spooky," on which Roy Yeager played.

"We just wanted to put the group's faces on the cover, for a change," Mike McCarty said of the illustration. "We actually just took a photo of them walking down the street, and the

Outtake from the Candler mansion photo session. This photo would appear as a cover illustration on sheet music for "Spooky."

Note the position of Robert Nix (left) in relation to the other band members in this back-cover image seen on *Underdog.*

dog was added to the picture later. It was artwork by Diane Yarbrough and me, done from my photos."

The back-cover image was a painting of the band, done on black textured linen. It was based on a photo that was taken at one of Atlanta's Candler mansions (originally owned by the founding family of the Coca-Cola company). The huge residence was in a state of disrepair, so there was somewhat of a spook-house vibe to the image.

Curiously, Nix was posing in the picture by himself, leaning through a broken-out window in the left-facing (and closed) half of the double-door entrance, while the other five members were seen as a group through the open door on the right. Some observers might have speculated about some kind of hidden meaning in the layout (considering that this album was Nix's swan song with the band, and he was already gone when it was released).

However, any supposedly secret allusions (a la legendary clues on the covers of Beatles albums about Paul McCartney's rumored "death") are imaginary/nonexistent. Mike McCarty explained that the image has "no symbolism . . . just the way they were posed related to height, etc. This photo shoot happened during *Champagne Jam* time period, not during the *Underdog* time period, and at the time everything was great. We liked the photos and I used them as reference for artwork."

Many combos who were still in "bar band" status continued to appreciatively emulate the Atlanta Rhythm Section's hits, including the ones on *Underdog*.

"Some of the cover bands I played with covered 'Spooky,' 'So Into You' and 'Do It or Die,'" said the Kentucky Headhunters' Greg Martin. "A.R.S. songs were well written and had great arrangements and hooks. Not your typical 'Southern Rock'; the writing was pretty diverse and complex. That band had a definite blues element in their sound, but they could be just as comfortable playing a ballad. Their songs were very popular in Kentucky; the audience would always hit the dance floor when you kicked into one of their songs!"

• • • • • •

The Atlanta Rhythm Section would perform fewer shows in 1979. It seemed the huge events of the previous year had worn the band members and their associates out, and they had to break in a new drummer as well.

One hometown effort was a performance early in the year at Alex Cooley's new upscale venue, the Capri Ballroom, located in the Buckhead area of Atlanta, but that club didn't last long.

A CHAMPAGNE JAM

ATLANTA RHYTHM SECTION
Sat., May 12 at Eisenhower Hall Theatre, U.S.M.A.
8 p.m. Tickets at Eisenhower Hall Box Office.
Presented by The Dialectic Society
West Point, N.Y. 10996 914-938-4159

Influence of Smokey and the Bandit? Paul shows off his Pontiac Trans-Am to band members, Buddy, and Arnie. New drummer Roy Yeager is seen behind the vehicle in the center of the photo.

Over the year, the band also didn't travel long distances as often. They played in Milwaukee in early February, in Providence, Rhode Island, on April 28, and at the US Naval Academy in Annapolis, Maryland, the next day. In a tip of the headstock to another branch of the military, the boys performed at the US Military Academy at West Point on May 12.

Barry swears this Polydor publicity photo wasn't posed. He insists it was one of the rare moments where he was intentionally animated onstage.

For the most part, however, the A.R.S. seemed content to perform primarily in the Southeast. Some early March bookings with Louisiana's LeRoux in a supporting role once again were exemplary, and in May the boys shared a bill with Boston and Poco in Charlotte.

Not long after Roy Yeager began touring with the band, the Atlanta Rhythm Section's tour bus was rolling on an interstate in Missouri when a fiery traffic accident occurred right in front of their vehicle.

"We saw a tractor-trailer crash through a guardrail," said Steve Hammond, who was traveling with the band on that particular sojourn.

The tour bus quickly pulled over, and Ronnie, Steve, J. R., Roy, and road manager Sammie Ammons sprinted over to the rig.

"Diesel fuel was everywhere!" Steve recounted. "We opened the cab, and the driver, who had fallen asleep at the wheel, had a death grip on the steering wheel. Every one of us was yelling 'Get out—you're on fire!' But he didn't move; I think he was in shock. Instinctively, I grabbed him by the arm and snatched him out of the truck; he tumbled on top of us, and not a minute too soon. The truck burned to the ground while a hundred or more people stood and watched."

J. R. agreed that the driver was "possibly suffering from shock and may have had some relatively minor injuries. We put him on our bus and somebody went running across a plowed field to call the police and emergency medical help—this was in the days before cell phones. Presently, the cops arrived and shortly thereafter the medical help got there. I remember hearing one of the cops saying that they couldn't find the truck driver, who was on a couch covered up with my coat on our bus, so we showed them where he was."

It turned out that the truck driver was from Norcross, Georgia, a suburb of Atlanta.

"It was a rush like I had never felt before," Steve said of the incident, "but I had to get a new pair of shoes. Diesel fuel doesn't come out of leather!"

· · · · · ·

There were still some large, multi-act summertime shows in the offing in 1979, but the pace wasn't nearly as hectic as the previous year.

July 1 saw the boys performing for a crowd of 25,000 at Midway Stadium in St. Paul, Minnesota. Other participants included the Beach Boys, the Climax Blues Band, Ironhorse, and Jay Ferguson. Once again, the weather was so hot—even in the Gopher State—that fire hoses were used to cool down the crowd.

· · · · · ·

The third and final Grant Field concert, billed as "Champagne Jam '79," was another collaboration between Buddy Buie and Alex Cooley. Expectations for the July 7 event were high because the series had been building momentum.

The third all-day show was held in July because the Georgia Tech football team had scheduled a season-opening game for Grant Field a week earlier than usual, and new Astroturf was slated to be installed on the gridiron. The renovation was to begin a few days after the concert.

The Georgia Tech Police Department hosted representatives of the Michigan State University Police Department; that northern institution of higher learning had a similar event scheduled for later in the year, and the campus police came to Atlanta to observe the logistics involved with maintaining security at such a presentation.

Artists participating were Whiteface (whose bassist, Kyle Henderson, would later become a member of a pop/rock band called the Producers), the Dixie Dregs (the only Capricorn artists to ever perform at any of the three Grant Field festivals), the Cars, the Atlanta Rhythm Section, and Aerosmith. Once again, the Atlanta Rhythm Section lined up its coveted next-to-last performance slot.

A performance video was recorded at the A.R.S. sound check the evening prior to the show.

"The band came in the night before to shoot a video for "Spooky," said Jeff Jackson. "It was lip synched. I remember this because I had my parents come down to watch, so I knew it wouldn't be loud. We put a camera on the roof of the high-rise retirement home across the street. The opening shot is that camera with a wide angle panning on a slow zoom to the stage. They combined show footage with close-ups from the night before."

In spite of the high hopes for the third Grant Field mega-concert, the weather intervened on the day of the concert, albeit not in a manner that would be expected in the Deep South in July—the high temperature reportedly never got above seventy degrees, and the forecast was for rain all day. The precipitation never happened, but the weather was cold and dreary, and the crowd wasn't as large as had been expected. One authority would estimate the attendance at 43,000–45,000, while an Atlanta Rhythm Section spokesman cited figures of 45,000–50,000.

And while it might have seemed that the Cars, perceived as being in the "skinny tie" New Wave genre, would be out of place at a performance deep in the heart of Bubbaland, they went over well with the audience.

Roy Yeager was on drums for the Atlanta Rhythm Section set, which began at sundown again and was recorded. Once again, their performance was ecstatically received by the audience.

Ronnie's stage garb at the 1979 Champagne Jam concert was due to the unseasonably cool temperature. *Earl Wilkins, The Technique*

Aerosmith drummer Joey Kramer and vocalist Steve Tyler rock out during the final performance of the 1979—and final—megaconcert at Grant Field. *Blueprint, 1980*

Aerosmith was performing during what might politely be termed as its "pre-sobriety" times.

"Those guys were so pale, they looked like ghosts," said Dean. "Like walking death. It wasn't until later that they 'swore off' of everything."

"I can tell you that they weren't the most athletic-looking folks I've ever seen," Fern Quesnel added.

Once again, the Funky Fish—the Champagne Jam version—was seen on laminates/passes for the concert.

Gloria wasn't as upbeat about the '79 edition of the all-day event. "For me, that one didn't create the 'fire in the heart' that had happened at the first two, which had been magical to me; there had been a big adrenaline rush. But I wasn't backstage at the third one; I was in the V.I.P. area being a 'hostess,' so I didn't see all of the show."

Champagne Jam '79 wasn't financially successful, and another edition was never presented.

However, J. R. was effusive in his praise for how all three Grant Field events had been run.

"What I remember is that they were run as professionally as anything we ever worked," he said. "It was low key, and if there was a problem, it was handled efficiently. Everything was first class."

Passes for the three Grant Field megaconcerts.

The 1980 edition of the Georgia Tech yearbook would refer to the 1979 Champagne Jam event as "the South's largest drunken brawl and concert," but there had been only three arrests—two for drug sales, and one for criminal trespass—a fan had tried to gain entry by cutting on a fence with wire cutters.

Two weeks after the Champagne Jam concert, the Rhythm Section opened for the Allman Brothers at Madison Square Garden in New York City. Steve Hammond recalled seeing Geraldo Rivera hanging out backstage.

Barry doesn't have fond memories of that show, recalling that both bands sounded mediocre at best. The A.R.S. performance at Madison Square Garden was recorded, as had been the case with that year's Champagne Jam set and other shows, since the band had progressed to the point that they needed to put out a live album.

Unfortunately, the sonic quality of the music, or the caliber of the musicians' performances at the venues where recordings were done, or both weren't up to the boys' expectations. Bailey recalled that the results of all of the live recording efforts were "less than album quality," and he thought the Madison Square Garden performance was the worst example.

"The live recordings that we had done were of such poor quality that they were unusable," J. R. agreed, "not to mention the fact that some of the performances were judged by everyone to be subpar, to say the least."

"We had a lot of feet of audio tape," Jeff Jackson averred, "but they were such perfectionists—and Buddy was, too—that the recordings didn't meet their standards. It was like 'Somebody was rushing things' or 'Somebody was dragging things' or "I didn't like the way I played.' Or maybe you'd hear something that was pretty good, but then there would suddenly be something like feedback from a monitor that would ruin the performance."

Bill Wendt replaced Fern Quesnel as the F.O.H. tech for Atlanta Rhythm Section in the fall of 1979. Quesnel began working at Studio One full time as an assistant engineer under the aegis of Rodney Mills, replacing an engineer named Tad Bush. Fern had already been getting to know his way around the studio even before he got off the road, not knowing it would later become his place of employment.

"When the band would come off the road and would go into the studio, I went with them," he said, "essentially as Rodney's assistant. When Tad left, they needed a second engineer. Rodney came to me and said, 'You need to be in the studio.'"

Fern initially hesitated, but Mills insisted on the change.

"He watched me in every aspect of me learning how to become an engineer." Quesnel said of Mills. Fern would work at Studio One for the rest of the facility's existence and would describe the differences between road sound work and studio work as "night and day—completely different other than some electronic equipment being involved."

••••••

And the fall of 1979 would ultimately see the release of the Atlanta Rhythm Section's first "live" recording, titled *Are You Ready!*, a double album. The title was taken from the introduction to a typical A.R.S. concert, usually yelled over the P.A. system by a member of the road crew.

However, the album was a unique type of live presentation, in that it was, for the most part, recorded live inside Studio One, not in front of an audience of tens of thousands of fans.

Such a type of "live" recording was actually done (and is still being done) quite a lot by famous bands and singers; sonic embellishments of so-called live recordings have been utilized for decades.

For example, most of the songs presented as "live" tracks on Big Brother & the Holding Company's iconic *Cheap Thrills* album, released in 1968, were in-studio tracks with prerecorded crowd noise and applause added (one of that band's guitarists, Sam Andrew, described such fare as "artifacts cobbled together from more than one source"). However, the final track, Janis Joplin's devastating rendition of Big Mama Thornton's "Ball and Chain," was reportedly an actual live recording from the Fillmore West concert hall in San Francisco.

Some rock bands have even had (in-studio) substitute musicians performing on their so-called "live" albums.

"We were under pressure, as I recall, to have the album ready by a certain date, so the decision was made to do it in the studio," J. R. said. "This was not particularly uncommon at that time. I don't recall any serious objections by anybody."

The approach to *Are You Ready!* was to record its material with everyone playing in Studio One at one time, just like a concert. The songs were performed more "aggressively" and louder.

Roy Yeager was already onboard as the drummer and had played the '79 Champagne Jam a bit earlier. However, he wasn't pictured in the photo spread on the inside album cover (nor was Robert Nix). Yeager was cited in the album's credits—"Special thanks to Roy Yeager for his fine performance on drums," but the omission of his picture is another indication that the band was on a deadline, including the album's design and layout.

The front- and back-cover photo is an overhead shot of the concert crowd at that year's Champagne Jam, taken by Mike McCarty. The two live group shots on the inside of the album cover, which were taken onstage behind the boys during their performance, are from the Texxas Jam at the Cotton Bowl in 1978.

Other liner notes cite Buddy Buie as the producer, but Rodney Mills is noted as associate producer.

A hint about how the album was recorded was placed directly under the list of the album's list of songs (i.e., not buried in the credits) and reads as follows: "Compilation of live recordings & special live studio sessions. All post-production done at Studio One in Doraville, Georgia." Farther down the credit layout (and in much-smaller print) is a list of audio specialty companies in Atlanta, Florida, and Rhode Island that had recorded the band "on location." However, how many of those recordings—if any—actually found their way onto the album is nebulous.

The bottom line for band members was that they considered *Are You Ready!* to have been recorded inside the walls of their home studio in Doraville.

"It was mostly just a demonstration of how those songs and performances could take on another life—*a harder-edged life*—when done in a live show environment," Barry said of the album.

J. R.: "For the most part, we just played the songs as we would have played them onstage, and I think we all were satisfied with the results under the circumstances."

And the results were impressive—most of the songs on *Are You Ready!* did indeed have a harder edge, and "Another Man's Woman" took the reworked extended version heard on *Red Tape* even further—Paul's devastating, iconic bass solo on the version that appeared on *Are You Ready!* would become indispensable listening for many aspiring bass players in the ensuing decades, and the back-and-forth/trade-off segment between Barry and J. R., the latter of whom was playing slide, was much more raucous than any previous studio interplay.

The reception among fans was enthusiastic, and *Are You Ready!* was indeed a kick-ass live album—there just hadn't been an audience in attendance when it was being recorded.

Are You Ready! was released in October, and a twenty-page, slick-print, large-format (10 inch x 12½ inch) tabloid devoted exclusively to the Atlanta Rhythm Section appeared as a special insert in the October 27, 1979, issue of *Record World* magazine. The front cover of *Are You Ready!* also served as the cover for the tabloid.

In a combined interview in the leadoff "Dialogue" article, Buddy and Arnie told the story of the Atlanta Rhythm Section up to that point. The band members were profiled (including Roy Yeager; Robert Nix's recent departure being duly noted in the article), and ancillary persons involved in support roles for the band also were profiled, including Gloria Buie, Rodney Mills, Bill Lowery, Alex Cooley, and booking agent Alex Hodges, among others.

Block ads were on display from many music industry businesses that worked with the band, including their music publishers in Japan and Scandinavia, as well as the Macon firm that created and licensed Atlanta Rhythm Section tour merchandise.

Articles on the Champagne Jam concerts and the White House performance were included, as were salutations from numerous Polydor and Polygram record executives.

••••••

Just over four months after the final Champagne Jam at Grant Field, the Atlanta Rhythm Section performed on the Georgia Tech campus again, this time at the Alexander Memorial Coliseum, a.k.a. "the Dome," on November 2. The concert was a unique collaboration between Georgia Tech and nearby Georgia State University, with both colleges putting up expenses to fund the show.

The show was promoted only on the campuses of the two schools; the perception/inference was that the concert was for students only, and a student representative of Georgia State opined, "If the A.R.S. wanted to play for all of Atlanta, then they'd play at the Omni."

Of the 9,000 tickets that were available, GSU received 6,000, since that school had put up two-thirds of the funding. The initiative was seen as good public relations for both universities.

J. R. takes it out front at the November 1979 concert that was a collaboration between Georgia Tech and Georgia State University. *Blueprint 1980*

The opening act for the concert was white-soul singer Delbert McClinton. While McClinton was a capable performer, the audience's reception to him was somewhat cool, since they were in a proprietary state of mind, expecting a slam-bang performance from the hometown band.

And the boys put on a rollicking show for the raucous crowd, as Ronnie prowled the stage while wearing a large cowboy hat. The band would do two encores of two songs each. By now, "Rocky Raccoon" had become a standard introduction to the encore presentation.

Coming soon after the release of *Are You Ready!*, comparisons of the concert to the new live album were obvious, and one concert reviewer grumbled that "Doraville" and "Angel," which had appeared on the album, were not performed in the Dome. Paul's bass solo received its usual praise in print.

An op-ed piece in *The Technique*, the Georgia Tech student newspaper ("The South's Liveliest College Newspaper") stated that the collaboration between that university and Georgia State had worked well, and further joint concert ventures were also encouraged.

On November 15, Georgia governor George Busbee presented Ronnie, J. R., Roy, Steve Hammond, and Sammy Ammons with the Georgia Safety Council's highest award, the Silver Badge of Courage, for their actions in saving the life of the tractor-trailer driver while on the road earlier in the year.

••••••

And as if to validate that *Underdog* had indeed been an experimental effort when it was released early in the year, Buddy was selected as "Best Record Producer" for 1979 in a year-end edition of the *Atlanta Journal And Constitution*. The citation noted that he had garnered the same award the previous year and had won it again for work on the somewhat risky yet innovative '79 album.

••••••

That same year had also seen a "breakthrough album" recorded at Studio One by Jacksonville-based rockers 38 Special. Following the discouraging sales of their first two albums, which were recorded and produced by musician Dan Hartman in his studio in Connecticut, the band got closer to home by opting to record their make-it-or-break-it/three-strikes-and-you're-out album in Doraville.

Boosted by his recent coproduction efforts of Lynyrd Skynyrd's *Street Survivors* album, Rodney Mills had been designated as the producer for 38 Special's recordings in Doraville. Buddy had some misgivings, but not because he thought Mills wasn't up to the task—Buie just didn't want to lose Mills's engineering prowess.

38 Special's *Rockin' into the Night* would be released in January 1980, and its title track would become a smash hit.

But just before 38 had begun recording that album at Studio One, lead guitarist Jeff Carlisi had stopped by the studio on his own. His observation independently confirmed Barry Bailey's focused and meticulous efforts at working out guitar passages for songs, even if it meant returning to Studio One when there were no other Atlanta Rhythm Section members around the facility at the time.

"One day I went out to Studio One," Jeff recounted, "and there was only Barry and Rodney Mills, working on guitar parts. I watched from the control room as they threw ideas back and forth, so Rodney was actually producing Barry instead of just engineering.

"I didn't stay long, but I really got a grasp on the discipline Barry had as a player, and how he 'played for the song.' So that was an important educational event for me, and it's fair to say his playing 'mentored me by osmosis.'"

Carlisi would eventually acquire his own Les Paul Deluxe goldtop guitar. He acknowledged that he had been so impressed watching Barry and Rodney Mills that he figured he wouldn't mind getting a similar model of instrument if and when he happened across an example that conformed to his own guidelines regarding tone and playability.

"It actually wasn't a matter of 'I've gotta have one of those,'" Carlisi detailed, "but Barry's guitar *did* influence my own purchase."

Like "Reb," Jeff's Les Paul Deluxe was a 1969 model, and Jeff remembered the transaction well.

"Pawn shop in the Buckhead area of Atlanta. Three hundred bucks," he said. "I was probably about four years into 38 Special. I didn't have it when we first started out, but it was first used on *Rockin' into the Night*. It just really had the tone I was looking for."

While he appreciates the fact that he and Bailey had similar instruments, Jeff emphasizes that a player's abilities are more important than brands and models of guitars.

"Whether it was great players like Barry Bailey or Larry Carlton or anybody else, it was what the player did with his hands," he said.

Larry Steele, who had played bass very briefly for Lynyrd Skynyrd during the band's formative days, had become stage manager for 38 Special, and he visited Studio One in the late spring of 1979, while *Rockin' into the Night* was being recorded. He recalled being impressed by the facility and was appreciative of the relationship that would be forged between the Rhythm Section and 38.

"As a musician, I was in awe," he said. "The A.R.S. guys just came and went, or sometimes just hung around, being guys. By then I knew their whole history, so I hung onto every word spoken, which was mostly joking around and offering their

Fern Quesnel took this photo of Jeff Carlisi plying his trade with his Gibson Les Paul Deluxe goldtop during a recording session at Studio One. "It looks as though it's about 3 a.m. and I'm really tired of playing," Carlisi said of the archival image.

congratulations. They were always very supportive of 38, and 38 had a respect for them that was immeasurable."

Rodney Mills would work with Atlanta Rhythm Section and 38 Special recordings for many years. As for his ongoing responsibilities with the A.R.S. in light of his newfound role with 38 as a producer, he remembered, "We kind of divided it up. Buddy would go in and would work with Ronnie Hammond on vocals at night, and I would go in during the daytime with Barry or Dean or J. R., and we'd do the instrumental parts. Buddy would listen to what we'd done and tell us whether he liked it or not. Most of what we had to tweak was just a matter of the mix."

Mills still had a stressful occupation, however, and he would survive a heart attack at age thirty-seven.

"Rodney was Buddy's 'rock' in the studio," Gloria said, "but Buddy might not have let him know it. Rodney also did some coproducing later, on some of the Rhythm Section stuff. I don't think Buddy could have done everything he did without Rodney Mills. Rodney was 'the patient one.'"

CHAPTER 11
1980: Cracks in the Seams

For the Atlanta Rhythm Section, the new decade would start out in a rough manner and wouldn't improve. Robert Nix's departure had called attention to other festering problems—the stability of the band was beginning to get rocky, and Ronnie's troubles, much of which were self-inflicted, were worsening. That said, Hammond usually behaved in a professional manner in the studio and onstage.

And more success meant more stress regarding songwriting. J. R. felt like the pressure to get more material to the record company in an expeditious manner wouldn't allow some of the compositions to become fully thought out if they had to be written quickly.

"I didn't complain about it," he said, "but I knew it was there."

As for Buddy's feeling any pressure regarding songwriting, J. R. recounted, "I don't think he thought about it as much as I did, or maybe he had been thinking about it but didn't say anything. Buddy was more oriented toward the business side—'You've got to get this done,' or 'It's got to be done now.'"

Perhaps a type of façade was in place for at least some of the band members, as dissension, hurt feelings, and infighting began to expand.

••••••

38 Special's stage manager, Larry Steele, recalled a February 1980 triple bill of the Atlanta Rhythm Section, 38 Special, and the New Riders of the Purple Sage in Passaic, New Jersey, when Ronnie toasted the late Ronnie Van Zant onstage and then called out 38 Special guitarist/vocalist Donnie Van Zant, younger brother of the late Lynyrd Skynyrd singer, for a boozy sing-along on "Rocky Raccoon." The same scenario transpired the next night in New Castle, Pennsylvania.

"Funniest version of 'Rocky' I ever heard," said Steele. "For the crews, it was one of those 'we gotta start hiding the liquor' moments."

••••••

Early in the year, Paul participated in the recording of a solo album by guitarist Kerry Livgren of Kansas. *Seeds of Change* purveyed music that was more complicated than what was usually proffered by the Atlanta Rhythm Section. The album contained the type of progressive rock arrangements that Paul loved and was considered to be a "Christian rock" recording.

Other contributors to the album include three other members of Kansas, Mylon LeFevre, then-members of Jethro Tull and Ambrosia, and even Ronnie James Dio, whose inclusion was probably considered controversial by some fans of Christian rock, since Dio was singing for the English doom-rock band Black Sabbath at the time.

The Peavey Papers

VOL XXX   NO 1   JAN 1982

Paul Goddard of the "Atlanta Rhythm Section"

Paul had stated on more than one occasion that he was an atheist, but apparently he didn't have a problem with participating in Livgren's album, since he was playing the style of music he had always sought to play.

Kansas bassist Dave Hope sang on one song during the recording sessions (but did not play bass). That particular track was not used, but Hope recalled being at the studio on one occasion when Paul arrived for his own session work:

"It was raining pretty hard, and I looked out into the parking lot, and Paul was getting out of his car. He hurried to the studio with his Rickenbacker bass—no case—over his head! He was using his bass like an umbrella!"

And why did Hope think Paul admired the music of Kansas and Hope's own bass playing?

"I honestly don't know," Hope said with a chuckle. "I just always thought of us as a bunch of high school kids from Topeka; it was hard for me to think of us in the context of being 'famous artists.'"

But further collaborations between Goddard and Livgren were not to be. The album was released but didn't make much of a dent in the marketplace.

"Paul was disappointed that [*Seeds of Change*] was not more successful," said Nan Jacobs. "He had wanted to work more with Kerry."

And around the turn of the decade, Paul switched to using Peavey basses in the studio. He appreciated the innovative circuitry that the company's original bass model, the T-40, offered, but he rarely used that model onstage, since its body, made from northern ash, was heavier than most other popular basses. He would, however, appear with a T-40 on the cover of the *Peavey Papers*, a promotional tabloid, in 1982.

• • • • • •

One midsummer show in 1980 turned out to be particularly dangerous. The boys were booked at a Pennsylvania racetrack along with Illinois rock band Head East, and the audience was in place when the show was abruptly canceled due to rain.

"The so-called fans rebelled," sound tech Bill Wendt recalled. "They stormed the stage, as well as the sound and light towers, and burned up a lot of Head East's stage gear and [sound reinforcement company] Clair Brothers audio equipment. A.R.S. management sent the road crew each a $100 check for 'Hazardous Duty Pay' when we returned home. I still have the framed letter."

• • • • • •

Released in August 1980, *The Boys from Doraville* was the first bona fide studio-style album for the band with Roy Yeager on drums.

Several of the songs on the album sounded downright countrified. While the *Urban Cowboy* movie was released the same year, the transition of mainline country to a more rock-oriented sound hadn't really gotten up to full steam yet, and one wonders what the reaction of longtime A.R.S. fans might have been to such newfangled tunes.

It's easy to imagine a group such as the Bellamy Brothers performing such strum-along-sing-along songs such as "Cocaine Charlie" and "Silver Eagle." Moreover, Dean's honky-tonkish piano on more than one tune simply underlines their down-home approach.

More than one individual named Charlie or Charles would proclaim that he was the person cited in "Cocaine Charlie," but Barry noted that, like "The Great Escape" on *Champagne Jam*, the person being referenced in the song is a composite personality.

"There was no one in particular that inspired either melodic character," the guitarist said of the two songs.

Country-music stylings aside, *The Boys from Doraville* included some straight-on rockers that are noteworthy. Propelled by Yeager's tom-toms, "Next Year's Rock & Roll" picked up steam in a frenetic but listenable manner that threatened to careen out of control.

Barry's pinch harmonics are all over the album, but such "squeals" never seem to get gratuitous. Instead, those guitar licks come across as exactly what was needed in a certain passage in a certain song.

Most guitarists—professional or armchair—would probably cite "Putting My Faith in Love" as a definitive showcase for Barry, J. R., and Paul, wherein some massive chops are proffered, but the song doesn't come across like the players are showing off. Paul's skittering bass licks between some of the lines of the verses demand attention from a listener, there's some brilliant harmony/twin-lead guitar work, and a snarling slide solo from J. R. wraps up the proceedings.

While Ronnie wasn't particularly content with his performance on the album's final song, "Strictly R & R,"—it was in a lower key than what he considered to be his preferred vocal range—the tune is a dependable upbeat number that might have made a decent single.

The album also included some close-to-home guests—Steve Hammond sang background on "Next Year's Rock & Roll" and "I Ain't Much," and Rick Maxwell played pedal steel guitar on "Silver Eagle."

"They had recorded all of the parts [for "Silver Eagle"] except for the final vocal for it," Maxwell recalled. "Rodney asked me if I played pedal steel, and I said 'Yeah,' and he said 'Well, bring it in tomorrow morning; I want to try something. He put it on 'Silver Eagle,' it worked, and they kept it."

Maxwell would also play steel guitar on that song onstage with the band on more than one occasion at the Fox Theatre and would be required to join the American Federation of Musicians (AFM) just to perform that one song.

"The Fox was special," he recalled. "I also played many other venues as the song was getting good air play on country stations as well. I joined the AFM so as not to throw any kinks. And yes, it was worth it."

The cover illustration for *The Boys from Doraville* was a black-and-white photo that was hand tinted. Mike McCarty kept it simple because "they were scrambling, so there wasn't a lot of time to come up with a 'concept.'"

One of the promotional efforts for *The Boys from Doraville* was somewhat tongue in cheek. Bob Seger & the Silver Bullet Band had released an album titled *Against the Wind* in February; that album would ultimately hit the quintuple platinum mark in sales and would reside in the #1 position on

Cover artwork for Bob Seger & the Silver Bullet Band's *Against the Wind.*

Ad artwork for *The Boys from Doraville*.

Billboard's album chart for six weeks. It would also spawn four singles that charted, and would win two Grammys.

The cover illustration for *Against the Wind* had displayed a herd of wild horses splashing through shallow water, perhaps along a shoreline. The animals were reflected in a mirrorlike image in the shimmering water in the foreground of the artwork.

Six months later, a similar illustration was released in music magazines as an ad to promote *The Boys from Doraville*. While utilizing similar fonts and artistic concepts, McCarty's image presented an assemblage of old pickup trucks barreling through the shallow water.

Local promotion in Atlanta was also implemented. *Weekend*, an entertainment tabloid / "leisure guide" published by the *Atlanta Journal and Constitution*, displayed a full-page ad that showed the album cover of *The Boys from Doraville*, promoting the sale of the new release at the Turtle's Records & Tapes retail chain. The ad copy included enthusiastic endorsements from local radio stations Z93, 96 Rock, 94Q,

The boys dig into vittles during a publicity photo shoot at the Varsity drive-in. The band members reportedly ate so much that it would be a long time before any of them returned to the legendary restaurant.

and WQXI. Z93 seemed to be on target with its "back to the basics" remark about *The Boys from Doraville.*

Sales for *The Boys from Doraville* were disappointing, and the hit radio-oriented single that was released, "I Ain't Much," stiffed. It appeared that the so-called "Southern Rock" phenomenon had apparently run its course in the minds of many radio stations and consumers, so getting airplay even on AOR stations was an arduous task.

And the Atlanta Rhythm Section was still being pigeonholed in the "Southern Rock" category.

• • • • • •

August 4 saw the A.R.S. playing at the Wollman skating rink in Central Park yet again, with the Derringer band opening. The 1980 edition would be the final installment of festival performances at that venue; the stage for the Dr. Pepper Music Festival would be moved to New York's Pier 84 in 1981.

However, the 1980 swan song in Central Park was notable for the Atlanta Rhythm Section for more than one reason—a reporter from the *Atlanta Journal and Constitution* accompanied the band from Hartsfield Airport to the Big Apple show, preparing an "on the road" article about the band for the *Weekend* tabloid. Buddy was along for the trip, as well.

Moreover, George Martin, the iconic producer of Beatles albums, was on hand to listen to the band's performance. The band members were huge fans of Martin's, who remained backstage after the show to offer his compliments and converse with the boys.

"That's probably what I remember the most from all of those [Central Park] concerts," said Barry. "He was the epitome of what you might call 'perfection in production.' I was somewhat in awe before the show and after the show, but I just did what I normally did during the show. I remember Ronnie being more 'intense' [about Martin's presence] than me."

Reportedly, some preliminary conversations/overtures eventually took place—not necessarily at the Wollman skating rink—about Martin collaborating with the Atlanta Rhythm Section—and one wonders if Buddy was involved in such discussions, or how Buddy would have reacted if such an initiative had transpired, or how Buie would have been involved with Martin had such production work taken place. However, such a collaboration never happened.

• • • • • •

Following the New York show, the boys then traveled to the Midwest, where they performed at the ChicagoFest again (Michael Stanley Band opening) followed by gigs in Sioux Falls, South Dakota, and Mason City, Iowa. They returned to Illinois to perform at the state fair in Springfield (supported by the Dirt Band) before flying halfway around the globe for the band's first-ever concerts in Japan.

The three-concert sojourn to the Land of the Rising Sun was a fascinating experience for band and crew members, most of whom had never been to Japan. Promoted and coordinated through the Van Planning company, "Japan Jam 2" featured a mix of American and Japanese bands in three single-day concerts (two in Yokohama and one in Kobe, with a three-hour ride on a hyperswift "bullet train" connecting the two cities).

AUGUST JAPAN JAM 2 1980

Front cover illustration for the Japan Jam 2 souvenir booklet.

The previous year, "Japan Jam '79" had featured the Beach Boys, Heart, Firefall, TKO (a hard-rock band from Seattle) and Japan's own Southern All-Stars, a pop/rock sextet.

The headline act for 1980's Japan Jam 2 was Cheap Trick. That band was riding a huge wave of popularity due to its 1979 breakout album, which had been recorded live at Tokyo's Budokan arena (*Cheap Trick at Budokan* would eventually go triple platinum).

Other artists included Kalapana, a Hawaiian multi-ethnic soft-rock band, and Japanese bands Spectrum (a jazz/fusion octet with horns) and, once again, the Southern All-Stars.

The slickly produced souvenir concert booklet, which featured caricatures of participating band members on the front and back covers, had an introductory page in English and Japanese by Ichiruo Fukuda and had numerous photos and profiles (in Japanese) of musicians who were in the show.

Curiously, full-color artwork on the inside front cover showed the bands again, but the Atlanta Rhythm Section illustration showed Robert Nix instead of Roy Yeager. However, photos of Yeager appeared in the profile section of individual band members.

Obviously, the cultural differences in the (southern) United States and Japan amazed the band and crew.

"The whole Japanese trip was quite an experience," J. R. recalled. "The hotels, the bullet train, the venues, the food; all of those things were quite interesting, and in some ways surreal to a Southern boy who was born at the close of World War II.

"Japanese fans are like no other—somewhat restrained and maybe even intimidated at the gigs, possibly because of very strict security, which was kind of spooky. But they were almost rabid everywhere else. There seemed to be a fascination for almost all things American. And I never saw so many photographs taken, almost everywhere we went.

Artwork on the inside front cover of the Japan Jam 2 booklet shows Robert Nix with the band. The drummer at that time was Roy Yeager.

"There were even local Japanese 'country and western' bands, complete with western hats and boots, singing Hank Williams and other American country-music standards phonetically correct, *but they couldn't speak a word of English.*"

Steve Hammond confirmed the behavior of the concerts' attendees, recalling, "The stadiums had huge video screens, and the audiences just sat there politely and would applaud after each song. It was different but not by choice—they were not permitted to stand, and that policy was strictly enforced by a lot of security guards.

"English was a second language there, so we got around okay," Hammond added.

Soundman Bill Wendt snapped this photo of Ronnie, Roy, and Paul on the giant video screen during one of the 1980 concerts in Japan.

Ronnie's brother also noted the focus-on-the-music onstage approach of the Atlanta Rhythm Section and how such a presentation went over with Japanese audiences (particularly since Cheap Trick was a very active and visual band onstage).

"By that time, Ronnie was as polished as he would ever be, so he was the frontman," Steve said. "Granted, there still wasn't a lot of stage performance from the other guys, but they had a great stage presentation as a group. Each member of the Rhythm Section contributed a very unique and individual stage presentation, but to me, it was the energy they projected—sonically—combined with their very unique and different style of music. If you play that way, you didn't need a lot of stage presence for the Japanese audiences, who appreciated the music."

Paul would discover that he was considered to be a musical icon in Japan, due to a bizarre legend among some fans that had been promulgated by a popular Japanese radio station.

"He loved the Japanese tour," said Nan Jacobs. "The word on the street was that the reason his belly was so big was he had been struck by lightning in his stomach, and he was called 'Thunderbelly.'"

"The guys from Cheap Trick were super nice to us," said Jerry Coody. "Rick [Nielsen] is a little quirky, but in a funny and entertaining way, not in a bad way. And of course, they're a terrific band live."

Coody and the rest of the road crew appreciated their dealings with the Japanese stagehands, in spite of the language barrier. A Van Planning associate who spoke fluent English was assigned to the Atlanta Rhythm Section roadies as the go-to guy for stage and shipping logistics.

"The Japanese stagehands worked their butts off, but you couldn't talk to them," Jerry recalled. "The interpreter guy from Van Planning took the road crew out to dinner one night; we went to a sushi restaurant in Tokyo. It was in a high-rise building with a different restaurant on each floor. I'd never seen that before.

"And it's really true—when you go into one of those kinds of restaurants, you're supposed to take your shoes off and leave them by the door. Well, we left several pairs of big ol' cowboy boots there, and the Japanese customers were fascinated by them; they were looking and pointing at our boots and talking among themselves . . . but I couldn't understand what they were saying anyway. They were probably saying something like 'Who would wear something that big?'"

One of the Yokohama concerts was recorded for a Japanese radio show.

"Buddy, Gloria, and I went to a studio in Tokyo," Bill Wendt recalled, "kind of late at the end of one of the nights to try and remix the tape. They were only able to record sixteen tracks so we had to make a lot of quick decisions on what ended up on tape. We were not used to only sixteen tracks for live or studio recordings, but I think we made the best of it. It was a great learning experience for me, and we had a ball."

Van Planning was pleased with the attendance and the performances of the bands. The Japan Jam 2 concerts were considered to be the only successful shows of that country's 1980 outdoor concert season.

••••••

The return from Japan on August 29, gave the band a little over a week to recuperate from any jet lag before they began a three-night, sold-out booking at the Fox Theatre, which would comprise their first performances in Atlanta in over a year.

Before the Fox shows, however, the extended profile of the Atlanta Rhythm Section, including a report on the Wollman skating rink performance on August 4, appeared as the cover story in the *Atlanta Journal and Constitution*'s August 23 edition of *Weekend*.

Accompanied by nine photos, the straightforward article detailed the efforts of crew and musicians in presenting the show. Most of the band members provided honest and eloquent observations—not all of which were upbeat—about life on the road. Moreover, Paul was still grumbling about his preference for progressive-rock music, and Ronnie claimed to have stopped drinking the previous week.

The early September booking at the Fox was enthusiastically received by fans and the local press. One article noted that Ronnie's voice was somewhat ragged at times, speculating about whether the trip to Japan had affected his pipes.

●●●●●●

A definitive episode—call it a turning point—that would permanently affect the attitude and commitment of the band members happened in mid-November, when the A.R.S. was on a relatively rare tour in western states (and it helps to remember that the incident happened in the days before cell phones and text messaging).

The boys were in California and were about to head to Moscow, Idaho, to perform at the University of Idaho on Friday, November 14, as part of that college's 1980 homecoming festivities.

Ronnie chipped a tooth, and instead of seeking dental help in his current locale, he decided he wanted to go home—immediately—to Atlanta to have his own dentist fix it. A phone call to Buddy in the middle of the night resulted in Buie begging Hammond to stay, but the producer also admonished Hammond regarding the singer's financial obligation if he bailed.

Gloria: "Buddy said, 'If you do this, you will pay back every dime of what the band could have gotten, and what the promoter would have paid. I don't think you want to do that, Ronnie.'"

When Ronnie opted to leave, the other band members figured they wouldn't be able to perform without their lead singer. They decided to go home as well and were taken to the airport.

This development was unbeknownst to the road crew, who had already traveled to Moscow and performed a standard setup of the band's gear in the university's gym. At around 2:30 that afternoon, Jeff Jackson was informed by a university representative that he had a phone call from Gloria Buie, which Jackson took as an ominous sign—Gloria didn't call road crew members at show venues.

"It was actually Buddy on the phone," Jeff remembered. "He said, 'The band's at home.' I told the guy who had booked the show for the university that Ronnie had had some major dental problems that was causing him some extreme pain. We had four or five shows left, all at state universities in the Pacific Northwest, and we had to cancel all of them. The show before the canceled University of Idaho concert had been the breakeven point of that western tour."

Legal action ensued against Hammond, and eventually the plaintiffs (a consortium of colleges where shows were canceled) prevailed.

"Ronnie had lots of money deducted from his royalties for years," Gloria said succinctly.

Buddy would recall that "by 1980, the Atlanta Rhythm Section was coming apart at the seams . . . the band and I were at each other's throats."

CHAPTER 12

The Rest of the 1980s: Frustration, Departures, and Realignment

In early 1981, Jeff Jackson left the Atlanta Rhythm Section organization to take a job as the production manager of 38 Special. The initial contact had been sort of a two-way street, as Jeff was trying to get in touch with that band's stage manager, Larry Steele, and at the same time Steele was looking for Jackson for the same reason.

••••••

The A.R.S. performed at Six Flags over Georgia, Atlanta's mega-size amusement park, in early June. The gig was a two-performances-in-one-night booking that was part of that facility's salute to graduating high school seniors, not unlike the Disney World "Grad Nite" event that the boys had played three years earlier. The shows were slated for 9 p.m. and midnight, but the weather played havoc with the concert.

A crowd of about 7,000 attended the first show, which had to be stopped for thirty minutes about halfway through the set due to a cloudburst accompanied by thunder and lightning. The midnight set had about 4,500 attendees and had to be shortened by ten minutes when another thunderstorm blew in.

The band did not play any songs from their upcoming album, slated for release in late summer, and in spite of the interference of the rainstorms, park officials were satisfied with the turnout and the reception to the band's music.

••••••

The Atlanta Rhythm Section would change record labels after *The Boys from Doraville* had run its course.

"In those times, your relationship with a record company seemed to be based on one or two people there believing in you," said J. R. "But once those kind of people left a record company—as they often did—you then had to deal with someone who didn't particularly have the same opinion of you. That had happened to us with Polydor; Arnie had stepped out of the picture."

Arnie Geller: "I had resigned on good terms from Polydor in 1977, and they had been supportive when I told them I was going to look after the band. Later, I renegotiated our contract to add eight albums at half a million dollars per album, which was a good deal.

"Not long afterwards, I approached Polydor again, about a Polydor/BGO joint label for other artists on BGO Records, which was separate from the Rhythm Section deal, and they agreed. As was typical in the record industry, new executives preferred to develop their new artists, because they didn't get credit or recognition if their success came from existing artists on the label.

"At some point, the bloom was off the rose between Polydor execs and the Rhythm Section, making it time to look for a new company. Being familiar with the details of the record contract, I found that Polydor had missed picking up their option in a timely manner, so that was a way out that would open the door for exploring other labels."

The A.R.S. then signed with the Columbia label, owned by CBS. Their first album on that label would be *Quinella*, released in August 1981, which begat the final hit for the band.

"Alien" had been originally written by Buddy Buie and Mose Jones members Steve McRay and Randy Lewis about a year earlier. The song was recorded by that band in 1980, for their second album on RCA, but that follow-up album to *Blackbird* had been shelved by the record company.

However, Buddy's ears picked up on something in "Alien" that made it sound like the Atlanta Rhythm Section could also do it justice.

What's more, Mose Jones's keyboard player would actually play on the A.R.S. version, in spite of the presence of Dean Daughtry right there in the studio.

"Buddy called me at home one night and said that the A.R.S. needed one more song to record for their new album they were working on," McRay recalled. "The guys had heard our Mose Jones recording of 'Alien' that we wrote with Buddy, and really liked it, so Buddy asked me if I would mind coming to Studio One and showing it to the band.

"I said, 'Yes, of course; when do you want me to come by?'

"He said, 'Well, we're here now'—I think it was about 11 p.m.—and I said 'So do you want me to come on over?'

"I went to the studio and they all thanked me for coming out. I sat down at Dean Daughtry's Rhodes piano in the control room and started to play the song. J. R. Cobb and Barry Bailey started going over the chords with me, Paul Goddard started playing the bass parts, and Ronnie Hammond and Buddy and I started singing the song.

"Pretty soon, it was sounding like a record. Rodney [Mills] looked at Buddy and someone said, 'Let's cut it!' So I looked at Dean and started to get up and show him the keyboard part, and he said, 'No, that sounds good; go ahead and play it with them.' I asked Dean if he was sure; it wouldn't have taken but just a minute to show him what I played. That's the kind of guy Dean is.

"So we recorded 'Alien' that night, and then a few days later Ronnie called me to see if I wanted to sing with him on the background vocals, and of course, I said I'd love to sing those parts with him. Ronnie could have done it all himself, but he asked me, so that always made me feel good."

Buddy had forewarned McRay that "Alien" might not make the final list of selections for the album, but later advised that the song sounded strong to him, and that the band, Rodney Mills, and a Columbia executive who had visited the studio and heard the song all felt the same way. Nevertheless, Buie cautioned McRay not to get his hopes up; a final decision had yet to be made.

Buie continued to make update calls to McRay, first advising that three Columbia A & R (artists and repertoire) executives really liked "Alien," so the tune would probably be included on the album.

A week later, Buie called McRay with the news that Columbia had decided to release "Alien" as a single.

Shortly before the release of *Quinella*, Polydor officials heard an advance copy of the album, which was slated to be released by the Atlanta Rhythm Section on another label.

According to Arnie, Polydor took legal action to prove that the band had breached their contract, and to show that the *Quinella* album legally belonged to Polydor. With *Quinella*'s release pending, a judge ruled on a Friday afternoon that the trial would begin the following Monday morning.

During the proceedings, it was pointed out that Arnie had saved the envelope that contained Polydor's affirmation of picking up their contract option with the Atlanta Rhythm Section. However, it was not postmarked until the day after the option expired. Within three weeks, the judge decided in favor of the Buie/Geller Organization.

"If they hadn't thought the record was going to be a hit, they never would have sued," Geller said of Polydor. "I remember celebrating when we read the federal court judge's comments stating that none of the Polydor witnesses were credible. It was a major triumph."

••••••

Quinella was adventurous, but wasn't as all over the map as *Underdog* had been a couple of years earlier.

The leadoff track, "Homesick," had a definite Lynyrd Skynyrd influence and would become a concert favorite of many fans. Its hard-rocking, clap-along style included innovative drum fills by Roy Yeager.

"I guess 'Homesick' qualified as a bit more straight-ahead 'Southern Rock' than some of our other songs or recordings," said Barry. "I do remember enjoying recording it. [It was] a good J. R. Cobb and Buddy Buie rocker."

"We knew there would be the 'Skynyrd comparison' like there always was whenever we did a tune like 'Homesick,'" J. R. averred, "but we didn't really mind. We were trying to write something with a little harder edge that would be fun to play onstage, and we tried to do that pretty often, with varying degrees of success. I think we had all gotten used to the 'Southern Rock' label, and I guess by then we knew it just kind of came with the territory. I always enjoyed playing that tune, and I wish it had been even more popular."

And "Homesick" would also be respected by other musicians. About a decade after the release of *Quinella*, country-rock singer Travis Tritt later would cover the song, and a decent amount of mutual respect would develop between Atlanta Rhythm Section members and members of Tritt's band, particularly guitarist Wendell Cox.

Originally from Cumming, Georgia, Cox grew up in a musical family. He first heard the Atlanta Rhythm Section when WQXI in Atlanta played "Doraville."

"My brother David was a drummer in a band that opened for them at Lanierland Music Park in Cumming in 1976," Cox recalled. "He had a few of their albums at that point, and I was wearing out many needles listening to them religiously at the age of nine. I was at the show and blown away by how much the A.R.S. sounded like the records. Needless to say I was hooked. Barry Bailey was a huge influence on me, but actually all of them were. Their sound and the way they put it together in production was captivating."

Cox and Tritt met in Marietta before Tritt had a record deal.

"Some friends recommended that we meet," said Cox, "and his vocal style matched what I played perfectly. From then on it's been the same. When Travis and I got together and started figuring out the influences between us, I immediately brought up the A.R.S. He liked them too, and I turned him onto a couple of songs I really liked; he would do the same with artists he was into. Once he got his deal off the ground, he surprised me by saying he was going to record 'Homesick.' Once we recorded 'Homesick' we instantly became friends with the A.R.S., so I was on a cloud! Later on, we would record 'Back Up Against The Wall,' that was featured in a Steven Seagal movie called *Fire Down Below*."

The Atlanta Rhythm Section never played a co-bill with Tritt, but Cox sat in with the A.R.S. on numerous occasions.

The Charlie Daniels Band would record its own version of "Homesick" for a 1999 album called *Tailgate Party*. C.D.B. lead guitarist Bruce Brown was a fan of the original A.R.S. version, however.

"It has a lot more of the tough swagger of a Southern Rock track than many of their other tunes," said Brown, "but they sounded right at home."

On the other hand, the title track of *Quinella* as well as "Going to Shangri La" loped along in a semi-reggae style, and several others, including "Alien," were presented in the band's typical and dependable laid-back groove format.

"You're So Strong" started out in a jazzy style with impressive backing vocals, only it shifted gears to a raucous tempo somewhat like "Next Year's Rock & Roll" had done on *The Boys from Doraville*.

After several photography-based album covers, Mike McCarty returned to an artwork concept based on the horse-racing theme of the title. Racing thoroughbreds and roses adorned the front cover, while a cigar-chomping, well-dressed canine (which appears to be a greyhound) was found on the back, brandishing a winning ticket. The cover design was unique and befitted the title of the album.

Publicity for *Quinella* included a release party held at a bona fide horse farm in Alpharetta, an upscale community just north of Atlanta. Ox drove his beloved LaSalle to the event, and the classic automobile was an obvious attention-getter.

The coming-out party for the album was organized by Bill Lowery and publicist Mark Pucci, who had a previous association with Capricorn Records in Macon. Pucci now had his own public-relations firm, which had a unique affiliation with the Lowery organization in Atlanta, and was handling the publicity campaign for *Quinella*.

"Lowery Music was my first client when I opened my own business in early 1980," Pucci detailed. "As part of my deal with Bill, he gave me some office space in the Lowery building so I could also work with other clients—some Lowery-related, others not. When *Quinella* came out I was hired by the band to do PR for that album, apart from whatever I did with Lowery and my other clients."

Pucci was appreciative of the professional attitude of band members in publicizing *Quinella*.

"We got some good press on the album," he said, "and I never had any problems working with the guys in the band, contrary to some other experiences with other major bands that I worked with."

The publicist was also delighted with the album cover for *Quinella*.

"Mike was *the* graphics guy for the Atlanta Rhythm Section," said Pucci. "He had such a great sense of creativity about what he did. He was a perfect fit for the A.R.S. You could just look at his stuff and tell that it was Mike's."

One positive development in the musical marketplace was that "Alien" seemed to be one of the band's stronger singles.

"As far as Ronnie's singing goes, I think that one just really kind of 'hit his wheelhouse,' vocally," studio manager Rick Maxwell enthused. "And the guitar playing just kept climbing and climbing. The original, unedited version had at least two more minutes of Barry's guitar part. 'Quinella' was a good song, too, and there are a lot of 'pretty' songs on that album."

"Alien" would peak at #18 on a Mainstream Rock chart and at #29 on a Pop Singles chart. *Quinella*'s highest ranking on the album charts was #70.

The boys toured the West Coast with the Marshall Tucker Band in the fall of 1981 (in some respects, as an underlying/subliminal effort to make up for the chipped-tooth debacle the previous year). Another live effort was recorded—this time, in front of a bona fide audience—on October 27, at the Savoy Club in New York City. For nebulous reasons, it would be nineteen years before it was released. The lineup of the band was the same that had recorded *Are You Ready!*

• • • • • •

Early in the decade, Barry attended a National Association of Music Merchandisers (NAMM) show in Atlanta, where he got into a mutual-admiration jam session in the Gibson guitar exhibit with Cars guitarist Elliot Easton. However, the over-the-top riffing by the bassist who was also participating alienated Bailey.

Easton recalled that the bassist "just seemed to be soloing the whole time, insanely overplaying, and he was way too loud. Barry just pulled his cord out of the amp and walked off the stage. Feeling stranded, I followed him off a minute later."

"I was sort of being led around by a publicist who wanted to be there more than I did," Barry explained. "I thought a lot of the Cars; Elliot's playing was very clever and original. I sure didn't mean to leave him stranded there, though. What I don't remember is anything that inspired me to want to play in that kind of setting—a booth with a small stage—or maybe I just wasn't in the mood."

• • • • • •

The year 1982 saw Roy Yeager's departure after some three and a half years with the band.

Yeager had broken his foot in Daytona Beach prior to a show, and one of the techs was quickly called in to substitute. Roy did not return to performing with the A.R.S., and the first regular replacement on the drums was Danny Biget. Keith Hamrick later took the drummer's seat for several years.

That same year, BGO Records had another huge hit single and album on the Columbia label with "Pac-Man Fever" by Buckner and Garcia. Not long after, Arnie Geller and his family moved back to New York, where Geller became involved in the management of Cyndi Lauper's career for half a decade.

Arnie later formed Premier Exhibitions, Inc., a publicly traded company that globally toured *Titanic: The Artifact Exhibition* and *Bodies: The Exhibition*. The Buies remained close friends with the Gellers.

••••••

Another potentially ominous sign for the Rhythm Section as well as "traditional Southern Rock" bands (many of which were associated with the Capricorn label, which had filed for bankruptcy in 1979) was the advent of new and quirky music (conveniently dubbed "alternative rock") that had germinated in Athens, Georgia. Frontline purveyors of such oddball sounds included R.E.M., which had a unique, mysterious, and listenable pop sound (and a frontman who mumbled cryptic lyrics), and the B-52s, whose publicity photos made them look like 1950s models predicting futuristic clothing and hairstyles. The B-52s' initial album had been released in 1979, and R.E.M.'s first full-length effort debuted in 1983.

Such fare definitely wasn't blues 'n' boogie, and didn't bode well for veteran Deep South combos. The times, they were a-changin', y'all.

••••••

The follow-up to *Quinella* had been recorded with a working title of *Longing for a Feeling*, although some sources claim that the title was to have been *Sleep with One Eye Open*. Both proposed titles were also titles of songs on the album; i.e., one of the two tunes would have been a title track.

However, clashes developed between CBS/Columbia officials and Buddy over which songs were going to be on the album. The company reportedly turned down at least two songs that had already been submitted from Doraville, and demanded alternate material from the band. The fracas led to the abrupt cancellation of the album by record company executives.

"I didn't know what to think," said Rodney Mills. "It might have been a pushback from the record company, because there was some good material on that album. However, the band was really starting to get shaky around then; they'd get together in the studio to record basic tracks, but a lot of times it would just be one guy in the studio at a time doing his final part."

"I thought it was a good record; I don't think it was their *best* record," said Rick Maxwell, "but the whole climate of the music business was changing at the time. The 'outlaw' movement in country had started, and rap was coming out. A lot of Atlanta Rhythm Section fans were getting older, and they were starting to have babies and raise families. They were more focused on making the next house payment instead of seeing the next concert."

J. R.: "Maybe the chemistry wasn't there, or the songs weren't strong enough, or—speaking for myself—burnout could very well have been in evidence, and on and on. Who knows?"

"I'd heard that there was a difference of opinion between Buddy and CBS about whether or not the album was finished," said Barry.

Dean: "It's a pretty good album, but to me, *Quinella* is a better album."

Steve Hammond thought the unreleased album had "strong songs in the typical A.R.S. style."

●●●●●●

As for the contents of the album itself, the band seemed to be playing it safe, for the most part. A majority of the songs were dependable, medium-tempo rockers of the type that the band had always done well. There were a decent number of crunchy, chord-based riffs on the album, and the guitar breaks were appropriate. The tone of Paul's bass was particularly noticeable on "Bad Situation."

The somewhat different exceptions to such generalizing were the first track, "Sleep with One Eye Open," a snappy semi-funk number (that still interpolated guitar power chords), and "Higher," in which Ronnie's vocals lived up to the song's title—his singing was in a higher range than his usual performances, and while he handled the vocals in a decent manner, some fans who weren't used to that style may have thought that Hammond's presentation sounded a bit strained.

Then there was the final track, "Wine with Dinner," a cover of a Loudon Wainwright III tune. Wainwright had been a One-Hit Wonder in 1976, with a goofy novelty song called "Dead Skunk," but he had composed numerous other sarcastic/ witty songs, of which "Wine with Dinner" was exemplary.

The Atlanta Rhythm Section's cover version cranked off with a false start, followed by intentionally snotty singing by Ronnie regarding the perils of alcohol. Wainwright's lyrics included allusions to comic wino Foster Brooks, as well as to classic movies about alcoholism (*The Lost Weekend* and *Under the Volcano*). Obviously, the song, while humorous, was closer to home than anyone in the band would probably want to admit.

"Wine with Dinner" may have been a tongue-in-cheek song, but the A.R.S. wasn't particularly oriented toward whimsical music, and Barry wasn't a fan of his own band's version of the Wainwright ditty.

"I like Loudon Wainwright a lot, and we'd gotten to know him when he opened for us some years earlier," he explained. "I just didn't particularly like our interpretation of that song. It felt kind of flat to me."

Perhaps Columbia perceived a lack of diversity in the song selections and was alienated by the similarity of a lot of the material; i.e., one listener's "dependability" could be another listener's "monotony."

Or maybe the Atlanta Rhythm Section was still being stereotyped as a "Southern Rock" band by the record company. In its decision to shelve the album, CBS/ Columbia may have figured that "Southern Rock" was a fading/soon-to-be-extinct genre. Regardless of the reason(s), the release of the next album was off. In the ensuing years, its unpublicized nickname among the band members and business associates would be "the CBS reject album."

"It kind of put the brakes on their career," Butch Lowery opined, "and the other problem was that we couldn't get out of our contract. From what I remember, they toyed with us for months."

The band members didn't blame Buddy for the "CBS reject album" debacle. Nevertheless, one result of the disappointment was that the cracks in the commitment of band members to Buddy and to each other would grow larger, and the pace of personnel changes would pick up.

One of the more memorable songs that Buddy Buie ever cowrote was "The Day Bear Bryant Died." Being a huge Crimson Tide fan, he was obviously heartbroken when Bryant passed away on January 26, 1983. By the time the funeral was held, Buddy and Ronnie Hammond were in a cabin that Buddy had rented on Lake Lanier in Georgia.

And it would have been at one-on-ones like this that the producer and the singer began contemplating a solo direction for Hammond.

"We were taking a break," Buddy remembered, "and turned on the television as Keith Jackson's haunting voice narrated the scene of thousands lining Interstate 20/59 to honor their hero. Every overpass was packed with mourning fans and onlookers as we watched, mesmerized and misty eyed. Ronnie began softly playing a hymn-like melody on his guitar. At that point we forgot about our mission to write another rock-and-roll masterpiece and spent the rest of that day composing 'The Day Bear Bryant Died.'"

A demo was recorded but languished in storage for over two decades until the song was recorded as part of a University of Alabama CD for fans. Several Atlanta Rhythm Section songs were on the same album.

"It sounded like something Buddy would do," Arnie Geller said of the Crimson Tide–oriented project.

• • • • • •

Beset with personal problems, including increased erratic behavior, Ronnie Hammond quit the Atlanta Rhythm Section later in 1983, although he was still eyeing a possible solo effort overseen by Buddy.

The band immediately turned to its original lead vocalist, Rodney Justo, who substituted for a brief time. A singer named Andy Anderson was then hired to be the frontman.

Anderson, originally from Greenville, South Carolina, was an acquaintance of the A.R.S.'s then drummer, Keith Hamrick. He had worked with Billy Joe Royal since 1977, as a warm-up lead singer who would switch to background vocals when Royal took the stage; they had the same type of arrangement that Rodney Justo had with Roy Orbison in the mid-1960s.

"In those days, we played hotel clubs," Anderson said of his days with Royal. "The band did three dance sets; Billy Joe Royal did two shows. Billy Joe got me an audition [with the Atlanta Rhythm Section] in 1984."

Andy was a strong singer with an earthy, almost-raspy voice in a slightly higher range. He was also an exuberant performer onstage. The band sounded somewhat different when he was the singer—some fans liked the changes that Anderson brought, and some didn't. Some fans missed Ronnie, but Anderson stuck to his assignment in a professional manner.

"I thought Ronnie had an exceptional voice," Dean opined. "Nobody else really sounded like him, even the other guys who sang with us. And of course, Ronnie had also sung all the hits. But Andy did a good job; Barry and I were just trying to keep things going."

"I'm sure some of the comparisons may have rankled him," J. R. said of Anderson, "but Andy was an easy guy to work with. He learned the songs quickly and did a good job. I can't complain about anything that happened when he and I were in the band. He wasn't Ronnie, never could be Ronnie, and we didn't expect him to be Ronnie."

Anderson would come and go from the Atlanta Rhythm Section lineup more than once in the ensuing years and decades. Such redundancy usually happened when Ronnie would return on more than one occasion (from more than one stint in rehab), only to fall off the wagon again.

"Ronnie was up and down, back and forth a lot," Barry recalled. "The intervals of when he'd return and leave again varied."

Anderson also continued his association with Billy Joe Royal, appearing with the "Down in the Boondocks" singer if the scheduling didn't conflict with Atlanta Rhythm Section performances.

"It kept my chops up," Anderson said of his double duty.

Ultimately, Andy Anderson was probably considered to be unofficially "on call" as a substitute vocalist if and when Ronnie wasn't available. It was an unusual arrangement, but pragmatic under the circumstances.

"We weren't taking him for granted," Barry explained, "but he was the one we called if Ronnie wasn't up to performing. He was sort of our 'replacement by default.'"

And Anderson was actually a fan of Hammond's, noting, "I met Ronnie once; he was a big influence on me."

"He has always done an outstanding job, having been shuffled in and out of the band several times," radio veteran Lynn Sinclair said of Anderson.

* * * * * *

Turnover in road crew members also increased as the stability of the Atlanta Rhythm Section further deteriorated. Jerry Coody departed in the mid-1980s and compared the status of the band to a fictional combo satirized in a movie that was released in 1984.

"Nobody was happy about anything," Coody said. "I'd come in from off the road, and it was like *(This Is) Spinal Tap*. During that time, I didn't go to Buddy's and Gloria's offices anymore."

Coody eventually went to work at an Atlanta computer store, later got into memorabilia sales, then worked at a wholesale jewelry business.

* * * * * *

Michigan native Rick Campbell signed on as a truck driver / road crew member in 1982. The Rhythm Section was touring to support *Quinella* when Campbell joined up, and his first drive was to a concert in Toronto.

As performances became fewer (and at smaller venues) during the decade, the number of personnel on the road was reduced. Campbell subsequently diversified into more load-in chores, including stringing guitars. Sometimes three techs would go out with the band; sometimes two. Eventually, two techs and six musicians became the standard.

"We did a week at [Lake] Tahoe where it was just me and the soundman," Campbell recalled, "and we did a European tour with just me and the soundman. There was no steady road crew at the time, but there were local guys wherever we played that helped out."

* * * * * *

The band's relationship with Buddy continued to get more rocky as well, and his management association with his longtime protégés was discontinued. Another bone of contention was the fact that Buddy owned the rights to the Atlanta Rhythm Section name, meaning the boys couldn't use that moniker without his permission if they opted to record something.

"Buddy kind of washed his hands of us when people started to leave," J. R. summarized. "I wanted to keep going and get another manager, and we did, for a while. Obviously, Buddy was against that; he didn't think it was a good idea. He made it clear that we weren't going to use the name to get another record deal."

Turnover in management personnel also happened, as Sharon Lawrence took over the personal management of band members and more than one road manager would join up for a brief time then depart. Later, Paul Cochran would briefly manage the band.

Bill Wendt departed from the A.R.S. / Studio One organization shortly before Buddy relinquished management of the band, but Wendt would still sporadically do freelance work for the band when asked.

"I was called in to assist with sound engineering on various A.R.S. concerts after the band's management had changed, and Sharon Lawrence and then tour manager John Nixon—who had worked with Grinderswitch and Hank [Williams] Jr.—had taken over," Wendt remembered, "but not much was happening as far as major tours or recording deals for them. The band had already cut way back on touring, so there was no full-time pay or retainer opportunities for the road crew."

※※※※※※

Producer Chips Moman told J. R. that he might like to do some sessions in Nashville with the A.R.S., and Cobb presented the proposition to the rest of the band.

"Not everybody was crazy about it," J. R. recalled. "Paul wasn't, for sure. We went up there, but Chips had this 'country-music thing' hanging over his head, which didn't bother me, but Paul didn't like country music one bit."

Some basic tracks were recorded in Nashville for a proposed Atlanta Rhythm Section album on a proposed label called Triad, with Moman, producer / music publisher Buddy Killen, and erstwhile Capricorn head honcho Phil Walden as the trio associated with the project and the name. Rodney Justo was the proposed vocalist for this new edition of the band, but both Barry and J. R. recalled that the idea didn't get very far.

Mark Pucci was involved with publicity for Triad and recalled a 1984 kickoff at a Nashville country club, of which Killen was a member. Triad artists Jesse Colter and Tony Orlando were in attendance, as were several members of the A.R.S.

Mike McCarty recalled designing a cover for the ultimately canceled project, noting that the album title was *Hardball*.

"That was when they were butting heads with Buddy," McCarty said of the band. "J. R. sort of stepped into a leadership or spokesperson role to work with Chips. I turned the artwork over to Chips and Phil Walden, and they wrote me a check. I never saw the artwork again, and I have no idea what happened to it."

The Triad venture lasted less than a year.

Rodney Mills also observed the widening rifts between Buddy and the A.R.S.

"Buddy and Ronnie were looking at an idea that maybe Buddy could establish Ronnie as a solo artist," Mills remembered. "They were doing demos on their own, and some of it was going to be almost country. And Buddy and J. R. stopped writing songs together for a while."

Barry would recall that the notion of Buddy working with Ronnie on a solo career was "the main impetus for us going our separate ways back then."

"I do recall that Buddy did work with Ronnie for a while as a single artist and tried to get a deal for him, but never succeeded," Gloria confirmed.

According to Steve Hammond, however, his older brother didn't necessarily harbor any strong ambitions to be a solo artist, but he had written numerous songs on his own, as well as songs with Buie.

"I don't think he ever really aspired to having a solo career," Steve clarified, "but I think he aspired to write his own music, even outside of his relationship with Buddy."

• • • • • •

Frustrated by the direction the Atlanta Rhythm Section was taking, musically and otherwise, Paul Goddard left the band soon after the Triad sessions.

"The way I understood it, they were taking the sound in more of a country direction," said Nan Jacobs. "There were a lot of issues, but it was the music more than anything else. Had they grown musically—in his view—I think he would have stayed. But I can recall him saying, 'I think they're actually glad to have me out of the way.'"

Goddard would settle into his post-A.R.S. lifestyle by operating a short-range radio station in his own home (reportedly interpolating a "Mr. Microphone" toy) and briefly attempting to form his own progressive-rock band, to be named Interpol. He created numerous recordings, some of which were made under the supervision of famed producer Eddy Offord, who had worked with Yes and Emerson, Lake & Palmer, but the project never got off the ground.

Paul would later work in the computer department of a school supply wholesaler, which allowed him to work on electronic gear.

• • • • • •

And soon after the Triad initiative imploded, J. R. decided that he, too, had had enough, since he'd maintained a busy career since the mid-1960s.

"The band was coming apart for no shortage of reasons, and I was pretty burned out," he reflected. "I had a teenage son who my wife was raising virtually by herself, and I wanted to do some other things as well. There were problems with management, like there always is. I kept on writing songs and took a break from writing with Buddy, but eventually got back together with him.

"But I also worked with Chips's publishing company in Memphis and was writing and recording songs there for a while. I learned a lot about country music that I hadn't known before. Chips was a very popular producer at the time, so he'd get [unsolicited] tapes from a lot of people. I'd listen to them, forty to fifty tapes a day, from housewives or people who'd never written a song before, but we got some from professional writers, too. I would pass along something to him if I thought it was worthwhile. I got to where I could listen to a verse and a little bit of chorus, and I'd know whether it was good or not pretty quickly."

One of J. R.'s first recording projects in Memphis was the 1986 album *Class of '55*, featuring Johnny Cash, Roy Orbison, Jerry Lee Lewis, and Carl Perkins, recorded at the legendary Sun Studios.

Produced by Moman, the album's creation was also filmed by Dick Clark Productions.

"We sat in the studio and played but didn't use any of the equipment in there—all of the machines and electronics were in a truck out back," Cobb remembered. "I loved the way that album turned out."

J. R. would also record an album with award-winning actor Robert Duvall that was never released. Cobb described Duvall as "a great guy; he really got interested in country music because he'd done that movie (*Tender Mercies*). He worked awfully hard and wasn't bad at all."

Cobb later played guitar behind a country-music supergroup called the Highwaymen for five years. The singers for that band were Johnny Cash, Waylon Jennings, Kris Kristofferson, and Willie Nelson.

●●●●●●

Turnover of Atlanta Rhythm Section band members would continue, and some individuals were pretty much considered temporary employees or substitutes.

"It was kind of a hiatus, but somehow, Dean and I managed to keep the band together through the Eighties," Barry said. "Some [of the new band members] worked out better than others; some didn't last long at all."

Chamblee, Georgia, musician Steve Stone joined the band on bass just before J. R. left, but wasn't the first bassist to play in the band following Paul's departure.

Stone had been a teenager in the 1970s, and had attended both Champagne Jam concerts at Grant Field in 1978 and 1979, where he'd paid attention to the performances of Mose Jones, Mother's Finest, the Dixie Dregs, Whiteface, and the Atlanta Rhythm Section.

"I didn't stay for either ('78 closing band) Santana or ('79 closing band) Aerosmith," he detailed. "I left after the A.R.S. was done. I was really more of a fan of local bands, and as far as I was concerned, the other bands weren't quite as good."

Following high school, Steve had played with bassist Jerry "Wyzard" Seay of Mother's Finest, but that association lasted for only about a year. His initial connection to the Atlanta Rhythm Section was Dean, who Steve met through studio work. It helped that some of Steve's studio work was done at Studio One.

"J. R. and Barry were still in the band when I was working with Dean, and I told Dean—and I was pretty much joking—'Well, why don't you fire the bass player you have and let me have that job?' And a few weeks later, that guy quit. I learned the songs and borrowed Wyzard's Alembic bass.

"To me, the Atlanta Rhythm Section had always been about the songs," Stone emphasized. "Until I played with Barry, I didn't really 'get' the great guitar parts."

●●●●●●

Barry also had to function as road manager for the band for most of the 1980s.

"Barry had always been responsible in his musical job and with his talent," said Gloria, "which meant he didn't need a lot of maintenance, and he handled his new job well."

●●●●●●

After several years of estrangement, Buddy and the remaining original Atlanta Rhythm Section band members managed to reconcile.

"He loved them to a fault," Gloria said of the relationship between her husband and his longtime musical associates. "Once, when I was questioning some of the expenses, Buddy said, 'Honey, if they were business geniuses, then they wouldn't need us!'"

Gloria also likened Buddy's having to deal with the different personalities in the A.R.S. to University of Alabama football coach Nick Saban's accomplishments in dealing with the personalities of young football players.

"I'll have to give credit to Barry and Dean for holding the whole thing together," J. R. said of the remainder of the Eighties. "Then Buddy got interested in the band again, wanting to write some songs for them, and he also wanted to write with me again. But he didn't necessarily want to produce the band or manage them anymore."

• • • • • •

Gloria recalled that Studio One had never really been a moneymaker, but Buddy had eventually bought out each of his other partners' portions of the business.

"We made enough money from other acts to keep it open," she said.

"I never made a nickel on Studio One," said J. R., who had sold his part of the business to Buddy prior to leaving the A.R.S. "We didn't run it like a business, like we should have done. If you're going to run a studio you should run it like a studio, not like some place to hang out, because it won't work. You can't run a business that way."

The legendary facility was sold to Georgia State University in 1986, and went through a gradual phasing out before closing in 1989. Rick Maxwell returned to Griffin to work for a family business, later moving to Macon to work in the communications field.

"Buddy had been very open about how he was wanting to sell out," said Fern Quesnel, who had become the house engineer at Studio One. "He said he was getting out because he wanted to write songs."

Rodney Mills recounted his final trips to Studio One.

"I went out there in our Dodge Caravan with a kid who did yard work for me," the veteran soundman remembered. We got two loads of tapes out of the studio. I couldn't believe the stuff that was in there. Some of the tapes wound up at Southern Tracks, Bill Lowery's new studio down on Clairmont."

Mills later began working at other studios in Atlanta, as well as studios in other cities. Eventually, he opened his own mastering facility, Rodney Mills Masterhouse, in Duluth, and garnered an impressive roster of clients.

Fern remained on the site as an employee of Georgia State University and was considered an "instructor."

"Carter Thomas was the head of their Commercial Music and Recording department," he recounted, "and he was the one who was responsible for the purchase of the studio. I think it was Buddy who told Carter I could manage the studio. Carter really cared about his students."

Thomas left Georgia State, and the program subsequently stalled, eventually being terminated by the university. Quesnel would later work at another local studio before getting involved with computers. His business meant that he crossed paths with former A.R.S. bassist Paul Goddard, who was working on computers at a school supply wholesaler.

• • • • • •

The same year Studio One closed, Terry Spackman signed on with the Atlanta Rhythm Section as a roadie/tech. His stint would last ten years.

"I went to work for them right when 'classic rock' was coming back into vogue, including radio stations," Spackman recalled. "Barry ran the whole show on the road when I worked for them. He made sure we got paid; he'd set up hotel rooms, rental cars, and plane tickets if those were involved—made sure everything was set up right."

●●●●●●

In the late 1980s, the Buies' son Ben was in his early teenage years, but he wasn't necessarily headed toward a career in music, despite the early exposure to notable performers.

"I took many years of piano lessons and excelled at it, but then quit because it wasn't 'cool,'" Ben remembered. "I can still play, but not all that well anymore. I messed around at guitar but never got that good. More pragmatically, I always felt like I had a 'good ear' and would be great in the studio, especially as a producer. I remember Roy Orbison coming to our house when I was pretty young. Because I was so close to the A.R.S. guys, I didn't really consider them 'famous.' I didn't figure that out until later."

Hanging around Studio One when both of his parents worked there also meant that Ben's ears were sharpened to appreciate professional performances.

'I think it spoiled me, because the session musicians—including the A.R.S.—were so 'tight,'" he said. "Whenever I hear live music it is always a letdown by comparison. Truthfully, my focus was more on the electronics / computerized aspect of everything— the boards, etc. I was friendly with pretty much everyone, although I'm fairly introverted. I was kind of the 'child of the studio.' However, I do remember Ronnie Hammond being extremely kind."

Ben was also mentored in his interest in computers, which would become his career field when he reached adulthood.

"Greg Quesnel was a bad-ass engineer," he recalled, "and I learned a ton about computers from him. He convinced my mom to get me an Apple II and eventually a Mac. I probably owe my career to him. I wrote my first computer program at age eight."

●●●●●●

As the frustrating decade lurched to a close, the band (which included Barry, Dean, Ronnie, drummer Sean Burke, and bassist J. E. Garnett) managed to release *Truth in a Structured Form* on the Imagine label in 1989.

Since Studio One had changed owners and was being phased out, the album was recorded at Southern Tracks, Bill Lowery's facility on Clairmont Road. However, one track, "How Much Love Is Enough," had been recorded earlier at Studio One.

Buddy was listed as the producer of the album, while Brendan O'Brien was cited as associate producer and engineer on the Southern Tracks recordings. Rodney Mills received the same associate credits for the solitary Studio One song.

Steve Stone was listed as a member of the band but did not play on that album; instead, Brendan O'Brien played guitar along with Barry.

"[O'Brien] didn't want to go on tour with the band," Stone clarified. "That's when Barry asked me if I wanted to play guitar, and that's when I switched."

All but one of the songs on the album were written by Buddy and Ronnie, with the addition of John Fristoe as a third writer on "Awesome Love." "One Way Town" was penned by Brendan O'Brien and Chris Edmonds.

Truth in a Structured Form definitely took the band in a different direction. To many listeners, the album's production had a then-modern/slick/processed "power pop" sound, with loud, pounding drums, synthesizers, and grinding keyboards all wrapped in a slightly reverberating mix. To some listeners, it sounded like the band was trying emulate Bon Jovi and other 1980s "hair bands."

That said, there are some decent songs on the album, and Ronnie's singing sounds right at home in what almost comes off as an alternative genre for the band. Tunes such as "Neon Street" and "I'm Going Back" sounded radio ready for that particular era.

And not surprisingly, some songs such as "I'm Not the Only One" came across as stereotypical-for-the-times "power ballads." "What Happened to Us" sounded like it was inspired by John Waite's 1984 hit, "Missing You."

The front-cover art for *Truth in a Structured Form* seems to have a quasi–René Magritte vibe— set against a blue sky with wispy clouds, a full set of lips and teeth float above Barry's Les Paul Deluxe guitar, which is encased in a wire cube. Mike McCarty confirmed that the cube is in fact a cage, and is the "structured form" referenced by the title. The guitar is being played by a pair of disembodied hands. The neck of the guitar pokes out to the right, and a studious observer might ponder whether the hand on the fretboard would be able to exit the cube to play on the lower register of the instrument.

"That came about from the concept of a poster project I'd done years earlier at Bang Records, for a group called Pyramid," Mike McCarty detailed. "Buddy remembered it and told me he'd like to use the title for the next A.R.S. album, so I worked that illustration up."

Interestingly, only the initials "ARS" (no periods) instead of "Atlanta Rhythm Section" are found throughout the album, even where the list of band members is cited.

"We decided to just use 'ARS' because we thought it was just cooler that way," Dean said succinctly.

"From what I remember, the band was going to start going by just 'ARS' at that point, but it didn't seem to happen," said Steve Stone. "I think that was kind of a 'thing' at the time; kind of like how Kentucky Fried Chicken is now 'KFC.'"

"I think they were trying to switch gears and appeal to a different market," McCarty opined. "They wanted to go by 'ARS,' not 'the Atlanta Rhythm Section,' at the time."

That said, the reconciliation with Buddy, who owned the name rights to the Atlanta Rhythm Section, may have still been somewhat tenuous at the time, so the band was apparently trying to offer itself a marketing option by using initials only.

And *Truth in a Structured Form* was, at the very least, an acquired taste for most longtime Atlanta Rhythm Section fans, but some were alienated.

"That was when I lost interest for a while," an Atlanta fan said of the 1989 release. "It seemed like they had turned into something other than what we knew and loved, like when they were doing 'Champagne Jam' or 'Large Time' or 'Back Up Against The Wall.' Regionally, those songs had always been very popular."

"A lot of people said someone was trying to turn the A.R.S. into Def Leppard with that album," said Terry Spackman. "It got criticized a lot."

Mike McCarty described the contents as having "more of a hard edge that just wasn't them. It had some good songs on it, but it's not my favorite."

Opinions differed, however. *Truth in a Structured Form* did have its supporters among some longtime fans.

"I personally liked the sound of that album," radio programmer Lynn Sinclair. "It had much more of a raw, punchy sound. Other longtime fans weren't so welcoming because it was different from the smoother production they had been accustomed to. Brendan O'Brien, as coproducer, was responsible for the change."

One of the liner notes intones: "A special debt of gratitude is owed to Bill and Billie Lowery and the entire Lowery family and everyone at the Lowery Group for their belief in this music."

When Steve Stone changed over to guitar, his prowess meant that the band's approach seemed to switch from a loose "lead and rhythm" guitar concept to a "twin guitars" presentation.

"As a player, Steve was much more like Barry than I was," J. R. said. "I listened to him in the studio; he fit right in, and I'm sure he didn't have a problem learning my parts."

And Barry fine-tuned how Stone's guitar style fit into the band's performances, noting, "There really wasn't much 'playing off of each other,' in the sense of swapping stuff or improvising."

Band personnel at the end of the 1980s included, left to right, Barry and Ronnie in the front and J. E. Garnett, Dean, Steve Stone, and Sean Burke in the back.

CHAPTER 13
Journeymen: The 1990s

In late October 1990, Joe D'learo signed on as a member of the Atlanta Rhythm Section road crew, having been referred to the opportunity by Terry Spackman. He had worked with other bands and was assigned front-of-house mixer duties for A.R.S. concerts. He recalled his duties as well as assignments of the other tech(s), and what it was like working with a legendary band that wasn't selling out large venues anymore:

"In the beginning of my career with them, there were three crew guys. Me on F.O.H.; Rick Campbell, truck driver; and Terry as back-line tech. Later, a guy named Rusty Banks became the back-line tech.

"Then Rick started working in Atlanta, so we got a smaller truck that we could drive and did it two-man. Most of the time the venue had stagehands to help us load in. We would both set up the stage, then we would sound-check the stage for monitors. Then I would go out front and either Terry or Rusty would sound-check everything for me. It was a groove we had nailed down. The band never did a sound check; we never saw them until an hour before the show."

Joining as a road crew member at this point in the band's history—when Barry was handling road management duties—meant that D'learo was able to observe the behavior of the older and younger members of the band.

"Barry, Ronnie, and Dean were pretty wise," D'learo recalled. "It was a business to them. Ronnie's behavior never really affected them. He was the sweetest guy you could ever meet; a gentleman."

As for the duties of the two techs during a show, D'learo recounted, "I controlled the way the band sounded out front. The stage tech was up there making sure that everything was running smoothly, doing guitar changes and basic damage control during a live show. The stage guy would have his work cut out for him, keeping his eye on six folks at one time."

Rusty Banks, who had had earlier concert experience in lighting, joined the crew in February 1991. However, Banks's duties would be far more diverse than just illumination.

"I learned about guitars from Joe, after I had the A.R.S. gig," Banks recalled. "I remember meeting Steve Stone at Joe's apartment, and Steve kind of putting me at ease; he said it was real easy—"'E, A, D, G, B, E, except on 'Georgia Rhythm,' capo on the fifth fret, drop D tuning."

Banks was also advised of the importance of caring for Barry's amplifiers, particularly since they had been presented to the guitarist by Roy Orbison.

"I was intimidated as hell but learned out of necessity," Banks said. "After all, I knew who Barry was, and I was gonna be in charge of his equipment. I knew it was a good thing, if I could make it last. Lucky for me, Barry's setup was simple. And thank God that tone that is so revered came from him, and it wasn't up to me to dial up a bunch of effects or deal with a lot of 'extra stuff' to get his signature sound—straightforward, no bull****."

Steve, Ronnie, and J. E. onstage at Union Station in St. Louis, in 1991. *Harry Pilkerton*

Banks also befriended Ronnie fairly easily, due to common roots.

"To know Ronnie was to know a friend," he said. "Both of us being from Macon, we hit it off right away. One thing I learned pretty quick is that the time you spend together offstage can often be more valuable than the few minutes we spent together onstage. We are all doing a job, but it's the 'hanging out' time, the 'rental cars and airport bars' part that can't be understated."

The band did a European tour in 1991, including performances in Germany, Switzerland, the Netherlands, and Austria. Concerts included bookings with Meat Loaf.

"We did three weeks in September then went to Japan in October, and my wife got pregnant in between," Rick Campbell recalled with a laugh.

The Japan tour lasted from October 18 to 25, with four performances set for Tokyo, Nagoya, Osaka, and Tokyo again. The band and two crew members flew into Narita airport. As was the scenario in 1980, the Americans would not have trouble getting around, since most Japanese individuals

Japan 1991 tour poster.

associated with the promoters spoke fluent English, including a road crew that drove the band's equipment from town to town. English was also spoken by employees at tourist locations such as the Tokyo Tower, which the band visited on a day off.

"We had people to 'handle' us at the hotel," said Campbell, "and they made sure we got on the 'bullet' train to go to the next city."

While Campbell hadn't been on the band's previous tour of Japan some eleven years earlier, he quickly learned that the style and approach of presenting a concert in that nation had not changed, nor had the behavior of the audience.

"The thing about Japan that I remember is the efficiency of the crew," he said. "The first gig we got to, they took pictures of everything and what the settings were. Next city, everything was set up perfectly.

"The European audiences would want to get up and boogie. The Japanese audiences sat in their chairs and applauded politely."

Steve Stone, who had never been to that nation either, thought Japanese women were gorgeous, and, like Campbell, praised the efficiency of the local crews that set up equipment.

"Everything was set up exactly like we wanted it at every venue," he said. "I don't know if they measured things or what, but it was exactly what it was supposed to be.

"I watched people in the audience singing along with the songs like 'Doraville.' I was kind of like 'Really?' I wondered how well they could speak English . . . and how much they knew about Doraville."

The band also dined on traditional Japanese cuisine, and in conversations with their hosts, was asked more than once about the "you only live twice" lyric in "Do It or Die," since that phrase was the title of a 1967 James Bond movie (starring Sean Connery) that was set in Japan.

Both the European and Japanese tours were successful, and while the audiences weren't as large as they had been in previous Atlanta Rhythm Section sojourns to those markets, there was still a respect for the music by bands that would ultimately be dubbed as "classic rock" aggregations.

•••••••

Polydor Records would release a greatest-hits-style album titled *The Best of the Atlanta Rhythm Section* in 1991, proffering seventeen songs that had been on albums marketed by that label, from *Third Annual Pipe Dream* through *The Boys from Doraville*. As was the case for many "classic rock" bands, other "greatest hits"-style releases—manufactured and marketed by dubious businesses—would appear in subsequent years.

•••••••

Early in the 1990s, the Atlanta Rhythm Section brought in bassist Justin Senker, who remained in that position for almost two decades straight. His use of a five-string bass would add a potent new sonic dimension to the band's sound.

Senker had been raised in Atlanta, and while attending Georgia State University had met drummer Sean Burke, who would join the A.R.S. as drummer in 1987. Justin had gigged in a locally popular band called Follow For Now, and had hung out with Burke while *Truth in a Structured Form* was being recorded. He had even traveled on the road with the band.

His debut / self-described "trial by fire" with the Rhythm Section was on a flatbed trailer in Louisville, Kentucky. There had been no rehearsals; the first time he played entire songs with the entire band was in front of an audience in the Bluegrass State.

"A.R.S. took a date in late 1991, during a period of time that their [then-]current bass player had blocked out some time," Senker recalled. "I was asked to fill in. I had seen a couple shows hanging out with Sean and had heard their music almost incessantly on local radio growing up. So although I had never owned an A.R.S. album, I was pretty familiar with the music.

"About a week before the show, Sean finally got a cassette tape with the set of material to me. When Steve and I got together two days before the show to assure I knew all the parts correctly, we realized Sean's dubbing deck was dragging and I had learned several songs a half-step down!"

Justin also detailed his "coming-out show" in his hometown, at the Georgia Jam '92, held at the Lakewood Amphitheater on the southeast side of Atlanta:

"In May of 1992, I found myself in front of thousands of people at an amphitheater in south Atlanta playing with Lynyrd Skynyrd and 38 Special. It was here that I would meet Buddy Buie. Apparently, I passed his audition, too. With Buddy's seal of approval, I felt certain I would be the bass player for the A.R.S. for an indeterminable period of time into the future."

"Skynyrd was the headliner," Barry said of the show, "and because I already knew Skynyrd's tour manager, there were few limitations on rider 'dictates' regarding production, hospitality, guest or backstage passes, etc., at Lakewood. When we were onstage, we didn't get any boos or beer bottles or cans from any impatient Skynyrd fans."

For the A.R.S., the Georgia Jam show had an awkward moment right at the outset (as chronicled by a video of their performance), when Sean Burke broke his snare drum during the first song, but it was quickly replaced.

"Barry killed it," Rusty Banks said of Bailey's performance. "You can tell he's feeling it when he digs that toe in. He would move around, finding the sweet sounding spots, like a bird dog on point.

"I also remember Sean tried to throw a [drum]stick out into the crowd, but it hit the lighting truss and came right back to him. To his credit, he caught it, and kept playing. Couldn't happen again if you tried!"

••••••

Another memorable concert—for the entire band—happened a few months later. The Olympic Flag Jam, a grandiose event, was held at the Georgia Dome in Atlanta on September 17, 1992, to boost the upcoming 1996 centennial Olympic Games that were scheduled for Atlanta. The Olympic flag was officially transferred from Barcelona, Spain, the site of the previous Olympiad.

Overseen by Dick Clark and Whitney Houston, the event was attended by President George H. W. Bush and his wife.

"[That was a] cool gig at the Georgia Dome, in spite of the bomb dogs," Rusty Banks recounted. "President George H. W. Bush, Whitney Houston, Santana, Travis Tritt, Trisha Yearwood, Alabama, Garth Brooks, TLC, James Brown, and even Richard Petty were there. We met Dick Clark. Of course, there were also a ton of athletes; I had lunch with gold medalist Edwin Moses! Even got his autograph on a set of bass strings; it's what I had on me. One hell of a long day for one song, 'Champagne Jam.'

That place was packed, and it holds over 70,000. It was a filmed Dick Clark Production but was never released to the public, and that's a shame, because it was a great night."

Steve Stone: "That was the first big event held in the Georgia Dome. Since President Bush was there, I watched government snipers stationed up near the top. My most vivid memory of playing at the 'flag jam' was looking in the audience and seeing Coretta Scott King dancing along to us playing 'Champagne Jam.'"

Barry: "I remember that the 'production' staff didn't think that our speaker cabinets and heads—our whole back line, in reality—were up to TV aesthetic standards, so they tried to camouflage them as much as they could with draping. Actually, they were right; I was probably the worst offender. And it was an honor to be able to perform for another sitting president."

●●●●●●

Truck driver / road crew member Rick Campbell left the A.R.S. organization in 1993.

"I had a daughter who was born in '92," he said, "and what I was doing wasn't conducive to family life. There wasn't a lot going on with the band, anyway."

"Over the next several years, the band would work regularly throughout the concert season—generally Memorial Day through Labor Day—with the occasional weekend gig thrown in during the remainder of the year," said Justin.

●●●●●●

Buddy tried to work up some decent material for the A.R.S., and he still cowrote songs with J. R.

"In 1994, J. R. and I wrote a song called 'Rock Bottom,'" Buddy recalled. "I did a demo with the Atlanta Rhythm Section in an attempt to instigate a comeback for the band, and it was not the first time I'd done that.

"Tony Brown, president of MCA, liked the idea, but for whatever reason he never offered us a deal. I was disappointed, but I got a phone call from him about a month later. He says, 'Hey, man—sorry we couldn't make a deal on the A.R.S., but I'm cutting Wynonna Judd, and she wants to cut the song; would it be all right if I cut it?'

"I was very excited. Even though I was very disappointed that it wasn't being done by the Atlanta Rhythm Section, I was very excited that Wynonna was cutting it . . . it was a huge record for her."

●●●●●●

Macon was still a good market for the A.R.S., and the band usually played there at least once a year. August 1994 saw the boys performing at the Middle Georgia Music Festival in that musically iconic city.

One of the more dangerous performances for the Atlanta Rhythm Section in the 1990s happened on the first weekend of July 1995, when they played at a biker rally in Humboldt, Iowa. The event was known as the 11th Annual Freedom Rally. Around this time, Ronnie and his then-wife were trying to be the road managers for the band (although that assignment didn't last long).

The bands that were lined up ahead of the A.R.S. went through their respective paces onstage, on schedule. However, someone within the organization that was sponsoring the rally had given the band preceding the Atlanta Rhythm Section permission to extend its set.

"Usually, this would never happen, and if it did, it would only be by a song or two," Rusty Banks explained. "But these guys went forty-five minutes over their time!"

When the A.R.S. finally did take the stage, some of the rowdier members of the audience let the boys know in a vociferous manner that they had wanted the previous band to keep playing even longer, and Ronnie went ballistic, venting his frustration over the sound system.

The A.R.S. managed to get through their set, only to have their bus surrounded by seething bikers who demanded an apology from Hammond. Cooler heads eventually prevailed, and the bus got an abrupt Harley-Davidson escort off the property.

· · · · · ·

Atlanta Rhythm Section '96 was what the title said—in 1995, the band rerecorded thirteen of their songs (all cowritten by Buie) in Zebulon, North Carolina, for CMC International, a label that specialized in veteran bands. The collection was released the following year.

While better-grade recording gear may have been used (compared to the original recordings), Justin Senker described the collection as "a 'truck stop' record; a live-in-the-studio album that would be recorded and mixed with no frills and minimal overdubs in less than a week; intended for release in the barrel bins often seen at truck stops. The recording experience was a dash. Sean's parts and my parts were done within two days."

Barry agreed with Senker's pronouncement.

"It was, in fact, a truck stop–type recording," he said, "denigrating description or not. To take it a little further, I think it was pretty much a 'take the money and run' kind of scenario. One thing I do remember vividly, but somewhat sadly, is that Ronnie was in terrible shape."

"It seemed rushed," said Rusty Banks. "Nobody was really interested in re-recording the same songs in the same format, but it was relatively painless and was over in a hurry."

One interesting line in the (minimal) list of credits read, "Produced by Buddy Buie Productions." Rodney Mills was listed as engineer and Benny Dellinger was cited as assistant engineer.

For the first time, Mike McCarty wasn't involved in the cover design, which showed several buildings in downtown Atlanta.

To some extent, the somewhat no-frills approach made for some interesting listening—the slightly more intricate drums-and-bass interplay on "Champagne Jam" being exemplary. And while the Atlanta Rhythm Section had been through the live-in-the-studio route before, this time there wasn't any applause dubbed in.

That said, the album may indeed have seemed like a type of quickie/stop-gap measure. Sean Burke would depart soon afterward to play drums for the Outlaws. He would be replaced by Robert Jason "R. J." Vealey.

R. J. Vealey (rear center) replaced Sean Burke on drums soon after the recording of *Atlanta Rhythm Section '96*.

One of the first important gigs with R. J. Vealey onboard would take place on September 28, 1996, at Atlanta's World Congress Center, where the new drummer would find himself having to do an unexpected drum solo.

The Atlanta Rhythm Section was inducted into the Georgia Music Hall of Fame at that organization's eighteenth annual awards event. All of the members of the "classic" A.R.S. lineup were there for the ceremony—even Robert Nix and Paul Goddard. Plans were made to interpolate/integrate the past and current members into a brief set.

Singer/songwriter/actor Mac Davis was also inducted. The host for the ceremony was singer Bill Anderson. Georgia governor Zell Miller also attended and spoke.

In a delightful juxtaposition, Rodney Mills was inducted in the "Non-Performer" category the same year.

The band played "Large Time," "Voodoo" (which had yet to be released), and "Champagne Jam."

"I enjoyed playing with those guys again," J. R. said of the induction performance. "It didn't seem like Paul had lost a step at all; he played great, as usual, and Robert played well, too. It had been a long time, but it felt like old times for a little while. We all understood that it was a one-off and we probably wouldn't be doing it again, but it was fun—for me, anyway. I don't think that the new guys—who were probably not so new at that point—had any problems with us playing, and, as far as I could tell, the audience's reaction to the short performance was very favorable."

Barry agreed, recalling, "It was kind of fun having the newer members switch off with the 'old guys' during the performing of the songs."

An onstage power failure during "Champagne Jam" abruptly saw Vealey performing an unintended drum solo.

"R. J. had to vamp for what seemed like an eternity," said Barry, "but he did it very nicely."

"That was pretty surreal," Rusty Banks agreed. "Those couple of long minutes felt like hours. We were in a ballroom, so I had no idea where the power would have been located! R. J. played right through till the power came back, to roaring applause. He saved our asses that night."

For the record, other individuals who had been important or influential in the saga of the Atlanta Rhythm Section were inducted into the Georgia Music Hall of Fame in preceding and following years. This list also cites two more inductions for J. R. Cobb in addition to the A.R.S. induction:

Bill Lowery: 1979 (first-year inductee, along with Ray Charles and Lena Horne)

Joe South: 1981

Buddy Buie: 1984; Alabama Music Hall of Fame inductee, 2010

Emory Gordy Jr.: 1992

J. R. Cobb: 1993 (songwriting); Alabama Music Hall of Fame inductee: 1997

Dennis Yost & the Classics IV (includes J. R. Cobb): 1993

Mylon LeFevre: 2007

••••••

In 1996, guitarist Tinsley Ellis recorded a version of "Who You Gonna Run To" (from *Third Annual Pipe Dream*) at the Southern Tracks studio, with veteran producer Tom Dowd on the mixing board and Memphis legend Donald "Duck" Dunn of Booker T. and the M.G.'s on bass. While that track was never released, Ellis also recalled an effort by Buddy to get him to record "Mind Bender," the old singular chestnut from the 1970s by One-Hit-Wonder band Stillwater.

"Buddy Buie came to the Tom Dowd sessions at Southern Tracks," said Ellis, "and tried to get us to cut 'Mind Bender,' but I didn't want to have to drag a damn talk box around for the rest of my career."

••••••

A year later, the Atlanta Rhythm Section released *Partly Plugged* (Southern Tracks Records), and its promotion—as well as its album cover—tied in with the band's twenty-fifth anniversary. It contained ten tracks—four songs were new tunes (and three of them used electric guitars), while the rest of the album consisted of re-recordings of hits in a mostly acoustic format.

Barry described the album as jumping on the bandwagon of what had become known as the "unplugged" phenomenon, as popularized by appearances of artists playing acoustic versions of their songs in concert on the MTV cable channel.

"It was Dean's suggestion to do it," Steve Stone remembered, "because Eric Clapton and a lot of other people were doing those things. Buddy, J. R., and Ronnie had written some new songs they wanted put on there, but they weren't all acoustic songs; that's why it has the term 'partly.'"

Some music aficionados might have initially figured that the band's stereotypical laid-back-yet-focused style meant that the new acoustic versions would have been easily produced and recorded, but a smooth transition wasn't the case—the inherent differences in acoustic and electric stringed instruments meant that getting the desired musical results were not easily accomplished, but the band succeeded.

"Barry Bailey had to 'translate' all of his electric guitar parts to acoustic guitar," Rodney Mills detailed. "He couldn't rely on any sustain like you usually can with an electric, and he pulled it off brilliantly."

The quartet of new tunes, "Voodoo," "She Knows All My Tricks," "I Don't Want to Grow Old Alone" (which is an acoustic presentation), and "Child of the Video Age" were up first, followed by six classic A.R.S. songs presented in a primarily acoustic style.

"'I Don't Want to Grow Old Alone' was a demo Ronnie had done," Stone detailed. "We tried to do it in the studio, but it didn't sound as good, so that's actually the demo, with Ronnie playing guitar."

Some songs such as "Alien" and "Imaginary Lover" came off well in acoustic arrangements. Most listeners would probably have considered the unplugged version of "Angel" to have been the most ambitious undertaking, and while that song came across as a bit more intense than the other acoustic presentations, it was still a unique and listenable transmogrification.

"I played my twelve-string [guitar] on 'Angel' and 'Imaginary Lover,'" Steve remembered. "I liked the way those came out, and I felt that way about all of the acoustic songs."

And Ronnie sang the final track, a cover of "Do It or Die," in a soft and plaintive voice that served the unadorned presentation perfectly.

"I liked the opportunity to do those songs differently," Barry summarized. "I was satisfied with it, for the most part. It inspired me to buy a Taylor acoustic guitar."

"Buie thought the album might do something," said Rusty Banks, "so I remember being kind of excited about it. I was hopeful that 'Voodoo' might get some traction. Being a fan first, watching those guys work in the studio with Rodney Mills was pretty special for me, and hearing the old material played on acoustic guitars that I set up was really a gas. One thing I learned from those sessions was that Ronnie liked to cut his vocal tracks soon after he woke up because his voice felt fresher."

Referencing the twenty-fifth anniversary of the band, allusions aplenty to previous albums decorated the front cover of *Partly Plugged*. The ol' hound dog from *Dog Days* was now dressed in a tuxedo and white gloves, hoisting a glass of champagne in one hand—no surprise there—and brandishing a stogie (like the greyhound on the back cover of *Quinella*) and a piece of red tape in the other hand, as additional archival imagery hovered in the background.

"I was trying to get in a little something from each album, since they were re-recording older material," Mike McCarty said of the front illustration on *Partly Plugged*." The mushrooms and the castle from *Third Annual Pipe Dream* showed up. And the dog was portrayed as being older and more sophisticated by that point."

A special invitation-only event was held at the Hard Rock Café in downtown Atlanta to promote the release of *Partly Plugged* as well as the twenty-fifth anniversary of the Atlanta Rhythm Section. The occasion was one of the shows where Travis Tritt's lead guitarist, Wendell Cox, sat in, having been personally invited by Buddy; Cox noted that he was "deeply honored" by the opportunity.

Justin Senker recounted the live events to promote the album:

: A R S   C H A M P A G N E   J A M M I N ·   F O R   2 5   Y E A R S . . .

BILL LOWERY. BUDDY BUIE &
THE ATLANTA RHYTHM SECTION
INVITE YOU AND A GUEST TO CELEBRATE THE
25TH ANNIVERSARY OF
THE ATLANTA RHYTHM SECTION
AND
THE RELEASE OF THEIR NEW ALBUM "PARTLY PLUGGED"

TUESDAY. JANUARY 14. 1997
7-10 P.M.
HARD ROCK CAFE
DOWNTOWN ATLANTA

FEATURING A LIVE PERFORMANCE BY
THE ATLANTA RHYTHM SECTION AND AN ALL-STAR JAM

R.S.V.P. BY JANUARY 10 TO
THE HEADLINE GROUP. 404-231-9780

INVITATION IS NON-TRANSFERRABLE

"*Partly Plugged* was received warmly—although certainly not enthusiastically—by the music-buying public. After a couple of distribution hiccups, we managed to do a bit of a support tour for the CD. In scope, the tour resembled little more than the ongoing live schedule we had maintained the years before, although during these shows, the band would perform several songs acoustically, and the set featured our country-flavored new songs. *Partly Plugged*'s hometown release party and concert remain a career highlight—my only opportunity thus far to play Chastain Park."

And many other listeners considered *Partly Plugged* to be an overlooked gem in the unplugged genre.

"That album was amazing," said a longtime fan. "I can't believe it wasn't a huge success. The acoustic arrangements on it sounded hip."

While other "laid back" concerts to promote *Partly Plugged* were presented at venues such as Central City Park in Macon, Justin recalled that the band eventually dropped the acoustic portion of their performances. Nevertheless, the boys had been sufficiently motivated by the *Partly Plugged* sessions to look forward to making new recordings.

"Despite the lackluster success of *Partly Plugged*, it was as though a slumbering giant had awoken," said Justin, "and everybody involved was ready to begin another record. R. J.'s incredible skills behind the drum set had been fueling some amazing live performances. Dropping the 'acoustified' hits from the set and performing them electric once again boosted our show's energy and the band's confidence. [We were] a real band, not just another legacy act with several new members trying to hang on; a rock band with something to prove, and we were ready to prove it."

Buoyed by the positive feeling from creating *Partly Plugged*, the band geared up to record what was slated to be its first album of all-new material in a decade.

• • • • • •

Rusty Banks relinquished the roadie life for a day job in Macon in early 1998, but his last supporting role with the Atlanta Rhythm Section had a bit of "overlap" with his new employment opportunity.

"My last official gig with the band was a show I promoted with Stillwater as the opener, on February 21, 1998," he recounted. "Mercer University had offered me the technical director position at the Grand Opera House, a place I had worked when I was off the road. I couldn't think of a better transition than to have them perform there for my last gig."

The Grand Opera House had been built in 1884, and had been named to the National Register of Historic Places in 1970. In 1995, Mercer University had reached an agreement with government officials to manage the facility.

In an interview prior to the concert, Ronnie Hammond, who considered Macon to be his hometown, enthusiastically noted that he was looking forward to the show at the unique venue, recalling his last visit to the Grand Opera House at the age of four.

The Grand Opera House performance turned out to be a positive experience for the band as well as the audience, as Terry Spackman enthusiastically recalled:

"Ronnie was in good form; he had a lot of family and friends both onstage and offstage. His son Jesse was there. I asked Ronnie about his look that night—he was wearing black jeans, a white windbreaker, and a cowboy hat. He giggled and said it was his 'Garth Brooks' look. And you might've thought ol' Garth was there when the lights came up and Rusty introduced the band. The house went nuts! I was

Ronnie sports what he termed as a "Garth Brooks" aesthetic onstage at Macon's Grand Opera House, February 21, 1998.

stationed on stage right on Dean and Barry's side, so once again, I got a clinic on great guitar playing. [Stillwater guitarist] Mike Causey came up and they played 'Champagne [Jam]' together. I remember it was a good show, and it sounded great to be playing in a venue that lent itself to loud, meticulous, intricate playing."

Mike Causey also had an enthusiastic recollection of the show, remembering, "It had been a long time since our two bands had played together. We had been broken up for about fifteen years when we did that night, so that made it even more special. Of course, [jamming with the Atlanta Rhythm Section] was a thrill for me because of how much I thought of them. I not only thought that they were an incredible band, but I was a fan of their music as well, and to have a chance to play with them was an exciting moment for me."

• • • • • •

Curiously, the Atlanta Rhythm Section would play in Macon again just six weeks later, at a corporate-sponsored benefit for the football team of a new local high school. The poster to promote the April 4 event even used a photo from the February 21 concert. Mike Causey sat in again, but this time around, such participation by Causey as well as Big Mike and the Booty Pappa's, a local blues band, had been hyped prior to the show as a "jam session."

●●●●●●

Rodney Mills was also looking forward to working with the Rhythm Section on new material, and he recalled, "I had established myself as a producer with 38 Special, but Buddy wanted me to engineer this new album. Well, I wanted to help produce, too. The whole band went down to Eufaula to rehearse."

And *Eufaula* turned out to be the name of the album. It would be released on the Platinum Entertainment label; Buie and Mills would be listed as coproducers.

Buddy did not have a studio at the time, so the album was recorded primarily at Southern Tracks, with overdubs done at the same studio as well as Mills's Masterhouse facility, the Battery in Nashville, and "Buddy Buie's Lake House" in Eufaula.

"I really enjoyed doing that record," Barry recalled. "I liked most of the songs and was comfortable in the studio where we cut basic tracks, and in Rodney's home studio where we did overdubs. I especially appreciated the quality of cohesiveness that showed on all of the tracks, and I know that R. J. Vealey's drumming had a whole lot to do with that. Justin's bass playing didn't hurt, either."

J. R. Cobb had resumed writing songs with Buddy and with members of the band, and his name would be found in the songwriting credits for seven of the album's eleven tracks.

"J. R. was a big factor as to why I liked that album," said Steve Stone. "I *really* liked 'Unique.'"

"*Eufaula* really felt like a group effort," Justin recalled. "Steve and Dean augmented the songwriting efforts of Ronnie, J. R., and Buddy, who had really been churning them out. This time around the song ideas came to the band a lot 'looser' and not 'demoed' to death like the *Partly Plugged* tunes. R. J. and I were given more levity to create our own parts and supply the feel to the tracks.

"I had become a five-string bass player for the most part, albeit a rookie one. It was just beginning to feel comfortable and natural under my fingers. After finishing my bass overdub on 'Dreamy Alabama,' Buddy—who wasn't feeling great that day and had been lying on a sofa in the back of the control room during the recording— told me that I had just achieved my 'pinnacle performance' and that I probably didn't have a better bass part in me. Buddy's compliment during the recording fueled my confidence in the instrument and my ability to play."

⭘Lucent Technologies

Presents In Concert

ATLANTA RHYTHM SECTION

And a Jam Session with
Mike Causey of the Stillwater Band along with
Big Mike and the Booty Pappa's

APRIL 4, 1998 AT 8:00 P.M.
MACON CITY AUDITORIUM
$16.50

To purchase tickets call
TICKETMASTER — 752-1600
CENTREPLEX — 751-9232

As it turned out, the new album's contents would include new versions of two songs the band had previously recorded. *Eufaula* cranked off in an improbable manner with rearranged versions of "I'm Not the Only One" (from *Truth in a Structured Form*) and "Who You Gonna Run To" (from *Third Annual Pipe Dream*).

"From what I remember, Ronnie had started singing the lyrics of the chorus of 'I'm Not the Only One' on the vamp of "Imaginary Lover" when we would play live," Stone recalled. "Buddy heard how we were playing it and really liked it, so he decided we should redo it that way for *Eufaula*."

Listening to the separated-by-a-decade versions of "I'm Not the Only One" back to back highlights the 1980s-style mix of the first rendition, whereas the interpretation on *Eufaula* comes across in a strong and assertive manner.

As for "Who You Gonna Run To," Rodney Mills noted, "It's one of my favorite A.R.S. songs, and it got put in the mix because I had tried to pitch this to Gregg Allman when I was working with him, but no luck. So when we were looking for another song for the A.R.S., I brought it up to do a re-cut and we did it. I've always loved its infectious bluesy groove."

Barry was pleased with the do-over of "Who You Gonna Run To" as well.

"After completing the second version, I thought 'Well, this is even better than the first,'" the guitarist said. "Then I went back and listened to the original and found that it still held up, nicely. R. J.'s drumming on 'version 2' was pretty exceptional, though."

The new album also featured strong straight-ahead numbers such as "Fine Day" and the pretty-much-country "Nothing's as Bad as It Seems."

There was also the light, jazzy "You Ain't Seen Nothing Yet" with some bluesy piano and guitar licks.

More than one ballad-style track featured gorgeous string arrangements (done on keyboards) by award-winning Nashville musician Steve Nathan, abetted by heartfelt singing from Ronnie.

"Buddy and I went to Nashville and hired Steve Nathan to do the arrangements and performance on sampled strings from his library of orchestral stuff," said Mills. "[It was] amazing stuff, as always, from Steve, and a very emotional sonic enhancement to 'Dreamy Alabama.' I cried every time I heard it. There are some great songs on that album."

Steve Hammond cited the electronic effects on Ronnie's vocals as one reason "Dreamy Alabama" is a good song.

"It didn't really even sound like Ronnie's natural voice," he said, "but his singing fit the song really well along with the keyboard-synthesized sounds."

"I really liked 'Dreamy Alabama' and what I played on it," Barry said. "Same for 'Unique,' which Buddy was thinking of as a single . . . I think there were still 'single' releases, back then. 'You Ain't Seen Nothing Yet' was most challenging. It took me a large part of a night to figure out the chord progressions and to write a chord chart, but I like the way it came out, and I still like listening to it."

"When" was another lush example that interpolates Steve Nathan's sonic expertise, and the guitar solos featured both Barry and Steve.

"In the interest of giving credit where credit's due, Steve plays the first eight bars on the first solo of 'When,' and I finish the solo with the last eight," Barry detailed. "Same thing on the outro—Steve, the first eight bars, and I play the second eight. Then we play the melody—sort of—on the last eight bars of the chorus of the song, in harmony."

The album concludes with "What's Up Wid Dat?," a snappy three-minute instrumental. Its crisp and upbeat style indicates that it was a lot of fun to create.

Eufaula was also a favorite of Jerry Buie, who echoed Mills's "great songs" opinion, declaring that Ronnie Hammond's singing was "the best he'd ever done. I really liked 'How Can You Do This?'"

One fan who was an Alabama resident grumbled that the album was "criminally overlooked" when it was released, adding that he wept the first time he heard "When."

But despite the lack of interest in the musical marketplace, the bottom line for the band and producers was the satisfaction that *Eufaula* was an album they could be proud of.

Late 1998: Still gettin' it done onstage.

••••••

For numerous years, observers and fans of the Atlanta Rhythm Section probably thought the band was pretty much "going through the motions" in what was now obviously "journeyman" status. However, recording three decent albums in fairly quick succession with only one turnover in personnel had many folks, including band members, in an upbeat mood. It seemed the boys could still fire up some high-quality material, particularly if they were abetted by decent songwriting.

However, any positive developments and optimism about potential future projects crashed dramatically in Macon on December 28, 1998.

••••••

"Ronnie had been suffering from depression almost all of his life," Steve Hammond said of his older brother. "He was just never diagnosed. That's why he turned to alcohol; most people who are depressed are going to turn to something to try to make it go away."

"Ronnie being bipolar meant that when he was up, you couldn't ask for a finer, more fun person to be around," Terry Spackman averred. "It was an absolute joy, but when he would go through those dark periods, it was pretty tough."

The on-again, off-again lead singer of the Atlanta Rhythm Section had moved back to Macon. Although Ronnie had enjoyed the songwriting and recording experiences in the making of *Eufaula*, his lifestyle continued to be erratic, and his demons would overwhelm him just before 1998 came to an end. He had moved to a nondescript rental house on the south side of town around Thanksgiving and had become particularly distraught because a recent relationship had ended.

"He had hit rock bottom," Steve Hammond said succinctly.

Macon law enforcement officials were first called to his residence on December 19, when they received a report that Ronnie was threatening to commit suicide. That confrontation was resolved on the premises, but less than a week later, he began a drinking binge that lasted several days.

The police were called to the house again at 8 p.m. on December 28. A fire/rescue unit was dispatched as well. Disheveled and barely coherent, Ronnie confronted them in front of the house when they arrived. He was already bleeding from a self-inflicted cut on his wrist.

Brandishing a Fender Stratocaster guitar neck in one hand and a claw hammer in the other, Ronnie ignored the officers' commands to stop, snarling "You're gonna have to kill me!"

The wording of the police report about the incident was, as might be expected, somewhat terse: "He disregarded the officer's command and instantaneously lunged at the officer with both weapons raised over his head."

Officer Neil Smith, a Macon police veteran with twenty years of experience, had already drawn his gun and did exactly what he had been trained to do in such a scenario—he pulled the trigger on his weapon.

The .40-caliber bullet ripped through Ronnie's abdomen, exiting near a hip. He instantly fell to the ground and was quickly taken to the Medical Center of Central Georgia, where surgery was performed to repair the damage.

The slug was later recovered at the scene of the incident.

•••••••

"We always felt that Ronnie *wanted* to be shot," Gloria said. "We knew he was going through a rough period; we'd kept up with him through a friend of his, who called Buddy and told him what had happened."

The morbid message was quickly relayed through band members and associates.

"I got a phone call from Buddy around midnight," Barry recalled, "and both of us thought for a while that he was dead. Somebody did put out the word that he had died."

Rodney Mills also got a phone call from Buie, with the same initial message— Ronnie had been shot and was dead. A phone call from Buddy to his brother, Jerry, also carried the initial erroneous news that Ronnie had been killed by the police.

Buddy called Rodney back two hours later with an update that Ronnie had been shot but had survived.

"Knowing him all those years, I figured he'd reached 'the darkest of the dark,'" said Mills.

"I was asleep," Steve Stone recounted, "and Barry called and said, 'Steve, this is not a joke—Ronnie's been shot by the police. He may be dead; we don't know.' I went to Macon the day after and saw him in the hospital."

Steve Hammond and his brother Jimmy had to act as family spokesmen to the media.

"I went down to see Ronnie a couple of days later," Barry recalled. "We had some dates coming up, and we had to bring in Andy [Anderson] again. It was pretty traumatic."

A New Year's Eve show had to be canceled.

Marvin Taylor probably stated the opinion of a lot of veteran Atlanta musicians when he said that he was "shocked, but not really surprised. I'd watched Ronnie go through so many changes since we all lived in the same apartment complex way back when."

Macon-based musicians such as Mike Causey were also stunned, particularly since Ronnie had been slated to participate in an annual Stillwater concert.

"He was, as always, going to sit in with us at our yearly reunion show," Causey said. "I got a call from one of the local news departments asking me about Ronnie being shot, and I had not heard about it. I was devastated!"

"When he didn't make it that night, it was confusing," added Rob Walker. "When we finally heard what happened, it was horrifying. Ronnie was always such a soft-spoken, good-natured guy. It was surreal that he was shot for attacking a policeman. It just didn't seem possible."

••••••

Eufaula was released in late February 1999. Its front cover showed a country store near Lake Eufaula. Mike McCarty had not been involved in the cover design.

Eufaula

Atlanta Rhythm Section

Ronnie Hammond's recuperation—physical and mental—was arduous. He spent almost a month in the hospital and was released on the same day a Macon police review board exonerated Neil Smith—who had been placed on leave following the shooting—from any improper behavior in the incident; that is, Smith's actions had been justified.

Surprisingly, Ronnie began to work his way back into performing fairly soon; he considered such activity to be part of his recuperation. He would meet Neil Smith and apologize to the police officer almost a year after the shooting.

"When he got well, he came back," Steve Stone said of Hammond's return. "We did one show in Huntsville [Alabama] where Andy sang for most of the show, then Ronnie came on and sang a few songs toward the end."

A private performance to promote the release of *Eufaula* was presented on March 25 at Southern Tracks for 150 invited guests. The band set up in an outdoor tent, and the catered buffet included chili dogs from the Varsity. Local disc jockey Rhubarb Jones introduced the band, praising the spirit of the Atlanta Rhythm Section and the city from which the A.R.S. took its name.

As it turned out, the concert was terminated early by local police due to a noise complaint. Bill Lowery informed the attendees over the band's sound system that "It's either shut down or go to jail."

And Ronnie followed Lowery's announcement with an ironic statement of his own over his microphone: "You don't want to argue with the police."

Joe D'learo would depart from the Atlanta Rhythm Section organization in 1999.

Tragedy struck the band for the second time in less than eleven months on November 13, 1999, in Orlando, when drummer R. J. Vealey died after playing a concert.

The boys had performed for the 98.9 FM (WMMO) Fall Music Festival at the University of Central Florida. REO Speedwagon, Gary Wright, and Edwin McCain had been on the same bill. Attendance at the show was estimated at 10,000.

"When we first got to the gig, [Vealey] was lying down in the dressing room, saying 'Man, I am so tired; I'm as tired as I've ever been,'" Dean recounted. "Then he walked fifty yards to the stage and played the show."

The drummer executed a well-received solo before the band's final number, "Outside Woman Blues."

Following the performance, Vealey made his way over to the equipment truck, still grumbling about being exhausted. Dean recalled that Vealey also complained that he had a terrible case of indigestion.

"We had just finished, and Gary Wright was about to go onstage," said Steve Stone. "I was on the side of the stage, and I turned around towards our rental truck; R. J. was sitting there but all of a sudden he fell backwards and started convulsing. Several people came running over, including Geno Hocker, our soundman; Jason Shattles, our stage manager; and Geno Bishop, the guy that worked guitars for Edwin McCain.

"I screamed for [Bishop] to go get the medics, who were out in the field. None of us knew CPR. The medics that were on-site got to us in a few minutes. It wasn't long, but it just seemed like forever. They immediately started CPR."

Postmortem analysis indicated that such attempts would have been fruitless, since Vealey's heart attack had been so massive he had essentially dropped dead. He was thirty-seven.

"He died in Steve's arms," Dean said. "That was rough on Steve for a while afterwards."

CHAPTER 14
Journeymen: The New Century

Soon after the new century began, Barry Bailey decided to stop smoking—no easy task, considering he had consumed nicotine incessantly for thirty-five years. Many—if not most—of the publicity and concert photos of the Atlanta Rhythm Section over the decades had shown him with a cigarette in his hand or dangling from his mouth.

He even remembers the date he stopped: on March 25, 2000, he "retired" his habit with the help of a device called a nicotine inhaler.

Two weeks later, the A.R.S. was playing a gig at the Harrah's Casino in Cherokee, North Carolina, and Dean noticed that the nicotine device was working for Barry, and opted to try it himself. It worked for Ox, as well.

"I have not smoked anything—yes, *anything*—since then," Barry insisted, "although it took me about four months to wean myself off of the nicotine inhaler. Dean and I did offer support to each other during our transitions."

Asked if he ever got grumpy in the ensuing years about smoking, either because (1) he didn't like being around cigarette smoke, or (2) he didn't like seeing an old picture of himself with a cigarette, or (3) he still had a residual craving for cigarettes, Barry replied, "I get 'grumpy' only in the respect that I didn't quit sooner. Mostly, those photos remind me of how satisfying it is that I no longer harbor that addiction."

••••••

The Atlanta Rhythm Section would play in Eufaula two years in a row (at Buddy's behest, obviously), performing at the Eufaula Jam festivals in 1999 and 2000. Local media hyped the *Eufaula* album, which had been released in 1999, and chronicled the legend of all the songwriting that was done in the fishing trailer over the years.

One hardcore A.R.S. fan, George Piesch, was profiled in the local newspaper as planning on coming to the 2000 show from Vienna, Austria. In the article, Piesch proudly noted his Atlanta Rhythm Section music collection and his Atlanta Rhythm Section tattoo.

The back-to-back outdoor concerts were plagued each year by rain. When the band finally took the stage at the 2000 show following a delay due to a cloudburst, Ronnie compared the scenario to the Farm Aid benefit concerts, which also had to deal with rain on more than one occasion.

••••••

The 1981 live recording from the Savoy Club was released in 2000. It, too, was considered to be somewhat of a "truck stop" release, and in the ensuing years it would be marketed with different covers as well as at least one alternate title.

The band is in decent form on the recording, with a few embellishments and extensions of longtime favorites, as well as introductory performances of "Homesick,"

"Alien," and "Higher" from *Quinella*, released in 1981.

Once again, Paul easily demonstrates that he's a guitarist turned bassist, and the bright and beefy tone of his instrument does indeed reference the iconic sound of Chris Squire of Yes (even though the songs aren't as artsy as the music proffered by that British aggregation).

Moreover, while Barry's riffs are dependable, J. R.'s slide stands out noticeably on more than one track, as does Dean's exuberant piano, which gets a noticeable and expected workout on the set closer, "Long Tall Sally."

And Ronnie does a commendable job with his 'frontman' duties, bantering actively with the audience and introducing other band members when it's their turn for a solo.

Variations of the covers for the live album recorded at the Savoy in 1981 and released in 2000. Note that the drummer (Roy Yeager) is missing from the group photo on one example.

"I didn't even know it had been released in 2000 until [former A.R.S. roadie / truck driver] Jerry Coody sent me a copy," Barry said of the Savoy album. "The fidelity could have been better, but I was surprised at how well the band played. It probably could have used some tweaking. I didn't realize that it was that big of a deal until it was released."

"As I recall, we had known the gig would be recorded," J. R. Cobb remembered, "and I think we all played well."

In 2001, Ronnie Hammond left the Atlanta Rhythm Section for the final time, and his departure was intentional. He had agreed to sign on with a quasi-nostalgic concert venture that featured former singers with legendary bands in what was promoted as an all-star revue. Steve Hammond believes his brother made a conscious decision to quit the band for family reasons, and the all-star revue seemed to offer a less stressful scenario.

Did anyone ultimately think that Ronnie—who had come onboard as somewhat of a neophyte on the second Atlanta Rhythm Section album—had harbored any kind of an inferiority complex (at least, initially), given that the other five musicians in the band he joined had years of frontline professional experience?

"That may very well have been the case," J. R. opined. "He was one of those guys who could find the dark side in anything. It didn't matter how good things were going, he could find a reason to be depressed. He was a sweet guy when he was sober, but he was his own worst enemy."

"Whatever he did, he did it too much," Dean said of Hammond.

The A.R.S. turned to Andy Anderson once again. This time, he would be onboard for almost an entire decade.

"Andy covered Ronnie's stuff quite well, and I liked his stage presence," said Wendell Cox, guitarist for Travis Tritt. "I thought he did an awesome job fronting the band. And I always appreciated Andy calling me to come out and join them many times."

• • • • • •

As it turned out, Ronnie retired from the music business for good in 2002. A final concert billed as "Ronnie's Last Waltz" was held at the Whiskey River Club in Macon late that year. Among the backing musicians for the event were Dean Daughtry, Steve Stone, Justin Senker, and drummer Jim Keeling (who had replaced R. J. Vealey) from the Atlanta Rhythm Section, and Wendell Cox. According to Stone, the event wasn't emotional or melancholy.

"It was really more of a celebration," the guitarist said. "I didn't see anybody getting really sad. Michael Causey from Stillwater also sat in. A group of fans that call themselves Champagne Jammers came from all over the country. Even 'Southern George' from Vienna, Austria, made it for the event. But in my mind, I was thinking Ronnie would come back."

"I was planning on just playing a song or two, but Ronnie said he wanted me to play more, so I did," Causey said of his participation. "I wasn't sure about some of the chord changes on some of the songs. I just tried to stay out of the way and play when needed. I used my old adage 'When in doubt, lay out.' I certainly was familiar with every song, though, from listening to them for all these years, so I was fairly comfortable. Not to mention that all the guys playing in the band that night were so tight—Steve,

Andy Anderson. *Phantom Photography*

Justin, Dean. Wendell Cox played that night, and he just scorched it. It was such an honor to be with Ronnie and all the guys for his Last Waltz."

"We played as close and good as we could and had a large time, no doubt!" Cox enthused. "I did, however, walk off the stage with tears in my eyes, but I was so proud for Ronnie. It was an honor I'll never forget."

Ronnie Hammond's official last hurrah at the Whiskey River Club in Macon. Left to right, Wendell Cox, Hammond, Mike Causey, Steve Stone.

"I remember an interview Ronnie did in advance of his retirement concert," said Tinsley Ellis. "Ronnie said that the music he loved was no longer popular; that it had fallen out of style. I kinda know what he meant by that."

••••••

The new century also saw Dawn and Barry Bailey designing and building their own home on thirty acres of property in rural Georgia, about fifty miles from the huge I-285 circular interstate that surrounds the Atlanta area. It was a split-level design sheltered by woods and surrounded by pastures.

"I never really called it a 'farm,'" Barry said. "However, I took the farm tax easement, because Dawn and I bred horses."

They also built two ponds, totaling about three acres in size.

"We cleared away the woods, and they took about a year to fill up; they're being fed by two springs," Barry detailed. He stocked the ponds with bream, shellcrackers, and largemouth bass.

••••••

In August 2003, Dean played at Chastain Park in an ad hoc band that included Darryl Rhoades (who was also a stand-up comedian) on drums and Rex Patton on bass, backing iconic guitarist Chuck Berry, who was wont to use such "pickup" groups.

"I'd known Dean for several years," said Rhoades, "and he'd already played on several of my albums, so I was excited to play live with him as I was a fan since his days with the Candymen."

Steve Stone attended the gig but was not in the one-off musical aggregation, noting that he just wanted to watch Dean playing with Chuck.

"As with most of Chuck's gigs, there was no rehearsal," Rhoades recalled, "and we were warned by Rex Patton that it was basically every man for himself when Chuck started playing, as none of us had a heads-up on what was about to happen.

Chuck tore through his hits and occasionally even played in tune, which wasn't something he was prone to do, but hell—it was *Chuck Berry*, and I was glad to be backing him."

One of Berry's biggest hits was the double-entendre-laden "My Ding-a-Ling," and at the Chastain Park performance, the legendary guitarist referenced the song in citing Ox's keyboard abilities, announcing to the audience, "A man who tinkles the ivory like that must know how to play with his ding-a-ling."

Dean performs at Chastain Park with Chuck Berry.

The Atlanta Rhythm Section would record a live DVD in Stabler Arena in Bethlehem, Pennsylvania, on December 13, 2003, but Barry wasn't completely satisfied with the final product.

However, Barry had begun to feel some numbness in his lower extremities. After over a year of examinations and procedures, including MRIs (magnetic resonance imaging) and a spinal tap, he was diagnosed with multiple sclerosis in January 2005, but planned to continue working into that year.

But several months later, Dawn was diagnosed with an aggressive form of lung cancer. Barry immediately made arrangements to retire from the Atlanta Rhythm Section.

"She had surgery; lost a third of a lung," he said, "and went through a lot of chemo after that. She was supposedly cancer free, but it had metastasized into a tumor in her abdomen. Maybe it was a bit of a blessing that she didn't have to go on and on."

Dawn Vanderlip Bailey, Barry Bailey's life partner, breathed her last on Friday, July 7, 2006. She was fifty-seven.

••••••

When Barry retired, most fans of the Atlanta Rhythm Section knew the sound of the band would be different because of the loss of its founding lead guitarist, and

J. R. Cobb's recollections of Bailey's abilities probably spoke not only for fellow musicians, but average fans as well.

"Barry Bailey was Barry Bailey on any guitar through any amp, anytime, anywhere," Cobb said emphatically. "I've sat down and tried to play the exact same thing he played, on the same fret on the same guitar through the same amp, and it didn't sound anything like Barry. It was his hands and his touch and his taste, and it was like nobody else I'd ever heard. You could always tell it was him."

••••••

Following Barry's departure, Ox Daughtry was the only remaining original member of the Atlanta Rhythm Section who was still in the band.

••••••

By 2007, David Anderson of Huntsville, Alabama, had been added as a permanent member of the Atlanta Rhythm Section. In the 1990s, Anderson had played on the second and third albums recorded by a moderately successful Birmingham-based band called Brother Cane, and he was also active in creating his own recordings using loops and other sonic options.

"I was friends with Jim Keeling, who was the [Atlanta Rhythm Section] drummer at the time," Anderson recalled. "He and I grew up together, playing in bands. I did some studio work with Dean, and I got offered a job as a result. [There was] no additional rehearsal; I met a couple of the guys on my first gig with them, in a small town in Georgia—a town square festival–type show."

••••••

Barry would be honored in his hometown of Decatur in the summer of 2009, at a "Beach Party" sponsored by the Decatur Business Association.

"It was an idea from some of the guys and girls that were in my [high school] graduating class," he recalled. "They contacted me out of nowhere, and a couple of them came out to the house before the event. We had a nice time reminiscing and making plans."

At the ceremony on June 19, Decatur mayor Bill Floyd presented the now-retired guitarist with the key to the city and declared that date to be "Barry Bailey Day" in the Atlanta suburb.

••••••

Ronnie Hammond's struggles continued following his retirement, but an incident as violent and traumatic as the December 1998 shooting never happened again.

His last public performance was on June 26, 2010, at the grand opening of an outdoor performance stage at "the Big House," a large home on Vinings Avenue in Macon. It had been the headquarters of the Allman Brothers Band and the residence of several of its members during that band's earlier days.

Former Studio One studio manager Rick Maxwell had also moved to Macon and had remained in touch with Ronnie. Maxwell was also occasionally sitting in with a weekend warrior–type band called the Buckeye Band. Carl Pruett, who managed a radio station in Griffin, was an Atlanta Rhythm Section fan who also played guitar in that band.

"I was probably closer to Ronnie than I had been to anyone else in the Atlanta Rhythm Section," said Maxwell. "[Big House director] Greg Potter asked me if I could put together a group that wasn't local—someone that you didn't hear every

Friday or Saturday night in Macon—so I went to Carl regarding the Buckeye Band, then I asked Ronnie if he would like to join us, and he was all in."

"Ronnie had been quite reclusive after his incident with the law," Pruett said. "Rick stayed in touch with him all along, both being in Macon, and Ronnie did sing occasionally at church. He still had the pipes."

Maxwell: "I called Ronnie and told him what we were doing, and he said, 'I'll be glad to do it; when do you want me there?'"

Pruett: "We did maybe two rehearsals of A.R.S. tunes, but never with him. The night of June 26, we did a regular sixty-minute opening set around 7 p.m., then got with Ronnie in our motor home to discuss his tunes. It was funny—he popped up with 'Hey, do y'all know "The Weight?"' We did, so he wanted to add that to his part of the show's A.R.S. tunes.

"Ronnie came out and did one heck of a super show; he was amazing. There were hundreds of fans there; the whole lawn and backyard concert pavilion area was packed. Several guys went to their cars after the show to get their guitars for Ronnie and guys from our band to sign. Ronnie was covered up by fans for pictures and autographs for well over an hour. It was an incredible comeback night for him, and something he did not expect."

"He sounded phenomenal," Maxwell concurred.

"I thought it sounded really nice," said Steve Hammond, who was also at the concert. "At that point, Ronnie had not been using his voice like he had done for most of his life, and of course he was getting older. He had a lung condition, and he struggled to hit some of the highs on some of the songs, but he sounded pretty good and he enjoyed it."

Afterward, Maxwell and Pruett discussed the possibility of occasional future performances with Ronnie Hammond as a guest, but nothing ultimately transpired.

Ronnie Hammond's last public performance, June 26, 2010. Left to right: Marshall Woodruff, Hammond, Carl Pruett, Rick Maxwell.

* * * * * *

With All Due Respect, released in 2011, featured more new versions of Atlanta Rhythm Section tunes, as well as several unique covers of hit songs by other artists such as Steely Dan (to which the A.R.S. had already been compared on songs like "So Into You").

There might have been tendency for some fans or listeners to pronounce the album as being another "quickie" album, but David Anderson sought to differentiate.

"The thing that set this one apart is that we worked with Rodney Mills on it," the guitarist said, "so it was more legitimate than other 'truck stop CDs,' as I call them."

Andy Anderson finally got his shot as lead vocalist on a studio album, and his singing served the album well.

"I thought he did a great job," Steve Stone said of Andy's vocals. "He *is* a different singer."

Likewise, Jim Keeling and David Anderson were new participants on an Atlanta Rhythm Section album. Rodney Mills was the producer, and Buddy Buie was listed as executive producer.

Some of the cover tunes had innovative and intriguing arrangements, as exemplified by a shuffling tempo on "Bad Case of Lovin' You"—the original version by English singer Robert Palmer had been a flat-out rocker. Jody White, stage manager for the A.R.S. at the time, played drums on that track.

A resonator guitar / "dobro" (played by Wendell Cox) appeared on "Midnight Rider," and Dean's funky piano licks stood out.

Moreover, Ox also shines on the cover of Lynyrd Skynyrd's "Tuesday's Gone," which abruptly shifts to an interesting three-quarter/"waltz" tempo.

While there aren't any "unplugged" songs on the album, acoustic guitars make their presence known on more than one track, being particularly noticeable on "Rock Bottom" (and one wonders how many listeners were aware that the song that had been a hit for Wynonna was written by Buddy Buie and J. R. Cobb).

Steve Stone also liked the guitar interplay between David Anderson and himself on *With All Due Respect*.

"We switched off a *lot* on that record,'" he said. "On 'Sleep with One Eye Open' there are solos with both of us. I enjoyed how we worked together on 'Conversation' and 'Rock Bottom.'"

The band's ol' buddy from Mose Jones, Steve McCray, contributed some additional keyboard work, but one important development, particularly in the eyes of longtime fans, was the participation of three former A.R.S. members on the album.

Paul Goddard played bass on the leadoff track, "Sleep with One Eye Open," which had been one of the tracks on the early 1980s "CBS reject album," as well as a proposed title for that never officially released project.

And both former lead singers also chipped in.

"I got Ronnie to come up to sing on 'Conversation,'" Mills remembered. "My intention was to just get a verse out of him. When we got him in here, he literally could not sing without coughing. He said he could use some bronchial spray, so we went to the grocery and got him a bottle. Sure enough, it seemed to work, and when he sang the verse, it was like 'That's him.'

"I wanted him to sing more, so he sang the second verse, but when we got to the bridge, he couldn't get up to those notes at all. And that was it; he couldn't go any further, and that was the last recording of his singing. Rodney Justo came up later and sang the bridge and the other verses. Rodney also did some stuff on "So Into You" and 'I'm Not Going to Let It Bother Me Tonight.'

"But while Ronnie was here, he sat down and thanked me for helping invite him to be in the Atlanta Rhythm Section."

"I got to put a guitar solo on that song," David Anderson added. Unfortunately I never met Ronnie Hammond, but I can say we played together for his last recorded performance; we just were not in the same room at the same time."

With All Due Respect has a unique position in the discography of the Atlanta Rhythm Section, since it contains vocal contributions by all three lead vocalists from the band's history. It was released on May 23, 2011.

But Ronnie Hammond had died a little over two months earlier, on March 14.

With All Due Respect was well received by fans, but understandably the album seemed to fit into a nostalgia-type genre— and to some observers, the same might be said for the band itself, given that Dean was the band's only original member.

Hydra's Spencer Kirkpatrick noted, "The only thing I'd heard that might have been considered a negative—and they're aware of this—was that they were kind of along the lines of Lynyrd Skynyrd—[guitarist] Gary Rossington was about the only original one still there, and all of a sudden it's become a Skynyrd tribute band. Same thing for the A.R.S."

●●●●●●

Another musician who would use the term "tribute band" as applied to the "Dean as the only original member" incarnation of the Atlanta Rhythm Section was Rodney Justo, when discussing the return of Paul Goddard and himself to the band's lineup in 2011, not long after the release of *With All Due Respect*.

Rodney had retired from his beverage distribution job and was playing in the Tampa area with a casual but talented nostalgia combo called the Coo Coo Ca Choo Band.

"Dean and Rodney had started talking after Ronnie's funeral about getting back together, and then Paul had wanted to come back, too," Steve Stone remembered.

Paul's wife, Phyllis, had died less than a year before he began gigging with the Atlanta Rhythm Section again for the first time in decades.

"He had physically taken care of her for a long time," Nan Jacobs said of her brother. "She had breast cancer, brain cancer, [and] colon cancer, and he was her caregiver, 24/7. [Returning to the band] was a chance for him to live again."

Paul sat in with the Rhythm Section before officially returning, and Tinsley Ellis recalled the initial, tentative steps.

"I was at the Woodstock, Georgia, show when Paul Goddard took the stage with them for the first time in many years," said the blues guitarist. "There were literally thousands of grown men and women in tears. He was such a big part of their sound."

Dean remembered that Rodney returned to the A.R.S. first, followed shortly afterward by Paul. Over forty years after the Atlanta Rhythm Section was founded, the band now had three original members in its lineup.

The reaction about the return of Justo and Goddard and the departure of Andy Anderson and Justin Senker was, understandably, met with a few raised eyebrows when it happened.

"Of course they weren't happy about it," David Anderson said of Andy and Justin, "but they also understood that it's hard to argue with an original member coming back."

"I hadn't wanted to see Justin go," Steve Stone admitted. "As it turned out, I loved every minute I spent with Paul."

The band quickly assimilated Justo and Goddard, and both musicians were at home in their former turf. The vibe was so strong and positive that they began working up arrangements of lesser-heard Atlanta Rhythm Section material from the classic days, such as "Jukin'" and "Boogie Smoogie."

Paul was somewhat intimidated—for physical reasons—about attempting a comeback after decades. He had some nerve damage in his arms and had had a cancerous salivary gland removed a couple of years earlier. It had supposedly been easily treated, however, and he reportedly had a clean bill of health when he rejoined the A.R.S.

The verdict from Atlanta Rhythm Section members, ex-members, business associates, and fans about the return of the band's original lead singer and original bass player was unanimously positive.

Paul Goddard gets reoriented to an old, familiar assignment alongside guitarists David Anderson (left) and Steve Stone (right).

"They weren't playing the big venues, but it was good for him," Nan said of Paul's return, "and he loved Steve Stone like a brother. Steve had a great wit and so did Paul, and Paul respected Steve musically as well."

"When Paul decided to come back to the band, I think he had been thinking about the music he'd helped to create all those years ago, and had decided that it wasn't all that bad," Rodney Mills said. "I think he realized the importance of the contributions he'd made."

"In his later years, he said that he regretted that he had said he hadn't enjoyed playing the Atlanta Rhythm Section's music," said Gloria Buie. "He was really proud of everything that they had accomplished, and Buddy was thrilled when he came back. The first time we heard him after he'd rejoined was when Buddy booked the Rhythm Section at an ALS [amyotrophic lateral sclerosis; commonly known as Lou Gehrig's disease] fundraiser he'd set up in Dothan for a friend of ours. Paul was glad to be back; it was a very positive thing."

The ALS benefit, held on August 20, 2011, was part of Dothan's Downtown Music Festival. J. R. Cobb, Rodney Mills, Nan Jacobs, and Mike McCarty also attended the same event in "Circle City," and J. R. sat in with his former band for a couple of songs. He thought that Justo and Goddard sounded great.

"He seemed to really be happy," J. R. said of Paul, "considering how long he'd been out of music. He actually seemed to be enjoying it a lot more than he did when we played in the band."

"Paul was having so much fun it was unbelievable," said McCarty. "You've never seen somebody so happy up on that stage."

When J. R. sat in with the band, David Anderson briefly wondered if he, too, might be replaced by an original member of the Atlanta Rhythm Section, but another change in personnel didn't happen.

"I certainly wasn't going to argue when I thought J. R. was coming back," he said. "And I also would've been disappointed, but I would've understood."

In addition to the performance by the A.R.S., Buddy, J. R., Rodney Justo, and former Capricorn producer Paul Hornsby participated an open-to-the-public seminar about songwriting and performing. Hornsby was a native of a small Wiregrass town named New Brockton.

McCarty also participated in a meet-and-greet session at the Wiregrass Museum of Art.

••••••

Steve Stone would indeed develop a "kindred spirit" relationship with Paul.

"He was funny and quirky," the guitarist recalled. "He loved Yes, Kansas, and Renaissance. Since we both loved progressive rock, we'd often ride to our own performances together, listening to music through the car stereo, and we also went to see Yes at an amphitheater. They'd gotten a new lead singer, but we liked them. We talked about a lot of stuff; we became great friends."

The twosome had discussed possibly recording some progressive-rock-style music in the future, but nothing transpired.

⬤⬤⬤⬤⬤⬤

And two members of Kansas were also delighted to see that Goddard had returned to the Atlanta Rhythm Section, when their paths crossed on a cruise ship on which both aggregations had been booked.

"Kansas played on the 'Rock Legends Cruise II' in 2013," Richard Williams recalled. "We were being lined up for the lifeboat drill when [drummer] Phil Ehart and I saw Paul standing there. Paul was back in the Atlanta Rhythm Section, and he was all smiles. We ran right over to say hello.

"It was so great to see him back in the saddle. Afterward, my wife asked, 'Who was that? I've never seen you and Phil drop everything and rush to go say hello like that to anyone.' Like a little kid at Christmas, I told her, '*That is Paul Goddard!*' I don't know if Paul really knew how respected he was."

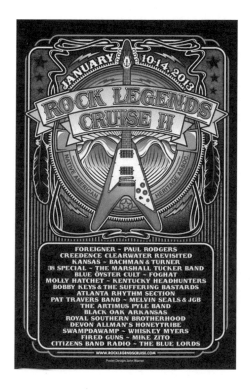

Paul is all smiles onstage during a Rock Legends Cruise II performance. *Rock Legend Photographers*

CHAPTER 15
The Road Behind

Hardcore Alabama Crimson Tide fans Buddy and Gloria had a decades-long football rivalry with Buddy's brother, Jerry, and his wife, Susie, who were big Auburn fans. Each year, the results of the "Iron Bowl" mandated that the losing couple took the winning couple to dinner, and the losers were compelled to wear hats with the logo of the winning team.

"The best I remember, I came up with that idea in an attempt to calm down the 'Iron Bowl war,'" Gloria recalled, "mainly because Buddy never grasped the concept of 'being a good sport' when it came to that game. It was so much fun and completely solved the animosity, because the loser always had something to look forward to as well!"

When the Buies opted to (semi)-retire, it wasn't surprising that Buddy wanted to return to Lake Eufaula.

"Buddy's dream was to live on the lake where he could fish and enjoy the lifestyle that he always wanted, including being around friends and family," Arnie Geller recalled.

However, Gloria balked, since she had actually grown to like metropolitan life in Atlanta.

"I was a small-town girl," she explained. "When I'd first got there, it was like 'Whoa—what have I been missing?' I loved the hustle-bustle of Atlanta, and when we'd come home to Dothan to visit, I'd be glad when we got back to the big city. Buddy grew up on the lake; I did not. His dream was always to come back to the lake. When I finally agreed, our son Ben said he'd give our marriage six months."

'Bama lost this year: Gloria and Buddy are shown in the kitchen of their Roswell, Georgia, home wearing Auburn "gimme" caps prior to taking his brother and sister-in-law out to dinner.

"I was not thrilled," Ben confirmed. "Mom has always been a 'city person.' I kind of felt like Dad was being stubborn, and Mom didn't have a lot of say in it. More than anything, I was worried it would age them, because they wouldn't have daily contact with people. However, I love taking my wife and kids there. Definitely a lot of great memories."

The Lake Eufaula property where the fishing trailer sat had been acquired by Buddy's sister after her husband died, and a member of her family had built a home there.

The Buies found another home in the same area at what was technically an Abbeville, Alabama, address, and moved in March 2003. The country store that had been on the cover of *Eufaula* was located nearby. Their new home would undergo numerous expansions and renovations in the ensuing years.

Once the Buies were settled in, Arnie Geller and his wife, Judy, visited more than once. Buddy and Arnie had stayed in touch after their business paths diverged. Geller remembered that Buie was pleased with Arnie's success in the "exhibition industry."

"He was for me all the way," said Geller. "It made sense to him because I was always in the business of selling tickets, and doing marketing and promoting."

Buie was known for driving his automobiles fast, and that propensity carried over to watercraft as well.

"Buddy took me out on the lake in his new boat and showed me how fast it would go," Arnie recalled. "Scared the hell out of me."

The Buies still maintained a music-oriented company called Buddy Buie Enterprises, and a couple of years after relocating to the lake, they founded, with Ben's help, a small, high-speed Internet service provider to serve the lakeshore area in which they lived. Ben developed the concepts and oversaw construction as well as upgrades such as high-speed streaming. The small business kept them active but still allowed Buddy to nurture any musical ventures at his own pace.

One personal project that Buddy pursued circa 2005 was the creation of a CD compilation of many of the hits he'd written or cowritten, produced, or both, accompanied by verbal introductions, details, and commentaries by Buddy. Not surprisingly, the just-for-friends-and-relatives anthology, titled *Music of My Life*, was so extensive (thirty-three songs) that it ended up becoming a two-CD set.

In addition to commenting about songs he had written and bands he had recorded, Buddy also lauded his business associates.

"I've been blessed with great partners over my life," he said on one of the spoken-word segments of the anthology. "Paul Cochran, Arnie Geller, Bill Lowery. But my most important partner is my wife, Gloria. Not just because she's been my wife for thirty-three years, but because she's been involved in every endeavor along the way. She handles the business end when I'm off being creative and crazy. She runs the office, has a degree in economics, and is an astute businesswoman. I'd be lost without her."

(Buddy was slightly off in his citation of his wife's education. Gloria actually had a business administration degree, with a focus on accounting, from the Mercer University School of Business and Economics.)

······

Buddy's lifestyle had never been exemplary regarding his health; he was diabetic and had weight problems, but he had managed to kick a decades-long cigarette habit back in the mid-1980s.

He underwent open-heart surgery (in Atlanta) in 2008, and wound up being in intensive care for three weeks. Gloria described his subsequent condition and appearance as "a shadow of his former self."

Two days after arriving home from Atlanta, Buddy developed a fever and was taken to a hospital in Dothan, where he was diagnosed with MRSA (methicillin-resistant staphylococcus aureus).

"It's a horrible infection," Gloria explained. "It's a killer, and they still don't have a cure for it. He'd picked it up in the hospital in Atlanta. Over the year, it got near his replacement heart valve, which was a pig's valve. The 'disease guy' at the Dothan hospital coordinated with the 'disease guy' at the UAB [University of Alabama at Birmingham] hospital, and they threw every 'cocktail' they could come up with at him to try to kill it.

"They told me he was going to die, but he survived it. It was long and it was hard, but what with his diabetes and everything else, he was never full strength again."

Buddy's extended recuperation left him frustrated and moody. Gloria struggled as well, because her husband was being kept down by the surgery, the illnesses, and their lingering aftereffects.

A trainer was hired to help Buddy work out; his legs were so weak he was having balance problems.

"He never fully recovered after almost dying from that infection," Ben said. "I think he realized he wasn't invincible, and that kind of took the wind out of his sails. For the first time in his life, he felt 'old'; he could see death on the horizon, and I think it bummed him out. Having said that, he seemed to be in pretty good health, aside from his type 2 diabetes, which he was able to manage. He just never had the same vigor after that."

And in spite of Buddy's travails, his old songwriting habits proved to be hard to break.

"We used to get together and write quite a bit," J. R. Cobb said of Buddy's (semi)-retirement years. "We wrote a decent number of songs, and maybe we'd make demos of some of them, but nothing ever happened. It was just an excuse to get together and hobnob. Sometimes we'd stay in the house that his niece built on the property where the fishing trailer used to be; his niece didn't live there all the time.

"And it got to where if we went there, I'd have to bring in the luggage and do all the cooking. Buddy loved to cook but he just couldn't get around anymore. He used a cane, but he should've been using a walker.

"One of the last songs we wrote together was called 'Remember This,' and he felt strongly about how good of a song it was. And even when his health started going down, you could ask him on any given day how he was doing, and he'd always say something like 'I feel great; let's go do this or that.' But when we were trying to write, he'd only be good for maybe two hours. Still, he was always upbeat, and even though I knew he had heart problems, he'd never admit to it. He always wanted to make you think he was going to live forever."

Circa 2005 déjà vu: seated in the Buies' kitchen on Lake Eufaula, J. R. and Buddy work on crafting yet another song. *robertoreg. blogspot.com*

······

In an effort that combined local history, art, and revitalization of an urban area, the city of Dothan had been contracting with artists to paint murals of local and area personalities for many years. The mural about Wiregrass pop and rock music, the twentieth of the series, was completed early in 2009, and was dedicated on June 11 of that year.

Among the personalities on the mural, painted by Wes Hardin, were Ray Charles, members of the Candymen and Beaverteeth, Bobby Goldsboro, and Martha Reeves. Band names and logos also floated behind the images of the musicians and singers.

And right in the middle was a larger-than-life portrait of Buddy Buie, sporting his inimitable enthusiastic grin. Hovering directly behind him was the classic Atlanta Rhythm Section logo and a picture of Dean Daughtry.

And Atlanta Rhythm Section music emanated from the P.A. prior to the start of the dedication ceremony, which was attended by Dean Daughtry, Rodney Justo, Bobby Goldsboro, Wilbur Walton Jr. of the James Gang, and David Adkins of Beaverteeth, among others. Buddy was among the speakers at the event.

······

In the latter part of 2010 and early 2011, Ronnie Hammond appeared to be getting back into shape, at least physically, and had also married again. However, Steve Hammond recalled that his brother "was never one to go to the doctor."

"Ronnie had lost a lot of weight," Steve said, "and had spent a few weeks working in my shop building a cabinet for his mother-in-law. During those few weeks, I had never seen Ronnie happier.

"We sat in the shop one day joking back and forth with one another. I had commented on what an excellent carpenter he was; he had spent some years building houses in his off time from music.

Music mural on display in downtown Dothan.

"He did mention to me that he thought he was very sick, and I shrugged it off and told him not to worry; he would be fine. He had been overweight for a few years and I thought he looked a lot healthier with the weight loss."

On Friday, March 11, Ronnie began having difficulty breathing when lying down. Steve recalled that over the weekend, his older brother wrote "a couple of letters to an old friend asking for forgiveness."

"It was almost as if Ronnie knew there was something seriously wrong," said Steve, "and it may have been his last chance to write these letters. He refused to go to the ER that Friday, Saturday, and Sunday because he had no insurance, and he didn't want to leave his wife, Tracy, with nothing."

By Monday, his condition had worsened to the point that seeing a doctor became mandatory.

"Tracy called me Monday morning and asked if I would come to the doctor's office to help her with Ronnie. He was very weak and unable to walk on his own."

While seated in the waiting room, Ronnie suffered a heart attack and went into respiratory arrest.

"By the time I arrived he had just passed," said Steve. "They had tried to revive him with CPR and chest compressions. The doctor's office did not have a defibrillator, the one thing that could have restarted his heart. I walked in the room where Ronnie was lying on the floor, just before the EMTs [emergency medical technicians] arrived. I kept trying to talk to Ronnie, asking him to please hold on and not leave us, over and over again, as if in some way he could hear my voice, in at least a spiritual way. It was too late. When Ronnie arrived at the hospital, the doctors told me his heart had never started again."

Ronnie Hammond was sixty years old at the time of his passing, on March 14, 2011.

The funeral was held at Maynard Baptist Church in Forsyth on March 18. Rick Maxwell gave the eulogy, and Arnie Geller read a memorial essay sent by California music industry analyst Bob Lefsetz. Buddy and Gloria, Barry, J. R., and Dean also attended, as did many other musicians and techs.

"Tracy, his widow, called me and asked me to speak," Maxwell detailed. "Her brother was a minister, and he was going to speak, but she also wanted someone who'd been around Ronnie for a long time."

Ronnie was buried in Monroe Memorial Gardens.

"He was just a sweet, kind human being," Gloria remembered.

"He was kind to a fault," said Maxwell. "He'd give you the shirt off of his back. He never played the 'rock star' part, and I miss him to this day."

"Ronnie was always a good guy to me, and I always liked him," said Rodney Justo. "We were always courteous to each other, and I always went to see the band when they were playing in the Tampa–St. Pete area; he'd always introduce me from the stage."

Lynn Sinclair had switched from radio programming to television work in 1990, but had remained a staunch Atlanta Rhythm Section fan and supporter.

"Ronnie never realized his own talent," Sinclair said. "I always thought that he sounded better and better with each record the A.R.S. put out. I think he just became more and more confident over the years with his singing, and with that, he became more confident on stage."

The cabinet that Ronnie had been building was unfinished.

"A few weeks later after Ronnie was buried, I finished the cabinet," Steve said, "and his mother-in-law came by to pick it up. Watching that cabinet leave my house brought me to my knees, and I wept to the point of not being able to stand. It was so heartbreaking for me, as this was the last art form he had done with his hands."

⁕⁕⁕⁕⁕

Robert Nix, the Atlanta Rhythm Section's original drummer, was residing in Batesville, Mississippi, on the eastern edge of the Mississippi delta, when word began to get around in early 2012 that he was seriously ill. Phone calls were exchanged; Rodney Justo called Nix, and Nix unexpectedly called Rodney Mills.

"A while before he passed, he called me out of the clear blue," Mills remembered. "We just had a normal conversation, but then he said, 'I wanted to call and tell you I've been listening to stuff we recorded over the years, and I never told you how much you contributed to our sound.' It was really touching; he'd never said anything like that back then."

Mills suspects that Nix knew that he was terminally ill at that time, but Mills himself had been unaware of Nix's condition.

Robert Nix died on May 20, 2012, in a hospital in Memphis. He was sixty-seven. Rodney Justo posted a memorial statement on the Atlanta Rhythm Section's Facebook page, and a notice was also placed on the band's website. The funeral was held at Batesville Presbyterian Church.

Mills had a conciliatory attitude about Nix's passing:

"A lot of the times when we were recording, Robert could be overbearing to the point of obnoxiousness, but he also pulled some really good stuff out of us; some of the songs benefited from his 'insistence.' I'm not as hard on Robert in my old age as I was back then. He had been in the studio a *lot*. I've looked back on the contributions that Robert made, and tried to weigh them against some of the times that were over the top. In the end, I've decided Robert was a very necessary part of that band. We made a lot of music together—not apart."

●●●●●●

Paul Goddard's return to the Atlanta Rhythm Section in 2011, and his performances in the ensuing three years had impressed a lot of fans and fellow musicians.

And not surprisingly, Paul would stay private about his terminal illness.

According to Nan Jacobs, her brother's salivary gland malignancy had metastasized to a lung, and there was no treatment. Although he smoked right up to the end (according to Barry and Dean), the very aggressive cancer in Paul's lung was reportedly different from the type that was caused by cigarettes.

"We knew he was sick, but we didn't know how sick," Steve Stone said. "I thought he had some small, cancerous thing that was being taken care of."

Dean had 20/20 hindsight about Paul's illness, noting that Goddard's original salivary gland malignancy may have been a subliminal factor in the original bassist's return.

Paul would chide Ox about weight loss, proclaiming he was shedding pounds while Dean wasn't. Daughtry would later come to the obvious conclusion that Goddard's weight loss was due to his malignancy.

The last concert Paul played with the Atlanta Rhythm Section was in his hometown of Rome in late March 2014, as he continued to stay private about his battle.

"A nice irony," said Nan. "He was barely able to play the concert. He was in and out of the hospital through April; he'd tell people that he was having some breathing issues. Steve [Stone] visited him a lot."

He finally contacted his sister about making some end-of-life decisions but was still denying that anything was seriously wrong. The day before he died, Paul told Nan what he wanted done with his basses and other personal items. Steve visited the hospital that day.

"I met with his cancer specialist, who had also been his wife's cancer specialist," said Nan, "and was told 'Your brother is dying and is in denial. The chemo I'm giving him is palliative, not curative.' I asked the doctor to go with me to talk to Paul, 'so he'll know that I know.'

"We went; Paul was very lucid and asked a lot of questions. The doctor started the ball rolling about having Paul transferred to Atlanta Hospice.

"They transported him to a hospice on North Druid Hills [Road] and put us in a family room while they got him settled into a room, but then a nurse came in and said 'He's going.' So he was only at the hospice maybe ten minutes."

The talented and eccentric original bassist for the Atlanta Rhythm Section passed away on April 30, 2014.

"Some of his nonmusical friends wanted a big 'celebration-of-life' event," Nan recalled, "but the more I thought about it, I was afraid it would become a circus, and his death had hit me harder than any other I'd been through, because it made me the last in my family."

There was no memorial ceremony, and Paul's remains were cremated. His ashes were taken to the mountains of North Carolina, where a priest who was a friend of Nan's performed a private committal service.

Nan cleaned out Paul's house. The effort was both a cathartic and revelatory experience for her "because there was so much of his life he didn't share with me." She opined that her brother's ultimate legacy is "probably the fact that an 'unlikely suspect' who doesn't read music can touch lives in ways that wouldn't have been thought possible, and to have people strive to play bass the way he played bass. I think he knew he had inspired a lot of bass players, but he didn't talk about it. I believe there were times when he was awestruck that a half-blind guy from Rome, Georgia wound up becoming a musical force to be reckoned with."

"Paul may have had his idiosyncracies, and he insisted on being himself," J. R. recalled, "but he had his own following when we were in the Atlanta Rhythm Section. There were people who thought he was as cool as could be."

"To me, Paul will always remain an enigma," said Justin Senker, who would return to the Atlanta Rhythm Section following Goddard's passing. "His brain operated on a level so far beyond mine, I usually couldn't 'get it.' [He was] a true genius. He was never unwilling to make you aware of his vast trove of knowledge and your relative lack thereof. He found that his skills at computer programming provided a much-better living than his amazing skills as a bass player ever had. During our rare face-to-face

Steve Stone with Paul Goddard's frontline bass.

encounters he was always engaging, kind ,and encouraging, but replacing a legend is impossible. I know and fully understand I cannot replace him."

••••••

The neighbors in the small lakeshore community where Gloria and Buddy lived would often have a cocktail hour at 5 p.m. on weekends. On Friday, July 17, 2015, the Buies were hosting such an event. Guests were still arriving as Buddy sat in a chair near the front door, delighting in watching the Buies' goldendoodle, Hampton, romp with a neighbor's dog.

Then Buddy gave off a loud "snort," and his head slumped forward. Gloria was in their home office, trying to make an adjustment on an Internet signal with one of the business co-owners, when a neighbor told her she needed to come into the living room.

"He was making an almost 'snoring' sound, which I'd never seen," she recalled. "Then he quit breathing, and we got him onto the floor."

More than one visitor began to perform CPR, and an ambulance arrived some twenty minutes later. Paramedics began their lifesaving protocols but had trouble getting any response. Buddy was rushed to a hospital in Eufaula to try to stabilize him and was then taken to a Dothan hospital, but he never regained consciousness. He was on life support, and Gloria recalled that her family was told that they "might have to make a decision." However, Buddy breathed his last on Saturday, July 18, at approximately 12:45 p.m.

"Buddy couldn't have planned it any better," his widow said wistfully. "He would have wanted to go exactly the way he did—at five o'clock with all of his friends around."

"Buddy lived life in the fast lane," said his younger brother, Jerry. "No question about that. He drove his car fast. When they called, my first thought was that he'd had a car wreck, until they explained that he'd keeled over. I was still shocked."

J. R.: "I knew he was going downhill, and I should have been expecting it, but I was devastated. I've told people that in my lifetime, I probably spent more time with Buddy than I spent with my wife."

Buddy even garnered a postmortem profile in the *New York Times*, and his passing was also announced on "shock jock" Howard Stern's radio show.

"I am a huge Howard Stern fan," Ben recounted. "The day after Dad died, one of my coworkers, who also listens to Stern, said they heard Dad mentioned on the Stern show. I thought he was joking; I was planning the funeral, so obviously I wasn't listening that day. Later, I found the clip on the Internet. I was blown away; I don't think I'd realized his death would register on a national level. It was a bright spot at a dark time."

Battling laryngitis, Arnie Geller gave the eulogy at the funeral. Ben Buie, Hunter Sheridan (Buddy's stepson), and David Michael Zell (Buddy's great-nephew) also spoke.

And J. R. participated, playing guitar while David Adkins played piano. Richard Burke, a singer with whom Adkins had worked, sang.

"Gloria had to find someone rather quickly," J. R. recalled, "because she had originally wanted Rodney Justo and me to perform together, but Rodney said that he was just too broken up to be able to sing, so Gloria asked David and Richard and me to do it instead. Richard did a fine job, as I recall."

"That's true," Justo said of his declination. "I know my limitations and knew I wouldn't be able to sing."

"Gloria told me that Buddy wanted two songs played at his funeral—'Traces' and 'Moon River,'" said J. R. "He and I had talked about what a great song 'Moon River' was, and I can see why he wanted it played. I played them and got through them, but it was the hardest two-song set I've ever done."

"It wasn't a 'show business funeral,'" Arnie clarified. "It was a family funeral."

"As far as funerals go, it was pretty great," said Ben. "I was moved by the turnout. I don't think I realized how many people he impacted during his life. The reception was great because it was like a party, which he would have wanted."

"Buddy always wanted a party at his funeral," Gloria reflected, "so we didn't have a visitation, just a reception at the Eufaula Country Club afterwards. Everyone was invited; there was an open bar and plenty of food! I will always be glad that we did that. He would have loved it."

Veteran journalist Kyle Mooty had become the general manager of the local newspaper, the *Eufaula Tribune*, in early 2015.

"I'd always been a fan of the Atlanta Rhythm Section," Mooty recalled, "but I did not know the Buddy Buie story."

Mooty had quickly become of aware of Eufaula's connection to Buie and the A.R.S. but did not meet the legendary producer/songwriter before Buddy died in July.

"When he died, a lot of folks told me about what a great guy he had been," said the journalist, "and I felt like they were one hundred percent sincere. They thought the world of Buddy Buie, because he was so good to Eufaula, even though he wasn't from here."

Mike Causey of Stillwater probably spoke for dozens of musicians when he spoke of Buddy's importance in the Southern music phenomenon.

"We owe a lot to Buddy for his immeasurable help and guidance with our songwriting," Causey said, "and all of his help with recording. He was one of the most interesting men I have ever known. He was very funny, very animated, upbeat, and just always had this glimmer in his eyes, which reminded me of a kid on Christmas morning. He was very positive to be around and very well read. Gloria, his lifelong love, was always so kind to us. They were like family."

Gloria didn't have time to grieve. A few weeks after Buddy's death, she was asked to work on a special version of "'Faula Fest," a local fundraising event for the Southeast Alabama Medical Center Foundation. Buddy had supported the foundation, so the slightly

robertoreg.blogspot.com

241

renamed "Buddy Buie's 'Faula Fest" was scheduled to be held in Eufaula on May 13–14, 2016. In addition to the annual golf tournament and other activities, the Atlanta Rhythm Section was booked to play.

"At one time, Buddy was working with the Medical Center of Barbour County," Gloria detailed. "He had always wanted people in Eufaula to give that hospital a chance, because he felt it was needed. A friend called me and asked if I'd consider doing something now, to honor Buddy. I went right to work, and I learned a lot of things about fundraising."

CHAPTER 16
The Road Ahead

In early March 2016, drummer Rodger Stephan replaced Jim Keeling in the Atlanta Rhythm Section.

"He had to make a very hard decision," David Anderson said of Keeling, his longtime musician friend. "He has a wife and young daughter that he missed on the weekends that we were gone. He wanted to spend more time at home, and he gets to do stuff like T-ball now."

Stephan, a Tampa resident who had extensive studio experience and had also backed up former Jefferson Airplane singer Marty Balin for around two decades, was also the drummer in Rodney Justo's Tampa-based nostalgia band, Coo Coo Ca Choo.

Accordingly, Stephan was onboard when the Rhythm Section performed at the "Buddy Buie's 'Faula Fest" benefit in May.

"I knew of Rodney's groups growing up," Stephan recalled, "but was always too young to get into the venues and had never met him until Coo Coo Ca Choo was being formed by Rodney and a couple guitar-playing friends of mine. I got the call one summer, showed up for an evening rehearsal, and it just clicked."

As for his affiliation with the Atlanta Rhythm Section, Stephan recalled, "Jim had decided to retire around the end of 2015. Rodney asked if I would be interested, and I think my response was something like 'Hell, yeah!' Jim agreed to continue with the A.R.S. until the end of February 2016.

"It was a little intimidating to be considered for an act with 'gold' and 'platinum' attached to the name. I'm very thankful to Rodney for helping me prepare, and I'm still knocked out by how welcoming they've all been to me."

The Buddy Buie's 'Faula Fest outdoor show went off smoothly, and Kyle Mooty noted how good the current incarnation of the band sounded.

"It was a great concert," the newspaperman said. "I was thoroughly impressed. It sounds strange to say, but some of those guys, at their age, sounded quite good, and I think a lot of fans may have been surprised. People attended from all over the Wiregrass; I met

Two days of GOLF n' Music
Benefiting the Medical Center Barbour Fund

Buddy Buie's
'Faula Fest

Featuring ATLANTA RHYTHM SECTION
May 13-14, 2016
Country Club of Alabama &
Eufaula Main Street Entertainment District

MEDICAL CENTER
BARBOUR
FUND

334-688-7000 ext. 7444 or 334-673-4150 | www.samcfoundation.org

Proudly Sponsored By:

ALABAMA POWER · M.G. DIXON LUMBER COMPANY · The Buddy Buie Family · Calendicare · E
Berney Office Solutions · Draffin & Tucker, CPA's · The Moring Family
Crowne Healthcare · Troy Bank & Trust · Robert & Susan Hewes · Rushton, Stakely, Johnston & Garrett
Jay & Lynnette Jaxon

The Atlanta Rhythm Section plies its trade at the "Buddy Buie's 'Faula Fest" concert, May 14th, 2016. *Eufaula Tribune*

fans from Enterprise, New Brockton, Dothan, Union Springs, and some from across the Georgia line."

"They knocked it out of the park," Gloria remembered. "It was a beautiful night in an open field."

"It was great seeing Justo and the band back in action again," Ben Buie enthused. "Amazing—they are still such a 'tight' band to this day; definitely carrying on the A.R.S. tradition of great musicianship. My two sixteen-year-old daughters were there, and it definitely isn't their type of music, and they still loved it. Great music is great music."

••••••

A celebration of Rodney Mills's seventieth birthday was held at the Red Clay Theater in the Atlanta suburb of Duluth (where Mills and his wife, Mary, resided and operated his audio-mastering business) on July 17, 2016. The event also noted his fifty-five years in the music business, starting with his teenage years in the Bushmen. The Atlanta Rhythm Section and Stillwater performed, along with other artists, and Jeff Carlisi was the emcee.

"They did 'Alien,' which brought back some great memories," said public-relations veteran Mark Pucci. Some thirty-five years earlier, Pucci had hyped *Quinella*, the album on which "Alien" appeared.

J. R. Cobb also briefly attended the ceremony.

••••••

Rodney Justo was now in the position of road manager whenever the Atlanta Rhythm Section performed.

••••••

Open since 1991, Eddie's Attic is an (obviously) upstairs restaurant / tavern / primarily acoustic instrument performance venue located in the downtown entertainment district of Decatur, Georgia, within walking distance of Agnes Scott College and Decatur High School (Barry Bailey's alma mater). The business's website touts Decatur as "a small artist-friendly town within the metro Atlanta area—a cultural blend of Berkeley and Mayberry."

The small "listening room" in Eddie's Attic includes a stairstep/bleacher-like seating section, and there was standing room only in the venue on December 9, 2016, for a performance by the Atlanta Rhythm Section. Most of the patrons were fans who came of age when the band was proffering hit songs and albums in the 1970s.

The lineup now consisted of Dean Daughtry, Rodney Justo, Steve Stone, Justin Senker, David Anderson, and Rodger Stephan.

A table set up in the lobby of Eddie's Attic stayed busy selling t-shirts and the Atlanta Rhythm Section's latest album, *From the Vaults* (Fuel Records), a two-CD set that includes archival material from the Candymen, a version of "Stormy" by Noah's Ark, and selections from the entire history of the band, plus a second CD of rare live tracks, which includes an example of Ronnie's quirky rendering of "Rocky Raccoon."

"Len Fico, who became our manager, put that together," said Justo.

Mary and Rodney Mills attended the concert at Eddie's Attic.

"The thing about the legacy of the Atlanta Rhythm Section is the longevity of the songs," Rodney said the next day. "They're still valid. You can listen to them after all this time, and they're still really good. Last night, Rodney Justo told me he'd had to study Ronnie Hammond in order to make those songs believable, and it works. I thought he really did a good job on 'Conversation.'

"And they still play really well; they're good musicians and a force to be reckoned with."

"You can tell the current band has a lot of respect for the original band," one fan said of the band's concerts. "Steve makes it clear that he was picked to take Barry's place; he's done a great job. However, you can also tell that he's not Barry, but he makes sure the sound, the chords, the tone, and the signature licks are all there. And Justin really pays homage to Paul. And on some of the songs, it's amazing how much Rodney sounds like Ronnie. And the chemistry between all of the musicians validates why they're there, and you can see it onstage."

Soon after the performance at Eddie's Attic, the band was booked for other appearances there in 2017.

• • • • • •

In mid-January 2017, the A.R.S. flew into the Ft. Lauderdale–Hollywood International Airport for a concert in the Miami area. Thirty minutes after they picked up their luggage, gunfire erupted at the same baggage carousel, as a shooter killed five persons.

Obviously, the carnage rattled the band when they heard about it via the news media. One member speculated that the shooter was probably in a restroom loading his weapon when they had been picking up their suitcases.

A March 30, 2017, press release touted a "Southern Rock Cruise" in the Caribbean, slated for January 2018. In addition to the Atlanta Rhythm Section, other bands scheduled included Lynyrd Skynyrd, 38 Special, Molly Hatchet, Wet Willie, Louisiana's LeRoux, and an Allman Brothers tribute band, among others. Instead of an at-sea concert, Skynyrd's performance was slated for a private barbecue on land in Montego Bay, Jamaica.

The A.R.S. was also booked for another cruise, this one in early March of the same year, proffered by the same promoter. The lineup for the "Rock and Romance Cruise" also included Styx, Michael McDonald, "and many many more soon to be added," according to the cruise promoter's website.

By the end of June, the "Southern Rock Cruise" had sold out.

Dean broke his wrist in a household accident in the spring of 2017 and was temporarily replaced for a few weeks by keyboard player Lee Shealey, who had been playing in an Atlanta Rhythm Section tribute band, according to Rodney Justo.

At a mid-May performance in Phenix City, Alabama (across the Chattahoochee River from Columbus, Georgia), Shealey fit in nicely, carrying off his substitute assignment without a hitch.

Dean "Ox" Daughtry

Rodney Justo

Steve Stone

Justin Senker

David Anderson

Rodger Stephan

The usual concert list for the band now included a lot of first tracks on albums, as typified by the Phenix City concert. There was "Doraville" (*Third Annual Pipe Dream*), "Crazy" (*Dog Days*), "Jukin'" (*Red Tape*—and Steve Stone and David Anderson excelled in harmony guitar parts on that tune), "Large Time" (*Champagne Jam*) and "Do It or Die" (*Underdog*).

"The set list may change a bit from show to show," said Steve Stone, "but the hits will always be played."

There were also some pleasant surprises at Phenix City, however. Rodney Mills's observation about the presentation of "Conversation" a few months earlier appeared to be validated, since the song did indeed feature plaintive vocals from Rodney Justo. However, the tune also had an unexpected, slightly different arrangement in which it was stretched out a bit, slowly picking in volume and intensity as the band chugged into an intriguing and very listenable jam/groove.

The encore song was "Homesick," yet another first track (from *Quinella*). "Another Man's Woman" was not performed simply because the band hadn't rehearsed it with their temporary keyboard player.

Dean returned to the band in late June.

Rodney would have to undergo spinal surgery on his C5 and C6 vertebrae soon after the Phenix City show. The side effects from the operation included a temporary inability to sing, so Andy Anderson was recruited once again to handle any performance during Justo's recuperation.

Rodney's battle back included therapy sessions with a speech pathologist. He described his situation as "only a setback. We're fortunate in that we've got guys who were former members of the band who've been willing to come back when we've needed them. That happened when Justin came back after Paul died, and it happened with Andy. I can't thank Andy enough."

All the time he had worked with the A.R.S., Andy had continued to work with Billy Joe Royal as well, if scheduling allowed. He had continued to work with Royal after his departure from the Rhythm Section in 2011. His last performance backing up the legendary vocalist had happened two weeks before Royal died in October 2015.

Anderson actually sang "Do It or Die" in concert for the very first time when he returned to the A.R.S. in 2017. Performances where Anderson had to sing included the return to Eddie's Attic in mid-August.

Justo returned to the band in October.

Anderson remained upbeat about his unique tenure with the Atlanta Rhythm Section. "I'm very honored to be a part of the A.R.S., and always will be," he said. "I'll be on call if I'm ever needed again."

•••••••

One indication of the staying power of songs recorded by the Atlanta Rhythm Section has been the fact that many of them have been rearranged and placed on sheet music for high school marching bands, youth jazz bands, and other musical aggregations.

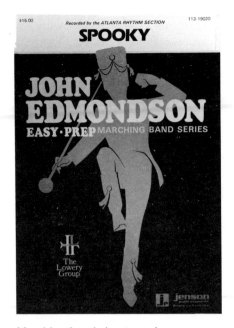

Marching band sheet music for "Spooky."

Young stage band sheet music for "Alien."

"Oftentimes, you relate songs to a time and the people in your life who still make an impact on you after all these years," said one fan who is in his fifties. "A.R.S. songs still have that effect on me, taking me to a really positive place with some of my fondest memories with my closest friends. Unfortunately some are not here today to share those memories with me, which gives the A.R.S. an even-bigger place in my heart."

••••••

Asked about what it felt like to be part of the Atlanta Rhythm Section in what is perceived as the band's twilight years, Rodger Stephan's response was eloquent.

"I feel very fortunate to have joined at this point," he reflected, "because the hard work is over. I would have loved to have been a part of the building process, but I never had to deal with the record labels, the brutal touring schedules, the pressure to come up with the next hit, or building a fan base. I'm not sure I would have survived all that. The music is great, the guys are great, the fans are great. I'm thrilled and honored to be part of the legacy and will ride this wave as long as they let me."

••••••

As the new century progressed, David Anderson's résumé had expanded even more, as he would perform with the Black Jacket Symphony, a Birmingham-based aggregation that specializes in intricate and precise live performances of classic rock albums. While he didn't participate in every presentation—the lineup of the B.J.S. would vary, depending on the album being reproduced—Anderson had been front and center on one of that band's most acclaimed presentations, which was their rendition of Pink Floyd's *Dark Side of the Moon.*

"He works somewhere all the time," Dean said succinctly.

Ox is also appreciative of David's guitar style, noting that Anderson also has the same "finesse" that Barry, J. R., and Steve have had.

A decade after he signed on with the A.R.S., David was appreciative of how Steve Stone motivates his own playing.

"Our playing relationship has grown over the years," Anderson reflected. "We have some bits that we have improvised during the show, and he certainly pushes me as a guitar player because he is so incredible."

••••••

Steve Stone marked thirty years with the band in 2016, and commented about his ongoing role, which had particularly changed when Barry Bailey retired.

"I took over most of Barry's stuff," said Steve, "but the sound and the mix make sure it's a 'two-guitar' band. On a certain song, I might play rhythm and Dave will play the lead, but we don't stick to 'you're the lead guitar player I'm the rhythm guitar player.'"

As for the future of the band, Stone said, "I'm not going to make any predictions, but when I joined in 1986, I was wondering if the band would even be around another six months! We play clubs, casinos, and festivals. And I'm still enjoying it."

"He does Barry's parts to a 'T,'" Dean said of Stone. "He does well 'on his own' but he also knows he's supposed to do the stuff that Barry did, and he does it perfectly."

"Steve's well-liked, and he's a very capable player," said former Hydra guitarist Spencer Kirkpatrick.

••••••

Decades after his employment at Studio One, Rick Maxwell still had some terrific memories of the A.R.S., citing three occasions at another Atlanta musical landmark, where he got to showcase his steel guitar talent on "Silver Eagle."

"The Fox was my holy ground," he said in a somewhat reverent voice. "I played three nights onstage with them there, although I did play some other concerts with them."

••••••

"I'm still a great fan of the Atlanta Rhythm Section," said Mylon LeFevre, who was now involved with a ministry in Ft. Worth. "I love 'em all, and I respect what they accomplished. They were my friends; we jammed together and did a lot of fun things together."

"They were a Southern band, but without the traditional 'southern sound,'" said radio and television veteran Lynn Sinclair. "Their hits were smooth; a couple were even rather tongue-in-cheek suggestive. Their music was different from anything that was out there at the time. They just happened to be from the South. They could've been from anywhere."

"There's never been anything like the synergy that the original members of that band had," former Mose Jones guitarist Marvin Taylor said of the Rhythm Section.

Taylor and other surviving members of Mose Jones had finally been able to release the 1980 album that was shelved by RCA some thirty years later. It hadn't been given an official title back then, so it was dubbed *Lost/Found*.

••••••

"I think of the A.R.S. as great players, with great songs," said Stillwater's Mike Causey. "Just ordinary homegrown guys with a hell of a lot of talent. To this day I love listening to them. I'll go on a trip somewhere or head somewhere to play, and you can bet I have all of their music on my iPod and cell phone. Looking back on my life, I must say if they hadn't had come along and did what they did, along with all of the Southern acts, we wouldn't have had a snowball's chance in hell to record, in my opinion."

"I think the A.R.S. brought a unique sophistication to Southern Rock," Causey's Stillwater bandmate Rob Walker said. "They were comprised of studio musicians, so there was an automatic polish to the sound they created. At the same time, they were all Southern boys at heart, so there was grit and funk in their music, too. Their music was a reflection of the city of Atlanta in the seventies—urban and southern at the same time. Buddy Buie's songwriting—his lyrics in particular—depicted the South in a very classy, 'down-home' way—'Dog Days,' 'Jesus Hearted People,' 'Champagne Jam'—as opposed to the more aggressive 'Southern Rock' sounds that were abundant at the time. It's not that there was anything wrong with the bands that had more of an edge, it's just that A.R.S. forged a 'Southern Rock' sound that rocked with a different perspective. I think that was their legacy."

• • • • • •

"Maybe people in the industry or radio had an opinion," said Wendell Cox, "but if you truly loved their work, there was no way you could ever look at anything of theirs as underrated. Those guys put 110 percent into everything they ever did."

Cox even engaged in some wishful thinking about recording another A.R.S. song with his decades-long employer, Travis Tritt.

"I would like to hear Travis cut 'Large Time,'" the veteran guitarist said. "We actually play around with that one every once in a while during our sound checks. I've always loved the 'spanking' Telecaster sound that Barry had on that track, along with J. R. Cobb's strong guitar track emulating the same guitar pattern. Truth be known, I'd say J. R. came up with that riff. He taught me as much as Barry did.

"I personally think that the Atlanta Rhythm Section will go down in history in many categories. Not just 'Southern Rock,' but contemporary, or 'pop with an edge,' if you will, because they certainly had power in their music. When I sat in with them, they weren't fooling around. As we say in the business, they were 'moving air' onstage, and I had heard it coming through the speakers on the radio as a kid.

"To 'label' A.R.S is hard for me because they did it all with a slick style but a hell of an edge. I don't think anybody will ever be able to do what they did again. I'm so glad they're still out there continuing to carry on the legacy. I'm their biggest fan."

• • • • • •

"The A.R.S. carved out a strong place in southern musical history," said Chuck Leavell, who was still gigging with the Rolling Stones in 2017. "They showed how putting together good material with good arrangements, coupled with strong professional musicianship, could result in a great band and a successful career. Their legend is secure."

• • • • • •

Some forty years after their bands were in the upper echelons of rock music (and had toured together), Kansas's Richard Williams hadn't forgotten his appreciation of Barry Bailey's tone and technique.

"I've known guitar maker Paul Reed Smith since his early beginnings," he said, "and on one of my visits to his factory we were discussing tone. Much of that conversation was about Barry and that sound. His Les Paul through that Marshall amp created— along with his hands—one of those 'Holy Grail' tones that most guitar players spend a lifetime searching for."

In 2016, the Atlanta Rhythm Section had played at a festival where the Kentucky Headhunters were also booked.

"I really enjoyed watching their show," said Greg Martin. "The songs and the band sounded great."

As for their place in music history, Martin opined, "I believe their legacy will be their songs. Each band member was strong, but collectively, they made a big sound.

"I have nothing but respect for the A.R.S. Their music is a part of my musical DNA. Even though I never tried to copy Barry or J. R.'s solos note for note, they both were an influence. I'm sure some of Barry's use of 'pinch harmonics' and tone rubbed off on me.

"The A.R.S. were mostly country boys, very much like the Headhunters. They did what they did well, found their own sound, and stayed with it."

Bassist Mark Egan pronounced the Atlanta Rhythm Section to be "great musicians that have crafted their playing and composing abilities, and have done it with a group sensibility. It's one thing to develop an individual style as a player, but to put it out there as a band identity is a very special accomplishment. The songs, arrangements, grooves, and group playing make for fantastic music.

"I know from playing and recording with the Pat Metheny Group and my solo recordings how much work it takes to create an individual sound. It's not only the musicianship of each player but the synergy of the group, coupled with great compositions and arrangements that creates the sound. This is what is special about the Atlantic Rhythm Section. They have a very recognizable style and are an important part of American music history."

"The A.R.S. was a combination of great songwriting, soulful singing, and a band of mature players that never let ego get in the way of what the song needed," said Bruce Brown of the Charlie Daniels Band. "Barry made every note count. What a band."

"The original lineup was hard to beat, guitar-wise," said Tinsley Ellis. "Barry Bailey is the greatest guitarist to ever come out of Atlanta. No one else even comes close. He's our Clapton here. He's got it all— tone, taste, and as strong of a melodic sense as any electric-guitar player anywhere. Like Carlos Santana, Barry knows precisely when to play low and slow, and when to turn up the heat and burn it down to the ground. 'Spooky' is a perfect example of Barry's genius—the song fades over some amazing guitar playing. I've always wished I could hear a version without the fade out.

"But like the Beatles, they will remembered for their songs. They came from an era when good music could make you famous. Nowadays, a musician has to bust out of rehab, run over someone with a car, and create some kind of ruckus in the media to get famous.

"'Conversation' is the forgotten ARS classic. Vocally, it's Ronnie's masterpiece. 'Alien' is also a forgotten classic; I can listen to it over and over. The Allmans had the stars. Skynyrd had the swagger. But the A.R.S. had the songs. And their songs have stood the test of time. I guess that's why they call it 'classic rock.'"

Having been a teenager in Atlanta when the Atlanta Rhythm Section was in its prime, and having later worked on the road for the band, Terry Spackman had a unique perspective:

"I always felt like they could make you think you had a chance, because these guys knocked down a lot of barriers and kicked open a lot of doors, and a lot of bands followed. Their albums were studio-engineered *way* beyond anything else that was coming out of Georgia at the time."

••••••

Asked about how and why the Atlanta Rhythm Section would be remembered, Dean Daughtry—who had rightfully become somewhat of a sage regarding the band and its history—said, "It was the music. We played our hearts out. Barry was a jazz guy, and J. R. was sort of a country player. Goddard was classical, and I don't know what in the heck I was. I think we were proud of the music that we helped to write and create."

The only continuous member of the Atlanta Rhythm Section was, like the band itself, going at his own measured and methodical pace.

"I still get royalty checks for songwriting, and I get checks from BMI for airplay," Ox said with a smile. "Just about any time I get in the car, I'll hear one of our songs, some of which I co-wrote, and some others, like 'Spooky,' which I didn't write. They still sound good."

Of all the songs he wrote with Buddy Buie, Robert Nix, or both, Dean's favorite number is somewhat surprising—it's "You're So Strong" on *Quinella*.

"Buddy and I wrote that," he detailed. "I like the way it just kind of builds up and rocks out, and it's one reason I think that's one of our best albums. But 'Dog Days' was his favorite song out of all of the ones that we wrote together."

••••••

"I talked with Buddy before I came back," Rodney Justo reflected, "because it was important to me that the legacy of that band wouldn't be 'just another band.' But we didn't want to just go through the motions, doing the same show with just the hits over and over again. That's why we worked up different concert arrangements of songs like 'Boogie Smoogie' and 'Conversation'—and I wasn't the original singer on those. I wanted people to say, 'Now I remember why I liked this band so much!'

"But the strength of the band has always been the songs, with their quality and emotion. If you don't have substantial songs, you certainly couldn't work forty-seven years like we have, and of course we owe Buddy for that. He was the 'editor,' and it was his concept. Everything we play these days feels like a homage to him.

"People talk about a 'Southern Rock' idiom and they always cite the Allmans, but stylistically, they were more blues-based, as were a lot of other bands. We're a Southern band that's created music that's very different and unique, and it's still 'Southern.'"

"So as far as our 'legacy,' I want to make sure that people realize it's Buddy's legacy most of all. Even though we had differences—and they were never personal—it was his vision and his tenacity that kept the band together, toughed out the songs, produced the recordings, fought with the record companies, promoters, agents, etc. Buddy used to say 'it's all about the songs,' and time has proved him right.

"Buddy is gone now, and I still find myself trying to gain his approval."

As for how much longer the Atlanta Rhythm Section will continue, both Rodney and Dean noted that they'd like to remain active, at least until 2020, which would mark the fiftieth anniversary of the band.

• • • • • •

Bert and J. R. Cobb celebrated their fiftieth wedding anniversary on January 21, 2017. They were residing in rural Georgia on a country road, and about the only times J. R. was playing guitar in front of others were occasional performances at his church.

"I still see a lot of nice things on Facebook about Barry Bailey, and how much he's missed." J. R. said. "Musicians appreciated the band and thought we did good songs and played them well. That's probably going to fade away, too. I'd imagine we will be remembered as a Southern Rock band that didn't sound like Southern Rock.

"We did a good job. For the most part, I thoroughly enjoyed it. The times I spent in the A.R.S. were, and are, some of my best memories, and I don't regret one day of it."

• • • • • •

About thirty miles northeast of the Cobbs' residence, Barry Bailey was making the best he could of his solitary rural lifestyle. He was determined to live as independently as possible for as long as he could, but he had made appropriate adjustments to facilitate his mobility—several four-wheel walkers were stationed at specific locations throughout his home, and in mid-2016 he added a lift chair to the stairs that lead to a downstairs den and office.

He was also wearing a push-button alert unit that contacts emergency medical personnel in case he falls.

"A lot of people, including most of my neighbors—who aren't exactly next door—are aware of my situation," he said, "and they do check in with me on a regular basis."

Barry still owns the Silvertone guitar he received as a birthday present in 1960. He also still has the Marshall amplifiers that served so well decades ago, but they're in storage. He usually plays his Taylor acoustic guitar if and when he actually feels like playing.

"I still play—not as much as I would like, but about as much as I'm able," he said.

And "Reb," Barry Bailey's legendary 1969 Gibson Les Paul Deluxe goldtop guitar, now rests quietly in its case in Barry's home. The instrument is a worn but proud and durable road warrior, also now retired.

References and Bibliography

PERIODICALS AND ONLINE ARTICLES

Abram, Malcolm X. "Atlanta Rhythm Section Is Back Again." *Macon Telegraph*, April 2, 1999.

"ARS Gets Platinum." *Record World*, September 30, 1978.

Atkinson, Terry. "Southern Rockers Loosen the Roots." *Los Angeles Times*, October 30, 1978.

Atlanta Constitution concert ad, May 25, 1975.

Atlanta Constitution concert ad, July 17, 1975.

"Atlanta Rhythm Section—Georgia Progressive Rock Pioneers, Buddie [*sic*] Guie [*sic*]—J. R. Cobb Songs Recorded by 200 Acts." *Billboard*, May 25, 1974.

"Atlanta Rhythm Section Is Returning Home with Three Performances at Fox Theatre." *Atlanta Journal and Constitution*, August 24, 1980.

"Atlanta Symphony Enters Final Week for Summer." *Atlanta Constitution*, July 13, 1975.

"Barbecue, Rock and the Chief." *Detroit Free Press*, September 27, 1978.

Barnes, Mike. "Paul Goddard, Bass Player with Atlanta Rhythm Section, Dies at 68." *Billboard*, May 1, 2014.

Berman, Pat. "Concert's Headline Act Played Second Fiddle." *Columbia Record*, November 4, 1977.

Bradberry, Brad. "The Atlanta Rhythm Section— Champagne Jams and Southern Dreams." *Goldmine*, August 6, 1993.

Browning, Allen. "Georgia Tech Hosts Rock Concert." *The Technique*, August 26, 1977.

Brunot, Luc. (Robert Nix interview) *Bands of Dixie* 65, November–December 2008.

"Buie, Geller Form Record, Mgmt. Cos." *Record World*, February 4, 1978.

Burgess, Steve. "The Atlanta Rhythm Section—Crazy." *Dark Star* 15.

Bussey, Bill. "GTPD Emphasizes Security as Champagne Jam Nears." *The Technique*, June 29, 1979.

Cade, J. D. "Symphony Rocks Out." *Great Speckled Bird*, July 10, 1975.

Cain, Scott. "Rhythm Section Gets Foot in Success Door." *The Atlanta Journal*, August 3, 1974.

Cain, Scott. "Rhythm Section: Things Hopping." *The Atlanta Journal and Constitution*, August 31, 1977.

Cain, Scott. "Atlanta Belongs to Rhythm Section." *Atlanta Journal and Constitution*, September 2, 1977.

Cain, Scott. "Oh, What a Grand Jam!" *Atlanta Journal and Constitution*, September 9, 1978.

Cain, Scott, "Carter Asks for Rhythm Section." *Atlanta Journal*, September 30, 1978.

Cain, Scott. "Billboard List Reveals Atlanta's Economic Woes." *Atlanta Journal and Constitution*, January 5, 1980.

Cain, Scott. "Rhythm Section Competes with Rain, but Packs 'em in at Six Flags Shows." *Atlanta Journal*, June 8, 1981.

"'Candy Power'—It's Heading Your Way." *Teen's Top Ten*, April 1968.

"Carter's Got Rhythm." *Atlanta Journal*, September 26, 1978.

Cassabonne, Jay. "We Had Us a Champagne Jam." *The Technique*, September 22, 1978.

"Champagne Jam Supplies Tech with New Turf." *Blueprint*, 1980.

"'Champagne' Pours Success for Atlanta." *News-Herald*, TGIF, March 31, 1978.

Champion, Patti. "Triumphs, Trials & Tribulations." *Hittin' the Note*, August 1977.

Clift, Eleanor. "Carter's Momentum." *Newsweek*, October 9, 1978.

The Collegian concert ad, September 15, 1978.

Cromelin, Richard. "Riding the Range of Musical Rock." *The Los Angeles Times*, February 4, 1977.

Crowe, Cameron. "Nicks' Coat Gets Nicked." *Rolling Stone*, August 24, 1978.

Dearmore, Kelly. "The 5 Most Enlightening Facts from the Texxas Jam 1978 Documentary." *Dallas Observer*, June 19, 2014.

"Decatur's Own Barry Bailey to Be Honored at Beach Party." *Decatur Minute*, June 9, 2009.

"Despite Odds, Atlanta's NARA Chapter Booms." *Billboard*, August 8, 1970.

Dog Days ad; including tour itinerary. *Billboard*, August 16, 1975.

Donlon, Cara. "ARS Singer's Shooting Ruled Justified." *Macon Telegraph*, January 20, 1999.

"Doraville Boys Play Georgia Rhythm; Santana Bops in for Concert at Fox." *Atlanta Journal and Constitution*, May 31, 1981.

Dukes, Billy. "Original Atlanta Rhythm Section Drummer Robert Nix Dies." www.ultimateclassicrock.com, May 22, 2012.

Dupree, Tom. (Review of *Third Annual Pipe Dream*) *Zoo World*, October 24, 1974.

Emerson, Bo. "Beatles' Atlanta performance Still Resounds 50 Years Later." *Atlanta Constitution-Journal*, August 17, 2015.

Ford, Dottie. "Tribute Concert to Benefit Commercial Music at G.S.U." *The Signal*, October 17, 1977.

Galloway, Derf. "Rockfest Proves No Dog." *The Technique*, September 23, 1977.

"Gold Clef Awards Show Lowery Publishing Rise." *Billboard*, January 20, 1973.

Griffin, Lance. "Buddy Buie Remembered for Music, Moments." *Dothan Eagle*, July 22, 2015.

Hall, Carla. "Barbecue and Rhythm on the South Lawn." *Washington Post*, September 26, 1978.

Harris, Art. "Rock Meets Rachmaninoff." *Atlanta Constitution*, July 23, 1975.

Harrison, Ed. "Paragon Shaping New Wing." *Billboard*, August 19, 1978.

Hebert, Joe. "A.R.S. Plays the 'Alexander,' Rowdy Crowd of 9000 Attends." *The Technique*, November 9, 1979.

Hill, Debbus. "Bronx Cheer to ARS; Country Joe Is Back." *Sunday Press*, March 26, 1978.

"In and around Town" (entertainment listing). *New York Magazine*, January 31, 1977.

Ingram, Debbie. "Mural Celebrates Local Musical Talent." *Dothan Eagle*, June 11, 2009.

"Inside Track." (column) *Billboard*, March 24, 1973.

"Keeping It Cool." *St. Paul Pioneer Press*, July 2, 1979.

King, Bill. "Rhythm Section—Musicians' Musicians." *Atlanta Journal and Constitution*, January 15, 1977.

King, Bill. "Artists Pay Tribute to Lowery." *Atlanta Constitution*, November 17, 1977.

King, Bill. "Stars Salute Bill Lowery." *Atlanta Constitution*, November 18, 1977.

King, Bill. "Atlanta Rhythm Section to Play at White House." *Atlanta Constitution*, September 21, 1978.

King, Bill. "BGO and Polydor Form New Atlanta-Based Record Label." *Atlanta Constitution*, September 21, 1979.

King, Bill. "Some Awards with Soul." *Atlanta Journal and Constitution*, December 29, 1979.

King, Bill. "ARS: New York's Fine, but It Ain't Doraville." *Atlanta Journal and Constitution*, August 23, 1980.

King, Bill. "ARS Is Back, Crowd Loves It." *Atlanta Constitution*, August 30, 1980.

Kirby, Kip. "Band's Enigmatic Image Shifts." *Billboard*, September 20, 1980.

Kovac, Joe, Jr. "Rock and Roll with a Bullet." *The Telegraph*, April 17, 2011.

Lanham, Tony. "ARS Leaders in Southern Rock." *Red and Black*, March 30, 1978.

Lawrence, Sharon. "'That Bitch Sharon' talks about the ARS." *Hittin' the Note*, August 1977.

Leonard, Larry. "Tech, Georgia State Sign for A.R.S. for Coliseum." *The Technique*, October 12, 1979.

Levitt, Howard. "A Rockin' Rise for Southern Sounds." *Record World*, August 10, 1974.

Little, Carole. "Studio One Sign of Atlanta Rock—Renowned Artists Drawn to City." *Red and Black*, September 25, 1973.

Lovejoy, Heather. "Drummer Robert Nix, Whose Career Began in Jacksonville, Died Sunday." Jacksonville.com/*Florida Times-Union*, May 22, 2012.

Makowski, Pete. "ARS in Cadillac Mooning Horror." *Sounds*, April 23, 1977.

Marsley, Leigh. "A.R.S. Lures Austrian Fan to Eufaula Jam 2000." *Eufaula Tribune*, June 7, 2000.

Mason, Jim. "Rock Group Is Good Theater." *Richmond News Leader*, April 26, 1978.

"Master Sound: Right in the Heart." *Billboard*, August 8, 1970.

McDonough, Jack. "Atlanta Rhythm: The Four-Minute Boogie." *Rolling Stone*, December 5, 1974.

McLane, Daisann. "A.R.S. Longa, Vita Brevis." *Crawdaddy*, May 1978.

McNeill, Phil. "A Sectional Analysis: The Blight of the Boogie." *New Music Express*, May 1978.

Mehler, Mark. "Timing Is Key to Success of Atlanta Rhythm Campaign." *Cash Box*, April 15, 1978.

Moe. "Rock at Midnight." *Great Speckled Bird*, March 19, 1973.

Moore, Roger. "Drummer Played until the End." *Orlando Sentinel*, November 16, 1999.

Mooty, Kyle. "'Faula Fest Music to the Ears of Gloria Buie." *Dothan Eagle*, April 16, 2016.

Moseley, Willie G. "Barry Bailey: Remembering the A.R.S." *Vintage Guitar Magazine*, December 2016.

Moseley, Willie G. "J. R. Cobb: Classic Bands, Classic Songs." *Vintage Guitar Magazine*, February 2017.

Moseley, Willie G. "Dave Hope: A Memorable Musical and Spiritual Sojourn." *Vintage Guitar Magazine*, April 2017.

Moseley, Willie G. "Southern Gold: Two Legendary Les Paul Deluxes." *Vintage Guitar Magazine*, October 2017.

Murphy, Jim. "ARS Takes the Stage at Cozy Grand Opera House." *Macon Telegraph*, February 20, 1998.

"New York, N.Y." (column) *Record World*, October 7, 1978.

"950 Attend Sugarloaf Concert." *FuTUre*, May 30, 1975.

Nix, Robert. "The Days of Love & Blood." *Bands of Dixie* 64, September–October 2008.

Overton, Gerry. "Doraville Band Is Proving They Have National Appeal." *The Signal*, January 30, 1975.

Palmer, Robert. (untitled review of Central Park concert) *New York Times*, July 12, 1977.

Paul, James. "Tech Hosts Champagne Jam, Reports Few Incidents." *The Technique*, July 13, 1979.

Perry, Scott. "ARS Comes Alive in Doraville, GA." *The Tennessean*, March 24, 1978.

Petty, Wesley. "Tech Houses Rock Shows; Four Bands Play for AA." *The Technique*, September 23, 1977.

"Pop Star of the Month." *Song Hits*, July 1977.

Pratt, Chuck. "Positively Bubbly—Atlanta Rhythm Section Tops." *Chicago Sun-Times*, March 26,1978.

Rudeseal, Ginger. "It's Just a Classic Statement, They've Got Atlanta Rhythm." *The Signal*, July 28, 1975.

"Rascals, Buie Sign with ATI." *Billboard*, May 23, 1970.

"Salute to Bill Lowery Scheduled." *Atlanta Constitution*, November 16, 1977.

Schruers, Fred. "'Champagne Jam' Toasts Rhythm Section." *Circus*, March 1978.

Sealey, Irving. "Jobs in the Music Business, Part Two— the Marketing Angle." *Rock*, September 1978.

"2nd Japan Jam Attracts Crowds in Good Weather." *Billboard*, September 13, 1980.

Sharoff, Robert. "More Georgia Boys at White House." *Detroit Free Press*, September 26, 1978.

Shaw, Russell. "Southern Rock—Where It's At." *Hit Parader*, February 1977.

Shaw, Russell. "This Trucker Hauls a Rock-Heavy Load." *CB Times*, September 1977.

"Six Groups Set to Play at Zoo in Birthday Bash." *The Oklahoman*, August 25, 1989.

Smith, Jack. "2000 Jam Brings ARS, Rain Again." *Eufaula Tribune*, June 21, 2000.

Squires-Smith, Barbara. "Committee Brings Atlanta Rhythm Section." *The Signal*, October 9, 1979.

Sundeen, Cat. "Rock Roundup in Texas." *Circus*, August 31, 1978.

Sutton-Smith, John. "Atlanta Rhythm Section." *Pacific*, March 1977.

Swenson, John. "Gone with the Trend." *Crawdaddy*, July 1975.

Swenson, John. "Carter's Campaign Jam—ARS Rocks the White House." *Rolling Stone*, November 16, 1978.

Thompson, Andy. "Six Hot Bands to Jam in July." *The Signal*, June 18, 1979.

Uhrinak, Bob. "Champagne Jam Cuts It for ARS." *Beaver County Times*, March 15, 1978.

Untitled review of *Champagne Jam*. *Tulsa Tribune*, March 22, 1978.

Untitled review of concert at the Electric Ballroom. *Cash Box*, August 10, 1974.

Ussery, Peggy. "New Mural Celebrates Local Musical Influences." *Dothan Eagle*, April 30, 2009.

Ussery, Peggy. "Downtown Music Fest Returns for Second Year." *Dothan Eagle*, June 20, 2011.

"Vandal Victory Pleases 15,000 Rowdy Fans." *Gem of the Mountains* (University of Idaho yearbook), 1981.

White, Cliff. "Baby You Can't Drive in My Car." *New Musical Express*, April 30, 1977.

"Writers Receive Lowery Awards." *Billboard*, December 10, 1977.

BOOKS

Bomar, Scott B. *Southbound: An Illustrated History of Southern Rock*. Milwaukee, WI: Backbeat Books, 2014.

Moseley, Willie G. *Smoke Jumper, Moon Pilot: The Remarkable Life of Apollo 14 Astronaut Stuart Roosa*. Morley, MO: Acclaim, 2011.

Shilds, Marti Smiley, and Jeff March. *Where Have All the Pop Stars Gone?* Vol. 3. Davis, CA: EditPros, 2016.

Steele, Larry. *As I Recall: Jacksonville's Place in American Rock History*. Jacksonville, FL: Larry Steele, 2016.

WEBSITES

www.atlantarhythmsection.com
www.daybeardied.com
http://paulcochran.com
http://robertoreg.blogspot.com
http://rocktourdatabase.com
http://sealplace.blogspot.com

OTHER SOURCES

A.T.I. Public Relations press release (May 6, 1970).

Polydor press release for *Third Annual Pipe Dream* (1974).

Polydor press release for *A Rock and Roll Alternative* (1976).

Champagne Jam press kit (1978).

All photos courtesy of Atlanta Rhythm Section publicity archives and (current and former) band members, associates, and fans except where noted.